Faiz

Also by the same author

Literary Non-Fiction

The Treasure: A Modern Rendition of Ghalib's Lyrical Love Poetry
Sahir: A Literary Portrait
Sahir: Har Pal Ka Shaa'yir (Hindi)

Fiction

Endless Life (A Novel)

Poetry

A Moment in the Universe

Translated Literary Works

Ghalib: Innovative Meanings and the Ingenious Mind
The Urdu Ghazal: A Gift of India's Composite Culture
The Hidden Garden: Mir Taqi Mir

Faiz

From Passionate Love
to a Cosmic Vision

SURINDER DEOL

RUPA

Published by
Rupa Publications India Pvt. Ltd 2021
7/16, Ansari Road, Daryaganj
New Delhi 110002

Sales Centres:
Allahabad Bengaluru Chennai
Hyderabad Jaipur Kathmandu
Kolkata Mumbai

ISBN: 978-93-91256-01-2

First impression 2021

10 9 8 7 6 5 4 3 2 1

Printed at Parksons Graphics Pvt. Ltd, Mumbai

CONTENTS

MANY FACES OF LOVE

Gopi Chand Narang

Time is the final arbiter of poetry's importance and its greatness. Both Mir and Ghalib complained about the lack of appreciation of their work by the people of their age. But with time, the mark of their greatness became clear. In this sense, time is not an abstraction. On the contrary, it is a determinant of the likes and dislikes of people with literary and artistic finesse. This includes the dynamic of the creators too. Many a time, it is through their ingenuity that the process of aesthetic appreciation and value judgement about the quality of art, literature and poetry goes through a change. From this point of view, Faiz is a poet of great merit and the most influential poet in the latter half of the twentieth century. There were other poets, but no one received as much popularity and accolade as Faiz. But fame is not the only measure of poetic greatness. The joy of poetry derives from many intangibles, but the poet's creative and distinctive golden touch plays a pivotal role and perturbs the literary canon. Faiz didn't get to the top in a day. He struggled and suffered a lot before he earned admiration and recognition. He started with *Naqsh-e Faryadi*, but it was with the second half of this collection and the subsequent poetry collections, namely, *Dast-e Saba* and *Zindaan Nama*, that he gained the extraordinary stature of being a poet with unique attributes. The reason for this success was neither biographical nor historical. If we look at the critical literary assessments among the progressives of those early years, Faiz was ranked twelfth or fifteenth. But then we come to the day when Faiz's metaphorical structure and aesthetic sensibility, as well as his stylistic lyrical uniqueness, coupled with his sweet-sounding poetic voice like that of a bulbul and rose, vanquished all contemporaries. The views of critics lost their vigour and Faiz's importance improved by the day. Faiz was accepted as a distinctive dominant voice of his age. Let us look at two of his couplets from a famous ghazal:

> Rapture now is the medium of discourse,
> all around, on everyone's lips.
> What has gained momentum
> can't be stopped.

> The style of expressing suffering
> I had invented in my confinement
> is now the way of chosen communication
> in the whole garden.

ab vohi harf-e junuun sab ki zabaan thahri hai
jo bhi chal nikli hai voh baat kahaan thahri hai

ham ne jo tarz-e fughaan ki hai qafas mein iijaad
Faiz gulshan mein vohi tarz-e bayaan thahri hai

अब वोही हर्फ़-ए जुनूँ सब की ज़बाँ ठहरी है
जो भी चल निकली है वो बात कहाँ ठहरी है

हम ने जो तर्ज़-ए फ़ुग़ाँ की है क़फ़स में ईजाद
फ़ैज़ गुलशन में वोही तर्ज़-ए बयाँ ठहरी है

The creative path zigzags, and it is filled with unknowns. In the same way, literary criticism generally takes time to unwind poetic curls and riddles. The creativity that is exclusive to a poet takes time to strike roots in its durability. The great verse then opens new pathways for its assessment. A great poet is either a rejuvenator of an established tradition or the fountainhead of a major departure from tradition. More often, he comes across as an innovator or a deviant who disregards the customary usage which others hold dear. He finds new ways of expression. He invents new poetic grammar. In this manner, the poet is either ahead of his time, or he becomes the representative voice of tragic events, pain and suffering or peoples' aspirations of the period in which he lives. Very often, he is the voice of his time. What was Faiz's miracle? When we look at his work in the proper context, we face several questions. Was he a revolutionary poet? Probably yes and no. Was he ahead of his time? The answer to this also is not an unqualified affirmation. The progressive movement was already underway.

Josh Malihabadi's thundering voice was ahead of everybody else. Even Faiz has admitted that it was Dr Rashid Jahan who put him on this path. As far as classical diction is concerned, Faiz's is a metaphorical extension of Ghalib and Iqbal. He said that he learnt from Ghalib the art of changing words into metaphors. Lyrically, Faiz uses the poetic language that was part of classic Urdu and Persian poetry, but he excels through the sensuous mellowness of his metaphorical voice, charming demeanour, restrained emotional connection, compassionate expression and the brilliance of his words that make a connection with the reader's heart. It is something that none of his contemporaries could claim. What was the secret behind this? There are themes like freedom, anti-imperialism, anti-capitalism, sufferings of the masses, protest against all forms of social injustice and oppression and aspirations for a better social order, which are not any poet's monopoly. These are universal socialist and nationalist themes, and as a matter of fact, they are a common denominator found in nationalist and freedom movements everywhere. Even in Urdu, these themes are found among all progressive poets. Faiz's view of life and his thoughts are in sync with other progressive poets. He is no different. But then where do we find his individuality and uniqueness? If we cannot separate him from others by thought and themes, then how could he achieve a distinctive place for himself? There is one possible answer: intellectual or ideological similarity is not the same thing as aesthetic sensibility, or the sparkling passion of love, or heart touching sensuousness.

A poet's thought structure or ideology is not just an abstraction: it comes into being through his creative expression. Every great poet moulds his thoughts in a peculiar vessel that is uniquely his own. Even if the poet does not invent a new language, he can delve deep into tradition to create his unique metaphorical and lyrical distinctiveness. The other aspect of this puzzle is that distinctiveness cannot exist without discrete thought and meaning because style is not merely a fixed formula, as there is no signifier without a signified. Those who think otherwise have a very restrictive understanding of the mystery that the creative style or structure of poetry entails. Stylistic qualities demonstrate the qualities of thought and reflection. They are not two separate things. If poetic expressions are different, then thought structure could also be different from others. It is true that Faiz may not have added any new words to Urdu vocabulary, but it is also true that he has definitely invented new metaphorical modes of expression, thousands of new word formations, brilliant images, similes and phrases that have become idioms of their kind, with innovative socialist and lyrical meanings. This is akin to creating new constructs which are different from the usage common through several centuries. This creative poetic thought structure is uniquely Faiz's own and is the basis of his individuality and greatness as a poet. Faiz has taken full advantage of what was alive in the classic tradition, but with the use of his highly sensuous metaphoric creative ability and magical touch, he never stops from inventing new meanings. This magic touch is something worth noticing. Literary criticism that is largely focused on palpable themes, given agenda topics and pronounced points of view, ignores the mystery of creative ability, new thinking and magical expressions, and it can never unfold the secrets of Faiz's delightfully glowing mellow verse. His poem 'Mulaaqaat' (Coming Together) from his collection *Zindaan Nama* is a case in point.

This poem is based on, as it is clear, the images of night and morning. Night, pain, sorrow, oppression, injustice—these are all metaphors. Morning's twilight sky is a sign of happy tidings. This linking of light and darkness and its social significance is nothing unusual. This is found in poems all around the world. From the thought perspective, it is not extraordinary. We do recognize that in the context of a prison cell, this is an exceptional poem. It is a blend of compassion and commitment. Although the symbols on which the poem is based are not highly inventive, it contains newness in the manner of its touching lyrical expressions and its thought pattern. Here, creativity and its interpretation are beautifully blended. The poet calls the night '*dard ka shajar*' (the tree of suffering and agony) which is higher than 'you and me'. It is greater because, within its branches, millions of caravans of flaming stars have come and lost themselves. Thousands of moons have lost their shine under this tree. 'Raat', 'dard' or 'shajar' are not new words, but the night which is '*dard ka shajar*', the caravans of stars, and moons losing their light are turned into exceptionally powerful and unique metaphors. They strengthen the pain of the night of human suffering. To say that the pain is more significant than 'you and me' is not a personal statement; it enfolds the pain and suffering of the others too. This metaphorical transformation is missed by most critics—how Faiz shifts his focus from the individual (you and me) to the communal (all of us) and eventually to the cosmic whole (all of creation, all beings). In these three spheres, he finds more that unites us than divides us, more that is strung by a common thread than existing in isolated silos. This common thread is signified by dynamic love.

One crucial skill that Faiz uses is that he lyrically transforms his revolutionary thinking into his aesthetic sensibility, and the two are never separated. He uses his creative touch to merge the two to create pure poetic enjoyment. This is something unique to Faiz in Urdu poetry. This distinctive imagist, metaphorical and aesthetic touch continues in the second part of the poem as well. The night of suffering is black, but the eyes of the beloved are a wave of precious gold, and as such, they are filled with glow and illumination that is the quintessence of inspiration and reassurance. Any other poet would have used the image of dawn after a night at a surface level. But this is where Faiz parts company with other poets. Towards the end, the poet even rejects the romantic vision of the morning, saying that those who are hurting, those who are in pain, their morning is not in the sky but 'where we stand'—a reference to the thought that one cannot stay away from one's love;

dawn's bright sky lies with the one that signifies love, rather dynamic love.

> The place where both of us stand
> is dawn's bright horizon.
> Here the sparks of sorrow,
> when they blossom,
> become pomegranate flowers
> of morning's twilight.

> *jahaan p ham tum khare hain donon*
> *sahar ka raushan ufq yahien hai*
> *yahien pe gham ke sharaar khil kar*
> *shafaq ka gulzaar ban gaye hain*

> जहाँ पे हम तुम खड़े हैं दोनों
> सहर का रौशन उफ़क़ यहीं है
> यहीं पे ग़म के शरार खिल कर
> शफ़क़ का गुलज़ार बन गए हैं

In a previously published article,[1] I had examined the structural foundations of Faiz's poetry. My main assertion was that Urdu poetry had advanced to a point where one could identify at least three or more triangles, i.e., structures of creative signification. Structuralism is the methodology that says that elements of culture (which includes literature) must be understood by way of their relationship to a larger system or structure. The theory works to uncover the structures that signify our thoughts, feelings and perceptions. It argues that there must be a

---

[1] Gopi Chand Narang, 'Tradition and Innovation in Urdu Poetry: Firaq Gorakhpuri and Faiz Ahmad Faiz', in *Urdu Language and Literature: Critical Perspectives*, New Delhi: Sterling Publishers, 1991. This article was also reproduced in Yasmeen Hameed, ed., *Daybreak: Writings on Faiz*, Karachi: Oxford University Press, 2013, pp. 65–74.

structure in every text, which helps the reader to interpret the author's work. Post-structuralism extends the argument by saying that it is not only important to study the text but also the system of dynamic knowledge that produced the text and how the meaning is dynamic and keeps evolving with the changing context.

Classical Urdu poetry was primarily focused on matters of physical love and beauty. This is the First Basic Triangle: Lover—Beloved—Rival. After an evolutionary process over a few centuries, another structure with a spiritual focus came into being. Some of the old themes like *'i'shq o sarmasti'* (love and joy), *'rindi o rusvaaii'* (drunkenness and infamy), *'sheikh o sharaab'* (sheikh and tavern), *'gul o bulbul'* (rose and nightingale), *'sham'a o parvaana'* (candle and moth) were used with metaphysical and transcendental implications. This is the Second Sufi Triangle: Mystic—Absolute Truth—Religious Orthodoxy coupled with the Ruling Hierarchy.

With colonial rule strengthening its roots in India, yet another structure emerged that had to do with social and political awareness, people's suffering and the freedom struggle. This signifies the Third Nationalist Triangle: Freedom Fighter—Freedom—the Colonial Power. This structure is visibly present in the works of early twentieth-century poets, such as Hasrat Mohani, Mohammad Ali Jauhar, Allama Iqbal, Jigar Moradabadi, Firaq Gorakhpuri, and subsequently in progressive poetry, which was inspired by Marxist or leftist ideology. The Fourth Progressive Triangle is an extension of the Nationalist Triangle in many ways, except that the progressives had a new enemy—the ruling class and the military dictatorship that opposed progressive ideology. These four evolutionary triangles are delineated in the table below:

1. The Basic Love Triangle		
Lover/Poet or Drunkard *aa'shiq, rind, shaa'yir*	Beloved *ma'shuuq mahbuub*	Rival or Disruptor *raqiib*
Love *i'shq*	Wine *sharaab*	The Other *ghair*
Legendary Male Lovers *Majnuun (Qais), Farhaad*	Legendary Female Lovers *Laila, Shiiriin*	Characters of Religious Orthodoxy Opposed to Love and Lovers *vaa'iz, naaseh, sheikh, mulla, zaahid, mohtasib*
2. The Sufi Love Triangle		
Mystic Lover, Mansur *aa'shiq, sufi, muvah-hid*	The State of Enlightenment *maa'refat, vahdat ul vajuud, hamaost, irfaan-e zaat, tasliim-e khudi, vahdat-e kul*	Religious Orthodoxy *u'lema, naaseh, muhtasib, mullah, sheikh, qaazi, mufti*
Poet, Speaking Voice, Protagonist *shaa'yir*	Divine Illumination *nuur, tajalli-e tuur*	Ruler, Establishment *haakim*
	Annihilation of Self *fana fi Allah, bekhudi*	Oppression *zulm-o sitam, jabar*
	Ecstasy *kaif-o masti, sharaab-e maa'refat*	Injustice, Murder *be-insaafi, qatl*

3. The Nationalist Love Triangle		
The Rebel, Freedom Fighter *mujaahid, baaghi, inqilaabi*	Freedom *aazaadi*	Colonialism, Imperialism *ghulaami, saamraaj*
Poet *shaa'yir*	Revolution *inqilaab*	Oppresser, Ruler *haakim, zaalim, jaabir*
	Self-Rule *swaraj*	Oppression *zulm*
	Patriotism *vatan-prasti, desh bhakti*	
	Sacrifice *sarfaroshi*	Prison, Execution, Chains, Executioner *zindaan, daar o rasan, zanjiir, qaatil*
4. The Progressive Love Triangle		
Freedom Fighter *aazaadi, inqilaabi, majnuun, baaghi, rind, aa'shiq, divaana*	Freedom *aazaadi*	Colonialism, Imperialism *sarmaayadaari nizaam*
Sources of Inspiration *maikhaana, mai, saaqi, sharaab, pyaala, jaam*	Revolution *inqilaab*	Oppression *taanashaahi*
Socialist/Marxist Ideology	Democracy *jamhuuriyat*	Ruler, Martial Law Administrator *zaalim, jaabir, haakim, saiyyaad*

Sunnat-e Mansur o Qais [the way of legendary lovers Mansur and Majnuun who gave their life for a cause or an ideal]	Dawn *sahar, savera*	Prison *zindaan, qafas*
	Spring Garden *chaman, bahaar, gul*	Accomplices *sheikh, mohtasib, naaseh, vaa'iz, mulla, maulvi*
	Social Justice *samaaji insaaf*	
Poet *shaa'yir*	Social Change *Samaaji tabdiili*	

All these triangles grow out of the Basic Love Triangle, and they can be coalesced and integrated with classical or contemporary words, images and metaphors, playing innovative double or multiple roles as creativity demands, producing layer upon layer of ingenious meanings, as we shall see in Faiz's poetry. There is no doubt that at a glance some of the words that appear in the above table seem customary because of their use over centuries. However, we cannot deny the fact that in contemporary poetry, at each stage, behind these words is hidden a whole structure of passionate love or social and political struggle in a new context. That is why several of these words or phrases were used as motifs during the freedom struggle. In Faiz's poetry, they create awareness of the need for independence or social change. When used as metaphors, these figures of speech became a fresh and a lyrical language of zealous poetic discourse, with Faiz's creativity in the lead. He distinguished himself in this endeavour because of his unique talent for creating metaphorical beauty through a magical creative fusion of Urdu and Persian that was outside the reach of the run-of-the-mill poets or poets with an agenda.

After the above structural analytical presentation, we can proceed to ask ourselves a fundamental question: what is the real secret of Faiz's aesthetic transformation? Love or romance apart, we have already seen that his aesthetic appeal is uniquely his own. It is something passionate and lyrical that we don't find in other progressive poets. Be it Josh, Makhdoom, Sahir, Jafri, Akhtar, Majrooh, Kaifi or Majaz, each was significant in his way. Some of them at one time were even considered much better, but slowly it came to be realized that Faiz's voice was the redeeming feature of the progressive era. From the margins, Faiz arrived at the centrestage of progressive poetry.

There is a view that the aesthetic feel that was present in Faiz's first poetry collection *Naqsh-e Faryadi* was lost in the subsequent poetry collections because he became involved in revolutionary poetry. This is not correct. We believe that the deep emotional lyrical touch that he showed in the later part of *Naqsh-e Faryadi* deepened further in *Dast-e Saba* and *Zindaan Nama*, and some later poems and ghazals. Let us look at two poems from *Naqsh-e Faryadi*. The first one is titled 'Mauzo-e Sukhan' (This Is What the Verse Is All About). This poem is significant because the poet artfully demolishes all boundaries between his love for the beloved, compassion for the suffering masses and his optimism for a better future, and meshes it all in one dynamic creative whole. But in the end, it is love that binds everything; and it is love with more than one face.

These are, and there might be many more subjects.
But think about the slowly opening lips of that
beauty.

And lo and behold, the faint outlines of her
alluring figure.
Tell me honestly where else you will find that
kind of magic.

This is what the inspiration of poetry is.
This is what the poet's native land is.
It is nowhere else, but here.

ye bhi hain aise kaii aur bhi mazmuun honge
lekin us shokh ke ahista se khulte hue hont
haae us jism ke kambakht dilaavez khutuut
aap hi kahiye kahien aise bhi afsuun honge

apna mauzo-e sukhan un ke siva aur nahien
tab'-e shaa'yir ka vatan un ke siva aur nahien

यह भी हैं ऐसे कई और भी मज़मूँ होंगे
लेकिन उस शोख़ के आहिस्ता से खुलते हुए होंट
हाये उस जिस्म के कम्बख़्त दिल-आवेज़ ख़तूत
आप ही कहिये कहीं ऐसे भी अफ़्सूँ होंगे

अपना मौज़ू-ए सुख़न उन के सिवा और नहीं
तब-ए शायर का वतन उन के सिवा और नहीं

Faiz wrote a two-part poem called 'Do I'shq' (Two Loves)
in which he described two 'loves', namely, the love that is
associated with fragrant tresses, ruby lips, glowing cheeks
and the enticing touch of hennaed hands, among other
unique attributes of beauty. This is the love of the beloved
as we find it in poetry. The second love that he describes
is the love of the country, its people, their sufferings and
aspirations, the need for freedom, social change and the
theme goes on. Faiz is apparently talking about the first
love, but he does it in a very subtle way. Starting with a
sad note, he unfolds different aspects of beauty, a beauty

that is not limited to a physical entity. The presentation is metaphoric until we reach the climax.

> I don't deny this i'shq or that i'shq
> I may have many scars on my heart
> but not the scar of any remorse!

> *us i'shq n us i'shq p naadim hai magar dil*
> *har daagh hai is dil mein bajuz dagh-e nadaamat!*

> उस इश्क़ न उस इश्क़ पे नादिम है मगर दिल
> हर दाग़ है इस दिल पे बजुज़ दाग-ए नदामत!

The Faiz that we meet in poems like 'Tanhaaii', 'Mauzo-e Sukhan' and 'Aaj Ki Raat' is also the Faiz that we find in 'Zindaan Ki Ek Sub-h', 'Zindaan Ki Ek Shaam' (from *Zindaan Nama*) and in 'Manzar' and 'Paas Raho' (from *Dast-e Tah-e-Sang*). Faiz doesn't talk about things like night, waiting for the beloved or memories of the days gone by in isolation. He weaves a net using these threads to focus his attention at 'pain' (dard) that lies submerged in the centre of our being. He sums it up beautifully in 'Mulaaqaat' ('Coming Together'). Faiz is a poet of the pain, suffering, agony, distress and discomfort that human beings go through in their lives. The lingering undefined suffering that Faiz talks about is his unique creative insight into human affairs. It is like a slow burning fire; it does not kill but it makes the person suffer on a continuous basis. Something that shows up time and again in his poems and ghazals is the word 'dard' and the multiple ways it expresses itself: '*dard aayega dabe paaon*' (pain will walk in silently), '*mere dard ko jo zabaan mile*' (if my pain could speak), '*bara hai dard ka rishta*' (the relationship of pain is the real thing), '*kab thahrega dard-e dil*' (when will the pain stop my heart), or '*juue-e dard*' (stream of pain), '*mauj-e dard*' (wave of pain), '*dard ke paivand*' (patches of pain), '*dard ka chaand*' (the moon of pain) and numerous other touching expressions.

We should be wary of thinking that pain (dard) is simply a negative force. There is a sublime, soulful side to it, namely, a creative tension, a force that impels an individual to do things for a bigger cause. Lovers suffer in love, but they also take pride in their suffering. Deprivation and suffering are sometimes states of pride as these are essential attributes of true love and commitment. We find evidence of this in classic poetry. Faiz does this artfully, in a unique way. From the depths of love's agony, Faiz's lover rises, projecting a feeling of 'this too will pass' since nothing in life is permanent. The evening of separation is long '*magar shaam hi to hai*' (but it is just an evening). The real challenge is to live a life for an ideal or a vision that is supreme. We can therefore say that Faiz makes an imaginative and soulfully elevating use of smoldering pain and suffering. It is a mix of conflicting routines and sublime or lofty energy, bringing us down sometimes, but also offering the courage to break the mold of oppression and do the opposite for a better life. The lonesome moon seen from inside the jail cell or on the crest of a roof; the vision of a blue still lake with the dreamy fleeting backdrop of the beloved; the image of a glowing glass of wine representing hope and longing that sustain life—these portrayals stay in the mind long after we have finished reading a poem. We have seen radiant nuances of this in the excerpts discussed above.

In this discourse of creativity and signification, one important point needs to be highlighted and elucidated. Isn't it puzzling that the second love triangle, which is the Sufi love triangle and signifies a transcendental spiritual (religious) structure, fuses perfectly with the third love triangle, i.e., the progressive (Marxist) triangle, which has predominantly material or secular signification? Isn't this a contradiction? How can polar opposites coexist? But in Faiz's poetry, they do coexist metaphorically. The Sufi terminology, especially references to the legendary Sufi martyr Mansur, are common in the larger context of Faiz's poetry. Time and again, he invokes the spirit of Mansur, such as, '*hamien se sunnat-e mansur o qais zinda hai*' (the tradition of the legendary Mansur and the historic Qais is alive because of our passion), or in the famous poem '*ham dekheinge, laazim hai ke ham bhi dekheinge*' (We shall see, it is certain that we shall see the day of judgement when justice will be done to one and all). There are references to the Holy Book and to the absolute truth, which are interwoven into the text and they blend and interact throughout Faiz's poetry in later years. These references are so frequent that for want of space we will restrict ourselves to quoting only two famous pieces, one qat'a and one poem, to make our point, and leave the rest for the reader to perceive how throughout Faiz's poetry this metaphoric creativity works and produces an all-inclusive cosmic sphere of signification. This is why we call it 'dynamic love' or 'visionary love', that which transcends all boundaries and all restrictions and encapsulates the whole humankind.

Qat'a
We create the commotion in the alley of madness.
Sheikh's garb and the royal crown of the ruler.
We keep alive the legends of Mansur and Qais.
We keep alive the love of flowers and the curved turban.

hamare dam se hai kuu-e junuun mein ab bhi khajil
a'ba-e sheikh o qaba-e amiir o taaj-e shaahi
hamien se sunnat-e mansuur o qais zinda hai
hamien se baaqi hai gul-damani o kaj-kulahi

हमारे दम से है कू-ए जुनूँ में अब भी ख़जिल
अबा-ए शैख़ ओ क़बा-ए अमीर ओ ताज-ए शाही
हमीं से सुन्नत-ए मंसूर ओ क़ैस ज़िंदा है
हमीं से बाक़ी है गुल-दमनी ओ कज-कुलही

The reference to the sheikh, the ruler and crown has definite implications not seen in realist poetry. Because of their power and influence, they are metaphors for the power structure that oppresses people. Mansur and Qais are martyrs in the cause of love: worldly or heavenly. Those who are fighting oppression have not lost their taste for the beauty of flowers or etiquette of magnificence, but their demands are of a different kind that can be met only with frenzy and self-sacrifice.

Here is the poem from *Mere Dil Mere Musafir*.

We shall see.
Yes, we must see.
The day that was promised.
That was written on the tablet of eternity.
When the towering mountains
of tyranny and oppression
will fly away like balls of cotton.
And under the feet of the oppressed
earth will quiver and quake.
When over the heads of cruel rulers
lightning will create a rumble and thunder.
When from the surface of loved lands
all idols will be removed.

And people like us
who are crushed and innocent
who have been excluded
from the holy sanctuary
will occupy seats of honour.
All crowns will be bounced in the air.
All thrones will be hurled down from
their high places.
Only God's name shall echo.
The one who is invisible,
the one who is present.
The one who is observed and the observer.
The cry of 'I am God' will resonate.
And the people will rule.
That is what I am,
and that is what you are.
And the humans created by God will rule.
That is what I am,
and that is what you are.

ham dekheinge
laazim hai ke ham bhi dekheinge
vo din k jis ka vaa'da hai
jo lauh-e azal mein likha hai
jab zulm o sitam ke koh-e giraan
ruii ki tarah ur jaaeinge
ham mahkuumon ke panv tale
jab dharti dhad-dhad dhadkegi
aur ahl-e hukam ke sar uuper
jab bijli kad-kad kadkegi
jab arz-e khuda ke kaa'be se
sab but uthvaa-ae jaaeinge
ham ahl-e safa marduud-e haram

masnad pe bithaae jaaeinge
sab taaj uchhaale jaaeinge
sab takht giraae jaaeinge
bas naam rahega allah ka
jo ghaiib bhi hai haazir bhi
jo manzar bhi hai naazir bhi
uthega anal-haq ka naa'ra
jo main bhi huun aur tum bhi ho
aur raaj karegi khalq-e khuda
jo main bhi huun aur tum bhi ho

हम देखेंगे
लाज़िम है कि हम भी देखेंगे
वो दिन कि जिस का वादा है
जो लौह-ए अज़ल में लिखा है
जब ज़ुल्म ओ सितम के कोह-ए गिराँ
रूई की तरह उड़ जाएँगे
हम महकूमों के पाँव तले
जब धरती धड़-धड़ धड़केगी
और अहल-ए हकम के सर ऊपर
जब बिजली कड़-कड़ कड़केगी
जब अर्ज़-ए ख़ुदा के काबे से
सब बुत उठवाए जाएँगे
हम अहल-ए सफ़ा मरदूद-ए हरम
मसनद पे बिठाए जाएँगे
सब ताज उछाले जाएँगे
सब तख़्त गिराए जाएँगे
बस नाम रहेगा अल्लाह का
जो ग़ायब भी है हाज़िर भी
जो मंज़र भी है नाज़िर भी
उठेगा अनल-हक़ का नारा
जो मैं भी हूँ और तुम भी हो
और राज करेगी ख़ल्क़-ए ख़ुदा
जो मैं भी हूँ और तुम भी हो

We gained freedom, but the country was divided. No revolution that progressives had expected occurred. Therefore, the progressives had to face the reality of the loss of a dream. Of all the contemporaries, only Faiz could write an extremely touching poem, 'Sub-h-e Aazaadi' in August 1947, which appears in the early pages of *Dast-e Saba,* opening with these memorable lines:

> This blemished sunrise, this daybreak of a night—
> mangled and mutilated.
> What we were waiting for, this is not the dawn.
> This is not the dawn in whose expectation friends set out
> in search of a journey's gratifying end, finding it somewhere.

> *ye daagh daagh ujaala ye shab-gaziida sahar*
> *voh intizaar tha jis ka ye voh sahar to nahien*
> *ye voh sahar to nahien jis ki aarzu le kar*
> *chale the yaar k mil jaayegi kahien na kahien*

> ये दाग़ दाग़ उजाला यह शब-गज़ीदा सहर
> वो इन्तेज़ार था जिसका ये वो सहर तो नहीं
> ये वो सहर तो नहीं जिस की आरज़ू ले कर
> चले थे यार कि मिल जाएगी कहीं न कहीं

And closing with these prophetic words:

> The time when the eyes and the heart
> find some solace has not yet arrived.
> Keep moving. We haven't reached the goal yet.

> *najaat-e diidaa o dil ki ghari nahien aaii*
> *chale chalo ke voh manzil abhi nahien aaii*

> नजात-ए दीदा ओ दिल की घड़ी नहीं आई
> चले चलो कि वो मंज़िल अभी नहीं आई

In Faiz's epic poetic journey, the graph shot up in the first three poetry collections. In the next three collections, he was recognized and heralded as a leading voice and redeeming feature of his age. Subsequently, the graph held steady. The last two collections were like summing up, with advancing age and worsening political conditions at home, but here and there is a smouldering fire and sparks in the ashes, coupled with his undying spirit of optimism. The voice of pain and hope had turned deeper and mellower with a touch of grief, as if that were coming from the depths of his psyche. The words are direct and straightforward with fewer metaphors and embellishments. They are self-reflective, as if he were getting weary of homelessness and wandering away from his country.

Here is a poem 'Dil-e Man Musaafir Man' (My Heart, My Fellow Traveller), which he wrote in London in 1978.

O dear heart of mine,
stay with me as we travel together.
Once again, there is a command
that we should leave our dear land,
with my heart forcibly separated from my roots.
We are wailing here and there.
Wandering to this town and that,
finding no trace of a messenger
who may take our message to our friends?
Asking every stranger that we meet
the whereabouts of our home.
At places unknown,
we spend days and nights
talking aimlessly to this person or that.
'How should I tell you
what the agony

of the night of separation is.'
No count of torments.
Had I made some name and earned some fame,
the suffering might have sufficed.
But as it is, 'Death was normal if that happened
just once, no more.'

mere dil, mere musaafir
hua phir se hukm saadir
ke vatan-badar hon hum tum
dein gali gali sadaaein
karein rukh nagar nagar ka
k suraagh koi paaein
kisi yaar-e naama bar ka
har ik ajnabi se puuchhein
jo pata tha apne ghar ka
sar-e kuu-e naa-shanaayaan
hamein din se raat karna
kabhi is se baat karna
kabhi us se baat karna
'tumhein kya kahuun ke kya hai
shab-e gham buri bala hai'
hamein ye bhi tha ghaniimat
jo koi shuumaar hota
'hamein kya bura tha marna
agar ek baar hota'[2]

मेरे दिल, मेरे मुसाफ़िर
हुआ फिर से हुक्म सादिर
कि वतन-बदर हों हम तुम
दें गली गली सदाएँ
करें रुख़ नगर नगर का

---

[2]The last two lines are borrowed from Ghalib.

कि सुराग़ कोई पाएँ
किसी यार-ए नामा बर का
हर इक अजनबी से पूछें
जो पता था अपने घर का
सर-ए कू-ए ना-शनायाँ
हमें दिन से रात करना
कभी इस से बात करना
कभी उस से बात करना
'तुम्हें क्या कहूँ कि क्या है
शब-ए ग़म बुरी बला है'
हमें ये भी था ग़नीमत
जो कोई शुमार होता
'हमें क्या बुरा था मरना
अगर एक बार होता!'

It is important to point out that revolutionary poetry often runs the risk of becoming outdated. There is a certain force that drives all revolutionary poetry. Once that force runs out of steam, it can take the verse down with it. Revolutionary poetry books often end up in the niches and recesses of our homes where they become food for insects. But if any part of the revolutionary poetry has come into being due to its inner 'creative jewel', it can cope with the force of time and survive. This is especially the case if the poet did not focus much of his attention on a given agenda, but instead metaphorically used drops of his heart's blood to write his verse. It is the poetry that comes with the inner glow, and it lives forever, rising above the struggles and the ebb and flow of time.

We have discussed more poems than ghazals, but Faiz's ghazals are equally important and significant. Faiz is the only poet of his era who achieved as much success in his ghazals as in his poems. In fact, some of the ghazals are even more popular and sung more frequently. They are like signatures of the poet's creativity among most people. Some ghazal couplets are quoted in public conversation to make a point. Let us look at two exceptional ghazals:

> When will the pain stop, O heart?
> How will I spend the night of suffering?
> I hear she will come in all glory.
> I hear that dawn's twilight will break.
>
> When will my breath transform itself into blood?
> When will my tear become a pearl?
> When are you going to have a hearing,
> O my tearful eyes?
>
> When will fragrance take over
> and when will the tavern get drunk?
> When will the morning of verse arrive?
> And when will I will see her?
>
> Neither preacher nor admonisher,
> neither counselor nor murderer.
> How will my friends and buddies
> have a good time in the city?
>
> How long do we have to wait for your arrival,
> the tall-statured love?
> What is the scheduled date for the doomsday?
> At least you will know this.
>
> *kab thahrega dard-e dil kab raat basar hogi*
> *sunte the voh aaeinge sunte the sahar hogi*
>
> *kab jaan lahu hogi kab ashk guhar hoga*
> *kis din teri shunvaii ae diida-e tar hogi*

kab mehkegi fasl-e gul kab mehkega maikhaana
kab sub-h-e sukhan hogi kab shaam-e nazar hogi

vaa'iz hai n zaahid hai nasseh hai n qaatil hai
ab shahar mein yaaron ki kis tarah basar hogi

kab tak abhi raah dekhein ae qaamat-e jaanaana
kab hashr mu'ayyan hai tujhko to khabar hogi

कब ठहरेगा दर्द-ए दिल कब रात बसर होगी
सुनते थे वो आएंगे सुनते थे सहर होगी

कब जान लहू होगी कब अश्क गुहर होगा
किस दिन तेरी शुनवाई ऐ दीदा-ए तर होगी

कब महकेगी फ़स्ल-ए गुल कब महकेगा मयख़ाना
कब सुब्ह-ए सुख़न होगी कब शाम-ए नज़र होगी

वाइज़ है न ज़ाहिद है नासेह है न क़ातिल है
अब शहर में यारों की किस तरह बसर होगी

कब तक अभी राह देखें ऐ क़ामत-ए जानाना
कब हश्र मुअय्यन है तुझको तो ख़बर होगी

The opening line speaks for the lover, but from the second line, the social context starts to unfold, one layer after another. Who represents the tearful eye? Who is waiting for a hearing? What is the significance of 'wait' here? The poet is waiting for a time when his whole being will transform itself into blood, when a tear will become a pearl. What kind of city is that which the poet is referring to: a city that has no 'vaa'iz', 'zaahid', no 'naaseh', no 'qaatil'? What kind of beloved is this tall-statured beauty? We know it from the last line that the beloved here is not that of blood and bones. She is something different. She knows when the doomsday will arrive. The doomsday itself could be the symbol of time when forces of oppression collide with the will of the people.

Faiz wrote a ghazal with the following matl'a: *'ham ne sab sh'er mein sanvaare the/ham se jitney sukhan tumhaare the'* (I metamorphosed and beautified in couplets all the love talk that I used to have with you). When you transform something into a couplet, you turn a thing upside down or inside out. The ability to do this is the inner urge of creativity to construct heart-pulling, everlasting poetry. It is not about the ability to have a conversation; it is about the ability to listen imaginatively, which is like climbing the first step on the stair of creative action. That is why when Faiz speaks, it is difficult to say whether he is addressing the beloved or the people or the country. Because he does this with the help of creative metaphors, the reader has to keep thinking of the subject that the poet is alluding to. But very soon, the reader becomes part of the brilliance of 'taghazzul' and the flow for social justice. One excellent and famous example of this is the following laconic ghazal.

Neither have you come,
nor the long night of waiting has ended.
Dawn was in search, and it has edged
time and again.

My engagement during the days
of my madness of love
had great purpose,
though my heart suffered badly
in the process.

The evening I spent listening to
the honorable preacher,
has certainly ended with my wandering
in the alley of love.

Imagine something that was not
mentioned in the story!
Sadly that very matter
has hurt the authority the most.

Neither flowers blossomed,
nor was there a meeting with her.
What a strange way to spend the spring!

I don't know what terrible things
the flower-picker did to the garden,
the gentle breeze was so restless
when it passed by my cell in the jailhouse.

tum aae ho na shab-e intizaar guzri hai
talaash mein hai sahar baar baar guzri hai

junuun mein jitni bhi guzri bakaar guzri hai
agarche dil pe kharaabi hazaar guzri hai

hui hai hazrat-e naaseh se guftugu jis shab
voh shab zaruur sar-e kuu-e yaar guzri hai

voh baat saare fasaane mein jis ka zikr na tha
voh baat un ko bahut nagavaar guzri hai

na gul khile hain na unse mile na mai pi hai
a'jiib rang mein ab ke bahaar guzri hai

chaman pe ghaarat-e gul chiin se jaane kya guzri
qafas se aaj saba beqaraar guzri hai

तुम आये हो न शब-ए इन्तेज़ार गुज़री है
तलाश में है सहर बार बार गुज़री है

जुनूँ में जितनी भी गुज़री बकार गुज़री है
अगरचे दिल पे ख़राबी हज़ार गुज़री है

हुई है हज़रत-ए नासेह से गुफ़्तुगू जिस शब
वो शब ज़रूर सर-ए कू-ए यार गुज़री है

वो बात सारे फ़साने में जिस का ज़िक्र न था
वो बात उन को बहुत नागवार गुज़री है

न गुल खिले हैं न उनसे मिले न मय पी है
अजीब रंग में अब के बहार गुज़री है

चमन पे ग़ारत-ए गुल चीं से जाने क्या गुज़री
क़फ़स से आज सबा बेक़रार गुज़री है

This is an exemplary ghazal, maybe one of his best. At one level, it is the lover waiting for his beloved and expressing his love and longing, but at another level it is all about social change and an uneasy longing for freedom. There are some other ghazals too that lend themselves to this two-way or multiple interpretations. Here are the opening couplets (matl'as) of some of the popular ghazals and we are leaving it to the reader's imagination about how they connect with them. These ghazals, when read in entirety, are extraordinary from the viewpoint of style, presentation and the hidden message.

1.

Let the breeze of the new spring
pour more colour into flowers.
I want you to come back
for the garden to glow more.

gulon mein rang bhare baad-e nau bahaar chale
chale bhi aao ki gulshan ka kaarobaar chale

गुलों में रंग भरे बाद-ए नौ बहार चले
चले भी आओ कि गुलशन का कारोबार चले

2.

Don't ask about the evening of separation.
It came and went by.
It was my heart that soothed
and it was my life that regained its balance.

shaam-e firaaq ab na puuch aaii aur aa ke tal gaii
dil tha ki phir bahal gaya jaan thi k phir sambhal gaii

शाम-ए फ़िराक अब न पूछ आई और आ के टल गई
दिल था कि फिर बहल गया जाँ थी कि फिर संभल गई

Maqt'a of this ghazal has a prophetic quality. It is from this
ghazal that the novelist Qurratulain Hyder took the phrase
'*akhir-e shab ke ham-safar*' for the title of her masterpiece
novel that fetched her the prestigious Jnanpith Award.

The fellow-travellers
of the later part of the evening—
Faiz, where did they go?
Where did we leave gentle breeze?
Where did morning go?

aakhir-e shab ke ham-safar 'Faiz' na jaane kya hue
rah gaii kis jagah saba sub-h kidhar nikal gaii

आख़िर-ए शब के हम-सफ़र 'फ़ैज' न जाने क्या हुए
रह गई किस जगह सबा सुबह किधर निकल गई

3.

Others are spreading the word
that I'm in love with you.
It is not something bad.
It is not a charge, it's an honour.

ham par tumhaari chaah ka ilzaam hi to hai
dushnaam to nahien hai ye ikraam hi to hai

हम पर तुम्हारी चाह का इल्ज़ाम ही तो है
दुश्नाम तो नहीं है ये इकराम ही तो है

4.

Bring forth the order of my execution,
In fairness, I should see it too.
Who are the ones whose signatures
are found at the top of the warrant?

laao to qatl-nama mera main bhi dekh luun
kis kis ki mohr hai sar-e mahzar lagi hui

लाओ तो क़त्ल-नामा मेरा मैं भी देख लूँ
किस किस की मोहर है सर-ए महज़र लगी हुई

This ghazal was written after the execution of Prime Minister Zulfiqar Ali Bhutto during the military regime of General Zia-ul-Haq. For Pakistan, the army takeovers and martial law impositions, one after another, and later the loss of its eastern part, were big historical shocks. Faiz captured the somber mood in his heart-rending ghazal-poem 'Dhaka Se Vaapsi Par'. In just in five couplets, the poet packs so much sadness that pulls at the heartstrings. Under the surface there are sparks of hope: 'we shall become friends again; we shall wipe out marks of blood'. This gives a new turn to a poem that is filled with despair. This is Faiz at his best. Hope, for him, is a higher vision of life. Losing hope is not only a personal loss, it is the death of the very process of creation and evolution.

We are aliens now
after so many pleasant encounters.
But how many meetings would it take
for us to be friends again?

When are we going to witness
the spring of spotless greens?
How many rainy seasons would it take
to clean the marks of blood?

Those were very painful moments when
the love affair ended.
Those were merciless mornings after
many delightful nights.

My heart wanted it but
its helplessness was acute.
We couldn't share our complaints
after we had prayed for long together.

Faiz, you said something
from the depths of your heart,
but what you wanted to say
was lost in the dissonance of voices.

ham ke thahre ajnabi itni mudaraaton ke baa'd
phir baneingein aashna kitni mulaqaaton ke baa'd

kab nazar mein aayegi bedaagh sabze ki bahaar
khuun ke dhabbe dhuleinge kitni barsaaton ke baa'd

the bahut bedard lamhe khatm-e dard-e i'shq ke
thiin bahut besabr subhein mehrbaan raaton ke baa'd

dil to chaaha par shikast-e dil ne mohlat hi na di
kuchh gile shikve bhi kar lete munaajaaton ke baa'd

un se jo kahne gaye the Faiz jaan sadqa kiye
an-kahi hi rah gaii voh baat sab baaton ke baa'd

हम कि ठहरे अजनबी इतनी मुदारातों के बा'द
फिर बनेंगे आश्ना कितनी मुलाक़ातों के बा'द

कब नज़र में आएगी बे-दाग़ सब्ज़े की बहार
ख़ून के धब्बे धुलेंगे कितनी बरसातों के बा'द

थे बहुत बेदर्द लम्हे ख़त्म-ए दर्द-ए इश्क़ के
थीं बहुत बे-मेहर सुब्हें मेहरबाँ रातों के बा'द

दिल तो चाहा पर शिकस्त-ए दिल ने मोहलत ही न दी
कुछ गिले शिकवे भी कर लेते मुनाजातों के बा'द

उन से जो कहने गए थे 'फ़ैज़' जाँ सद्क़ा किए
अन-कही ही रह गई वो बात सब बातों के बा'द

Faiz's thought process is revolutionary, but his poetic voice is not loud or thundering. It is artistic, mellow, soft and lyrical. He doesn't sound like a customary revolutionary poet. He is as much a love poet, an exceptional one for whom we can say *'barah na harf n guft ankamaal-e goyaa iist'*, meaning 'speaking loud or direct is not the insignia of excellence in creativity'. His tone is soft, as his heart is seared with the pain of love. His poetic presence can be compared to a dainty dimly lit lamp that is burning slowly. The pain of this slow smoldering is melting everything that has the potential to metaphorically create a deeply lasting form of turbulence. And with the intensity of the aesthetic beauty, the 'creative jewel' is fully illuminated.

Faiz's greatness lies in the fact that he did not sacrifice his aesthetic sense at the altar of partynost or a given agenda. Using his creative sensibility, Faiz produced verse that is a hallmark of beauty, magnificence, charm and demeanour, and more importantly, has its roots in shared culture; deep-seated compassion; empathy; tolerance; an all-encompassing, smoldering love and a profound yearning for a better tomorrow. All these elements put together have created a panacea for the renewal of the human spirit and dignity of humankind. Faiz makes a mark on the human heart. Some part of this may fall apart with time, but there is a significant portion whose brightness will never diminish. Faiz's work, we hope, will continue to radiate light and its creative force will forever guide the human spirit to search for a vision that is humanistic and cosmic. In his own words:

> I was serene and I stayed calm,
> not restless like the fervent Farhad,
> but is there anyone in the city
> who is exactly like us?

> *ham sahl-talab kaun se Farhaad the lekin*
> *ab shahar mein tere koi ham sa bhi kahaan hai*

> हम सहल-तलब कौन से फ़रहाद थे लेकिन
> अब शहर में तेरे कोई हम सा भी कहाँ है

Professor V.G. Kiernan (1913–2009) from the University of Edinburgh in the UK, a scholar of oriental languages including Urdu, was a close friend of Faiz and Alys. His seminal work *Poems by Faiz*[3] set a standard for both the translation and transliteration of Faiz's poems and ghazals. The success of that work depended on the fact that Kiernan placed Faiz's poetic contribution in its proper context, that included the literary and cultural history of the subcontinent and, more importantly, events in the poet's life. This kind of synchronization is important for

---

[3]V.G. Kiernan, *Poems by Faiz*, New Delhi: Oxford University Press, 1971.

understanding any poet's work, but it is especially important for Faiz, who spent several years in incarceration and many more years globetrotting for fear of returning to his beloved land that saw military coups and the imposition of severe restrictions on the free expression of views by writers and poets in his lifetime. Many other translators of Faiz that came after Kiernan did not follow his lead and, as a result, we have books that are missing the connection between the poet's life and his work. Also, because many of the translators did not delve deep into the metaphorical structures of Faiz's poetry, the results were less than satisfying. Surinder Deol has established himself as a highly proficient translator of Urdu verse through his translations of Mir, Ghalib and Sahir. More recently, his collaboration with me on my book *The Urdu Ghazal* required the translation of scores of Urdu poets covering three centuries. He places great emphasis on a true representation of the poet's voice, notwithstanding the challenges inherent in translating poetry from one language to the other. Further, Surinder provides useful insights into the evolution of Faiz's work, from its early days to the time of its full fruition, from its proverbial youthful passionate love to an all-embracing love of humanity and a holistic vision, with introductory notes on poems and ghazals that the reader would find extremely useful. Faiz's wizardry lies in his ability to combine love with reality, aesthetic sensibility with lyricism, a sense of grief with optimism, and worldly phenomena with a universal vision. Surinder's work keeps Faiz's allure alive and pulsating. It is a book that admirers of Faiz's poetry would love and cherish.

AUTHOR'S NOTE

At the end of my final year in college, the students organized a cultural evening, a celebration of the end of the academic year. As the function was reaching its conclusion, the name of a singer was announced, and a young, lean, turbaned Sikh boy came to the stage carrying a harmonium, which he gently placed on a small table. A tabla player soon joined him. He sang couplets and qat'as written by different poets, including some by Faiz, that got everyone's attention, especially with his mellow and flawless delivery of the poets' words. The college was DAV College in Jalandhar and the young ghazal singer was Jagjit Singh, who, in the coming decades, would redefine the art of ghazal singing. That was my early introduction to Faiz. Since I was already very fond of progressive poets like Sahir Ludhianvi, I promptly put Faiz in the same category—a progressive poet who also cared deeply about the well-being of workers and farmers. This perception, though simplistic, lasted for a long time.

It was only later that I had the chance to read some thought-provoking and perceptive articles by Professor Gopi Chand Narang on Faiz and to hear him talk about Faiz's poetic contributions, opening a new window for me to look afresh at the poet's work. Professor Narang's revealing findings and discerning interpretations prompted me to go back to Faiz's poetry collections, starting with *Naqsh-e Faryadi*. I discovered something that I had missed before: Faiz is a progressive poet, but he is also different from every other progressive poet. He talks about his *two loves*: love for the beloved and compassion for the deprived whose lives are filled with pain and suffering, and for each of these loves, he has created a world that is entirely different from the other. On one side, there is a world where the sun rises, spreading its golden rays and bringing with it a gentle breeze. The ambience is colourful: there is freshness coupled with luminosity; the air smells of blissful intoxication; dream-like pleasures are found everywhere; spring stays forever, filled with thousands of flowers in all colours and hues. Amid this natural beauty, there is the beauty of the beloved—honeyed lips, half-sleepy alluring eyes, tresses that hide constellations of stars. On the other side, there is a world where the sunrise is always blemished, and there are traces of pain and grief, which are found everywhere. There is an unsavoury profusion of sorrow, where nights are dark and deep, hiding an abundance of tears and sighs. If people raise their voices for freedom and social justice, there are jailhouses, shackles and hanging posts. Although these two worlds are very different, they coexist, overlap, intermingle, meld and mesh.

Professor Narang has dramatically enhanced our understanding by his close reading: that there is also a third side in Faiz's evolutionary love. This side of his revolutionary poetry lies hidden in the deep structure of his Sufi-inspired metaphorical language. This is the love of the beyond, the invisible, of the unity that connects all human beings and nature with one unapparent thread; it is the primal cry of the human soul for making a deep connection with the Absolute. It is the same fountainhead of love about which the rishis of ancient India wrote volumes, and saints such as Kabir, Baba Farid and Bhulleh Shah wrote ecstatic melodies. This third side of love was always present in Faiz's poetry, but it took the careful gaze of Professor Narang to discern it and to talk about it. I would have said more about

Faiz in the form of an Introduction or a Preface, but after reading the Foreword, I do not see any utility in adding those. Even this brief note does not add anything new that is not already covered in the Foreword.

Professor Narang gave me the honour of translating his seminal work on Ghalib into English.[1] That task, because of its complexity, took several years to complete. Even before that work was published in 2017, we started collaborating on another exciting project about the evolution and flowering of the Urdu ghazal.[2] Professor Narang is a transformational figure and I consider myself extremely fortunate that I got to know him well, and to have had the opportunity to work with him. During all these years, I have enjoyed his trust and friendship, which means a lot to me. Without his guidance, I would have never known Faiz as I know him now, and I would not have picked up the courage to write a book about him.

I am also grateful to Dr Syed Taqi Abedi, poet, critic and highly respected literary personality from Toronto, Canada. He was very kind to share with me his monumental research compilation on Faiz, containing dozens of articles, essays, critical analyses and accounts of people who had known Faiz as a person. I found those materials extremely useful. His willingness to help me as I was writing this book was quite reassuring.

I want to thank my wife and partner, Daler Aashna Deol, who makes it possible for me to have the space and time for these fascinating literary explorations. For this book on

---

[1]Gopi Chand Narang, *Ghalib: Innovative Meanings and the Ingenious Mind*, trans. Surinder Deol, New Delhi: Oxford University Press, 2017.
[2]Gopi Chand Narang, *The Urdu Ghazal: A Gift of India's Composite Culture*, trans. Surinder Deol, New Delhi: Oxford University Press, 2020.

Faiz and my earlier works on Ghalib and Sahir, she was an insightful critic, always challenging me to stretch the boundaries of what is possible, to realize something truly unique and exceptional.

To the reader, I would say that if you like great poetry, you have come to the right place. There is nothing in modern Urdu poetry as stimulating and electrifying as Faiz. When you read Faiz, you immediately fall in love with his lyrical taghazzul and his deep commitment to ending human suffering in whatever form it exists. The authenticity of his life's motto crossed all boundaries—national, ethnic, cultural, regional—to embrace the mantle of a true humanistic visionary. With the sheer magic and musical flow of his words, Faiz celebrates the sublimity and goodness of human spirit, and that is why he will always occupy a special place in the dazzling assemblage of Urdu's great poets.

September 2021   Surinder Deol
                                                Potomac, Maryland
                                                            USA

one

A MILLION DELIGHTS

In his first poems, Faiz appears as a bourgeois aesthete and a poet fond of decadence. I myself and most of the poets of our generation have experienced such a period. Among us, some have quickly come out of this swamp and some even now continue to struggle in it. Faiz's poems of this period are filled with images wrapped in pink muslin dresses, very tired with sleep and intoxicated with sensuality. They have no direct relationship with life. There is a gulf between them and life, a gulf called personal aestheticism, of which Faiz was unable to rid himself for a long time.

—Poet N.M. Rashed in his introduction to
Naqsh-e Faryadi[1]

The publication of this collection is a sort of admission of defeat. A few of its poems are perhaps tolerable, but a few tolerable poems don't make up a publishable book. In principle, I should have waited until I had accumulated poems of this kind in sufficient number, but it has begun to seem pointless to wait any longer.

—Faiz on his first poetry collection
Naqsh-e Faryadi[2]

---

[1]Carlo Coppola, *Urdu Poetry, 1935–1970: The Progressive Episode,* Karachi: Oxford University Press, 2018, p. 342.
[2]Hameed, ed., *Daybreak,* p. 54.

THE EARLY YEARS

Faiz didn't like to talk about himself and his life, but there were a few exceptions. One such occasion was his March 1984 talk to the Asia Study Group in Islamabad, which happened about eight months before his death.[3] He started his speech jokingly, saying that he had reached the age which Disraeli had called 'the age of anecdotes'. Any description of Faiz's early life must start with his father, Sultan Muhammad Khan, whom he called 'a nineteenth-century adventurer, who had a far more colourful life than I had'. Faiz was right about this characterization because the elder Khan was a character out of nineteenth-century fiction, who led a life that resembled a hero from a fairy tale: a rags-to-riches story with many rises and falls. Sultan Muhammad Khan was born in an impoverished landless family, but he was a young boy who was passionate about learning. While he cared about others' animals and took them to graze for a nominal reward, he artfully sneaked into a neighbouring primary school. Leaving his cattle to take care of themselves, he learned languages and other subjects. His efforts bore fruit and he earned a scholarship that took him to high school. Seeing no future for himself in Sialkot, a backward provincial town, he left for Lahore, where he lived in a mosque, doing odd jobs and learning to speak English. Then, as it happens in all adventure stories, one day, an Afghan diplomat, who also prayed at the same mosque, having been greatly influenced by the young boy's English-speaking skills, offered to take him to Kabul, Afghanistan, to be the interpreter of Emir Abdur Rahman,

---

[3]Sheema Majeed, *Culture and Identity: Selected English Writings of Faiz*, Karachi: Oxford University Press, 2005.

the country's dynastic ruler. During his stay in Kabul, the lucky boy met an Englishwoman, Dr Lillian Hamilton, the court physician.[4] The precise nature of this relationship is shrouded in mystery, but this woman played an important role in Sultan Muhammad's life. While he was close to the Emir and was even writing his biography, there were palace intrigues (some people perhaps didn't like an outsider having such great influence), and Sultan Muhammad found a good reason to flee Afghanistan and briefly returned to his village Kala Qader.

This stay in his native village was shortlived. The young adventurer soon showed up in London as Afghanistan's part-time ambassador and a part-time student at Cambridge University, where he earned a degree in Law and struck up a casual friendship with another student and aspiring poet from Sialkot, Muhammad Iqbal. Sultan Muhammad Khan completed a two-volume biography of the Emir, and as a result, he earned more by way of his salary and interestingly more goody bags from the new ruler, Emir Habibullah Khan. But again, like in most fiction, nearly all of the money was lost due to the sins of profligacy. Neither broke nor a rich man, Sultan Muhammad Khan returned to Sialkot and set up his legal practice. His wives and mistresses from Afghanistan joined him there. Because he had no male heir yet, he decided to marry again, this time, a young woman named Sultan Fatima, from a neighbouring village. This marriage fulfilled the intended purpose and four sons were born: Tufail, the eldest, rose to be a civil judge; Faiz

---

[4]Dr Hamilton published a book about her time in Afghanistan that provided useful information to English readers about an exotic country and its people. Lillian Hamilton, *A Vizier's Daughter: A Tale of the Hazara War*, London: John Murray, 1900.

himself; Inayat joined the army and attained the rank of a major and Bashir, the youngest, was both physically and mentally handicapped. He died a slow and painful death.

Faiz was born in village Kala Qader in 1911, but there was some confusion about his birth date. School records showed 7 January, while the municipal records mentioned his date of birth as 13 February. Faiz grew up in a household where Persian, Punjabi and Urdu were spoken. By the time he finished his education, he was fluent in five languages: English, Arabic and the three mentioned above.

Faiz mentioned three things in his presentation to the Asia Study Group that paved his way from his early years to be a lover of learning, a lecturer in a college, a poet and a journalist. First, next to his house in Sialkot, there was a bookshop that functioned like a lending library for a small cost. Most of his pocket money went into borrowing books. The books he read included Urdu novels by Abdul Haleem Sharar and Ratan Nath Sarshar, and European classics that included Dickens, Conan Doyle, Tolstoy and Hardy. Second, the fact that he was growing up in a town that had produced a poet like Iqbal was a source of great inspiration to be a poet himself. Third, there was a primary school nearby that became the venue of a mushaira once every month, and it was at this mushaira that he won a prize of one rupee for his foray into verse-making. Faiz left Sialkot after his matriculation and a faculty of arts (FA) degree for Lahore, a city that he loved until the last day of his life.

GOVERNMENT COLLEGE, LAHORE

In pre-Partition India, Government College, Lahore, had the reputation of being the most coveted institution of higher learning. Nearly half the professors were British nationals, and even the Indian professors were men of highest academic attainments. Faiz had followed the same educational path as Iqbal in terms of being a student at the Scott Mission School[5] and Murray College in Sialkot,[6] and he aspired to be a student at Government College in Lahore which Iqbal had attended 30 years before, but the admission into the bachelor's degree programme was not easy. This is where Sultan Muhammad Khan, Faiz's father, thought of using his brief acquaintance with Iqbal from when both of them had attended Cambridge. The distinguished poet obliged. Faiz took Iqbal's letter of recommendation to Qazi Fazal-ul Haq, the college principal. He got the admission, but to his dismay, Qazi Sahib didn't return the signed letter from Iqbal.

The year was 1929. Lahore was a modern city compared to Sialkot. There were cars on the streets and women moving around freely. For Faiz, this was a new world that offered a treasure trove of new opportunities. The college

---

[5]Faiz arrived in the sixth or seventh grade at the Scott Mission School in Sialkot. Allama Iqbal, another great literary figure produced by Sialkot, had graduated from the same school in 1893. Two teachers from the school who were highly respected Quranic scholars, namely, Maulvi Mir Ibrahim Sialkoti and Maulvi Mir Hasan, had a lasting influence on Faiz's intellectual development. Munshi Sirajjuddin, who was the patron of local poets, was not impressed by Faiz's initial forays into versification and strongly advised him to focus on his studies and not waste time writing poetry.

[6]Faiz spent two years at Murray College for his intermediate college degree. Early on, he drew inspiration from poets such as Ameer Minai and Daagh Delhvi, and under the influence of one of his professors, Yusuf Saleem Chishti, he started to write and recite ghazals. It was at one of the Murray College mushairas that Faiz recited one of his ghazals for the first time. The following couplet from the ghazal was the only one that stayed in the mind of one of his fellow students: *'lab band hain saaqi meri aankhon ko pila de/voh jaam jo minnat-kashe sehba nahien hota.'*

had a great learning environment, but the real gift for young Faiz was getting to know professors with whom he developed long-term friendships, and benefitted from their sponsorship later in his life.[7]

Faiz remained in the college for several years, earning a BA degree in Arabic, an MA in English and another MA in Arabic from Punjab University's Oriental College. But while he was in the second year of college, a great tragedy struck the family. During the wedding celebration of Faiz's younger sister Bali, his father Sultan Muhammad Khan died suddenly of cardiac arrest. It was one thing to mourn the loss of his father, but the added shock came in the form of the discovery that the family's financial prosperity was just a façade. His father had mortgaged lands and had run a debt of more than ₹80,000. The burden of supporting the family fell on the shoulders of Tufail, the eldest brother, and Faiz, who was a student and had no regular source of income.

Faiz didn't take long to show his poetic talent at college. *Ravi,* the college magazine, carried some couplets by him in its October 1929 issue. Gradually, Faiz also found a place in the college mushaira and other literary activities. Kanhaiya Lal Kapoor wrote an interesting article about it:

> I remember the day when Faiz rose like a black cloud and within a short period he had the whole literary world under his spell. This was probably an evening in

---

[7]Faiz met here three extraordinary teachers, Ahmad Shah Patras Bokhari (English), Sufi Ghulam Mustafa Tabassum (Persian) and Dr Mohammad Deen Taseer (English). Dr Taseer later ended up becoming Faiz's brother-in-law when he married Alys, the younger sister of Taseer's wife Christabel. The first poem written by Faiz titled 'Mere Maa'suum Qatil' was published in the Government College magazine *Ravi.*

July 1936 when Government College held its annual mushaira. Many senior poets like Dr M.D. Taseer, Sufi Ghulam Mustafa Tabassum, Hafiz Jalandhari, Hari Chand Akhtar, Akhtar Shirani, Charagh Hasan Hasrat and Ahsan Danish were present. Faiz was only 24 years old at that time. As per the rules of mushaira, younger poets were first called to present their kalaam. When Faiz's turn came, he read a qat'a 'Raat Yuun Dil Mein Teri [Khoii] Hui Yaad Aai' and his poem 'Mujhse Pehli Si Mohabbat [Meri] Mahbuub N Maang'. The listeners were mesmerized. When Faiz left the stage, everyone had just one question on their mind: who is this young poet? From where did he get this lyricism and this unique set of ideas? The next day all Urdu papers carried excerpts of Faiz's poem, and it created quite a stir.[8]

MAO COLLEGE, AMRITSAR

Faiz moved to Amritsar in 1935 to join the Mohammadan Anglo-Oriental (MAO) College as a lecturer in English. His stay in this city proved to be the most transformational in his professional and personal life. He soon became friends with Mahmooduzzafar (or Mahmood in short), an Oxford-educated ideologue who was in charge of the college in the absence of a principal, and his wife, Dr Rashid Jahan, a gynecologist, who was a dedicated member of the Communist Party. The post of principal was soon filled by

---

[8]Kanhaiya Lal Kapoor, 'Phir Nazar Mein Phool Mehke', in Syed Abedi, ed. *Faiz Fahmi*, Lahore: Multi Media Affairs, 2011. This short excerpt from the article, which was published in Urdu, has been translated, edited and condensed by the author.

M.D. Taseer, whom Faiz had known well at Government College. Taseer had gone to England in 1936 for higher studies and when he returned he brought with him not only a doctoral degree in literature from Cambridge (the first Indian to achieve this distinction), but also an Englishwoman named Christabel. As Taseer was a favourite pupil of Iqbal's, the latter, in spite of his ill health, spent time in drafting their marriage agreement and even acted as a qazi at the nikah ceremony. It was at Taseer's place that Faiz met Alys, Christabel's younger sister who was visiting her sister's adopted country, but got stuck there when war broke out in 1939. There was no way for her to safely return to England as the war had quickly gathered momentum and the world was suddenly a more dangerous place. When Faiz married Alys, Taseer, who was his teacher and boss, became his brother-in-law. Interestingly, 1939 was also the year when Faiz secured a place in a doctoral programme at Cambridge. Like Alys, his dream to go to England remained just that, a dream. But on the flipside, if both of them had gone to England at that time, they would have probably never married.

While in England, both Mahmood and Taseer had known Sajjad Zaheer and had contributed to the development of the idea that later fructified as the All-India Progressive Writers Association (AIPWA). Working with Sajjad Zaheer and Ahmad Ali, Mahmood and Dr Rashid Jahan had published a book of polemical stories titled *Angaarey* (Embers) which angered conservative Muslim clerics and their supporters. The effort didn't go very well; the book didn't have much literary value and the British were very keen to maintain their relations with the Muslim conservatives, and therefore they took no time in banning the book.

It was at the home of Mahmood and Rashid Jahan, that

Faiz met Sajjad Zaheer. The AIPWA held its first conference in Lucknow in April 1936, in which Faiz took an active part. Mahmood and Dr Rashid Jahan were also responsible for introducing to Faiz the communist ideology, especially Marx and Engels' work *The Communist Manifesto*. They also encouraged him to reach out to factory workers and farmers and teach them revolutionary ideas. This brought Faiz to the notice of the police establishment and a time came when he felt that he was no longer safe in Amritsar. In 1940, he decided to return to Lahore and took a teaching position at Hailey College of Commerce.

ADAB-E LATIF

One of the ideas that were discussed at the AIPWA Conference in Lucknow was related to creating new channels for communicating leftist and revolutionary thinking to the masses through new literary journals. These journals were also supposed to be platforms for writers (poets and storytellers) with leftist leanings, who found it difficult to get their work published anywhere else. This idea appealed to Chaudhry Bashir Ahmed who established a new journal called *Adab-e Latif* and asked Faiz to be its first editor. Faiz was reluctant to take up this responsibility in addition to his teaching and public outreach activities that he enjoyed, but he was pressured by friends into accepting this new role as a magazine editor. This assignment was short-lived, but it had a massive impact on Urdu magazine journalism. The 1941 annual edition of the magazine (saalnaama) made history because it carried within its pages writings that changed the course of fiction writing in Urdu. For example, it had stories the likes of which had not been written before in Urdu, and even if they had been

written, no magazine would have published them. These
were Saadat Hasan Manto's 'Kali Shalwar', Ismat Chughtai's
'Lihaaf' and Mumtaz Mufti's 'Badmaash'. Court cases for
publishing obscene materials followed. The magazine had
to be shut down. Faiz defended these works as 'masterpieces
of progressive literature', but circumstances forced him
to put this episode behind him as he decided to join the
Indian Army in 1942, a job that would move him from
Lahore to Delhi.

ALYS GEORGE

Alys George, born in 1913, belonged to a family of small
booksellers in London. There were three boys and two
girls. Alys, along with her elder sister Christabel, showed
early interest in theatre and other artistic activities. As
the family had no financial means to support the girls'
education beyond matriculation, they found avenues to
use their skills in jobs that paid little but satisfied their
leftist ideological interests. Alys worked as a secretary
for V.K. Krishna Menon, a brilliant mind but a man of
mercurial temperament and someone difficult to work
with. While working with India League, both Christabel
and Alys came to know several Indian intellectuals who
were dreaming up big things like the formation of the
AIPWA and it included Sajjad Zaheer, M.D. Taseer (who
Christabel later married), Mulk Raj Anand and Iqbal
Singh. M.D. Taseer came back to India in 1936 and
Christabel joined him soon after that. They were married
and had their first child in 1938—an event that brought
Alys to India for what was intended to be a short visit.
But no one knew that a war would erupt soon, making it
impossible for Alys to get back home according to plans.

As young Faiz was a frequent visitor to the Taseer household, he got to know Alys. In her words: 'We walked in the evening. Autumn had set in and winter followed, and in those sunny days and cold, starry nights, our friendship became something special.'[9] Alys took up a job, teaching girls English and French. It is not clear when and how Faiz proposed, but it is known that he faced opposition from his family and it took quite some effort on his part to convince them that Alys was the kind of girl with whom he would like to spend his life.

The wedding was set for October 1941. This was the time when Taseer moved from MAO College in Amritsar to be the principal of S.P. College in Srinagar. The wedding accordingly took place on 26 October 1941. (It is not clear what precisely happened that day.) The baraat consisted of just three people: Faiz, his brother Inayat and another friend. Faiz had brought some Indian clothes for Alys in a small suitcase, and of course, he had a ring for her, purchased with borrowed money. The nikah ceremony took place two days later, and it was performed by the Kashmiri leader Sheikh Abdullah. The marriage followed the contract that Allama Iqbal had prepared for the Taseer–Christabel marriage. Alys got the right to divorce and Faiz was prohibited from marrying again as long as he was married to Alys. While Faiz had to provide for Alys, any income that she earned was her own. When the newly married couple reached Lahore after a short honeymoon in Srinagar, Faiz's mother gave a new Arabic Muslim name to Alys: Kulsoom (meaning a girl with ruddy cheeks).

---

[9]Hameed, ed., *Daybreak*, pp. 318–19.

GHALIB AND IQBAL

Faiz's style of writing, his lyrical flair, his aesthetic sensibility, colourful imagery, the richness of his language that overflows with metaphors, similes and innovative word combinations owe a great deal to two great poets who came before him and who prepared the ground for him to attain greater heights of poetic brilliance. These were Ghalib and Iqbal. Unlike Ghalib, Faiz didn't create new poetic language, but he did learn a valuable lesson from him: the prolific use of metaphors not only helps the poet to attain a great depth of signification, but also to achieve ambiguity and layered innovative meanings that help in creating the text. This no doubt has a captivating effect on the reader. This is how Faiz assessed Ghalib's influence, in terms of bringing Urdu poetry closer to the threshold of modernity, with an emphasis on realism, modes of human experience and diversity of thought.

> Ghalib for the first time liberated the Ghazal from the tyranny of custom and usage, cut away ornamented frills and conventional trivialities, and in a diction all his own, with a montage of telescoped images and multi-associational meanings, made it into an all-purpose instrument of expression for both personal experience and abstract thought. The bewilderment this aroused at first, he treated with contempt ... The bewilderment with time gave place to comprehension and acceptance and his experiments gave to Urdu poetry completely new dimensions in expression— earnestly thoughtful, deeply truthful, wonderfully plastic and evocative, in diction, methodology of expression and analytical perception of experience,

Ghalib was the first of the moderns in Urdu poetry. For his models Ghalib turned to the great treasure house of Persian poetry, particularly to the poets of our own subcontinent, Bedil, Urfi, Naziri, thus restoring to Urdu poetry its broken links with this great heritage. He carried this process a step further by making the Persian language his vehicle for the expression of more expansive themes, descriptive, philosophical, discursive or narrative, an example, so eminently followed later by Allama Iqbal.[10]

Faiz closely followed the academic path that Iqbal had taken many years ago from the schools in Sialkot to Government College in Lahore. Although, as a Marxist, Faiz didn't agree with Iqbal's religious worldview, he deeply appreciated 'the world of man' that Iqbal depicts in his poetry. This is what he said about it.

> Inspite of Iqbal's deep devotion to religion he never mentions the other world or hardly ever mentions the other world except symbolically. There is very little talk of the hereafter in his poetry. There is no mention of any rewards or any punishments in the other world, for the simple reason that since he is the poet of struggle, of evolution, of man's fight against the hostile forces of nature, the forces hostile to the spirit of man, the hereafter in which there is no action, in which there is no struggle, is entirely irrelevant to his thought. Anyway, the ultimate thing is this theme, the theme of man and the universe of man, of man's loneliness and of man's grandeur. He speaks of man's loneliness because man is pitted against so many enemies. First

---

[10]Majeed, *Culture and Identity*, p. 158.

against the forces within him, like the forces of greed, cowardliness, of selfishness, exploitation and, secondly, the forces outside him like the forces of inanimate hostile nature. So he speaks of man as a small atom of passion set against the entire universe. He speaks of man's greatness, in that man is the only creature to accept the challenge of creation, man the microcosm of pain accepts the challenge of the stars and the moon and the sun and the universe. It is this great theme which elevates the verse of Iqbal, towards the end of his days, from the beautiful to the sublime.[11]

NAQSH-E FARYADI

Before we talk about *Naqsh-e Faryadi*, Faiz's first poetry collection, it is appropriate to have an overview of the totality of Faiz's poetical contributions. The following table provides the names of all his poetry collections, their year of publication and the number of compositions each one of them contained. We can see that *Naqsh-e Faryadi* had more poems than any other collection, while *Dast-e Saba*, published after a gap of 12 years, had more ghazals, qat'as and couplets. These publications spanned a total period of 44 years that included tumultuous events like India's Independence, Partition, the creation of Pakistan, jail time, globetrotting and pleasantly receiving some rare honours like the Lenin Peace Prize.

---

[11]Majeed, *Culture and Identity*, pp. 176–7.

Poetical Works by Faiz

Title	Year	Poems	Ghazals	Qat'as	Couplets
Naqsh-e Faryadi	1940	31	14	4	8
Dast-e Saba	1952	21	17	8	16
Zindaan Nama	1956	11	15	7	14
Dast-e Tah-e Sang	1965	15	11	7	14
Sar-e Vaadiye Saina	1971	30	7	6	12
Sham-e Shahr-e Yaaraan	1978	30	8	4	9
Mere Dil Mere Musafir	1980	27	3	2	4
Ghubaar-e Ayyaam	Posthumous	15	7	3	6
Complete Works					
Sare Sukhan Hamare	1982	A numbered collector's edition published in London by an admirer.			
Nuskha Haae Vafa	1984	Includes all poems, ghazals, qat'as and miscellaneous poetical writings.			

Source: Dr Syed Taqi Abedi[12]

Faiz used some metaphoric innovations of Mirza Ghalib as titles of his book. Translating these titles into English however is a challenge. For example, *Naqsh-e Faryadi* has

---

[12]Syed Taqi Abedi, ed., *Faiz Fahmi*, Lahore: Multi-Media Affairs, 2011, pp. 1348–51.

been translated as *Complaining Image*,[13] *The Image of One Who Laments*,[14] *Image of the Supplicant*.[15] Needless to say, these translations do not convey the sheer elegance and philosophical depth of Mirza's expression. Similar problems arise with titles like *Dast-e Saba* and *Dast-e Tah-e Sang*. In this book, therefore, all Faiz book titles are presented in their original form, without any attempt at translation.

Chaudhry Bashir Ahmed, the publisher of *Adab-e Latif*, who had persuaded Faiz to become the first editor of the magazine, also became the first publisher of *Naqsh-e Faryadi* and he used the imprint Maktaba Urdu for the first edition. At the suggestion of his brother, Chaudhry Bashir Ahmed chose a young calligrapher named Mohammad Husain to do the kitaabat. He also took care to select a good quality paper that had not been previously used for Litho printing, a process common at that time. For the cover design, he approached the famous painter Abdur Rahman Chughtai (1894–1975). There was also a proposal to gain Chughtai's commitment for an illustrated edition of Faiz's complete works, on the same lines that he had done for *Divan-e Ghalib,* but this plan was shelved after Faiz was arrested in connection with the Rawalpindi Conspiracy Case.[16]

Naqsh-e Faryadi was an instant hit with both readers and the critics, because these constituencies got something to be excited about in the book. The first half of the book had a lot of romantic poetry that appealed to most readers. The second half was more mature and some critics called it an example of 'romance mixed with reality'. There was

---

[13]Kiernan, *Poems by Faiz.*

[14]Ali Madeeh Hashmi, *Love and Revolution, Faiz Ahmed Faiz, The Authorized Biography*, New Delhi: Rupa Publications, 2016.

[15]Coppola, *Urdu Poetry.*

[16]Siddiqa Begum, ed., *Adab-e Latif*, Faiz Number, Lahore, 1985, pp. 43–8.

a call for social awakening and political change, but it was wrapped in a silky smooth voice, unlike the rumble of thunder associated with traditional revolutionary poetry. Faiz himself talked about the two clear strains in the book.

> The two epochs of the creation of *Naqsh-e Faryadi*, I feel that from 1920 to 1930 and then from 1930 to 1940—these two eras are different from each other, in terms of literature, political conditions and the attitudes and emotions of people. The poems of the first half of *Naqsh-e Faryadi* were written between 1928 and 1934, my student days. Most of these were influenced by the first era (of the 1920s to 1930s). The second half contains poems written after 1935 when I was teaching, and most of them were written in Amritsar, and these relate to the second era (of the 1930s to 1940s).[17]

Abu Mohammad Sahr, in a review of Faiz's poetic style points out, 'After *Naqsh-e Faryadi*, he paid a great deal of attention to life's starkness and bitterness using the niche of reality. He never said goodbye to love. Until the end, he stood at the shore of love and reality.'[18]

This chapter contains a number of selections from *Naqsh-e Faryadi*, starting with a famous qat'a.

QAT'A

Your lost echo reverberated last night—
like spring silently returns to the barren lands;
like the morning breeze glides gently over deserts;

[17]Hashmi, *Love and Revolution*, p. 102.
[18]Abedi, ed., *Faiz Fahmi*, p. 452.

like someone ill recovers without a known remedy.

raat yuun dil mein teri khoii hui yaad aaii
jaise viiraane mein chupke se bahaar aa jaae
jaise sahraaon mein haule se chale baad-e nasiim
jaise biimaar ko bevajh qaraar aa jaae

रात यूँ दिल में तेरी खोई हुई याद आई
जैसे वीराने में चुपके से बहार आ जाए
जैसे सहराओं में हौले से चले बाद-ए-नसीम
जैसे बीमार को बेवजह क़रार आ जाए

◆

QAT'A

My heart is a prisoner of the sorrows of the world
today.
Every part of my being is insatiably touched by a
cry of pain today.
The gathering place of existence is too desolate.
Where is the sadness of the absence of my friend
today?

dil rahiin-e gham-e jahaan hai aaj
har nafas tashna-e fughaan hai aaj
sakht viiraan hai mahfil-e hasti
ae gham-e dost tu kahaan hai aaj

दिल रहीन-ए ग़म-ए जहाँ है आज
हर नफ़स तिश्ना-ए फ़ुग़ाँ है आज
सख़्त वीराँ है महफ़िल-ए हस्ती
ऐ ग़म-ए दोस्त तू कहाँ है आज

◆

'GOD FORBID THAT I SHOULD SEE THE DAY'

This poem appears at the beginning of *Naqsh-e Faryadi*. Faiz wrote it during his student years. It has the feel of a prayer and is very heartwarming for that reason. The flow of words seems to arise from the great depths of the forlorn lover's heart, and they touch the reader with their sincerity, truthfulness and candour. The language is at a low level of complexity compared with the poet's later work, but this simplicity and directness is something that makes the poem more appealing. Coppola[19] guesses that stylistically this poem shows the influence of poets like Hasrat Mohani and Akhtar Shirani, and by implication not of poets like Ghalib and Iqbal, who became major influences in later years. Coppola even reminds us that N.M. Rashed, who had written a foreword for *Naqsh-e Fariyadi*, was correct to point out that 'in his first poems, Faiz appears as a bourgeois aesthete and a poet fond of decadence... Faiz's poems of this period are filled with images wrapped in pink muslin dresses, very tired with sleep, and intoxicated with sensuality.'

> God forbid
> I should see the day when you are desolate—
> when you find your untroubled sleep tainted,
> when your long-lasting joyfulness comes to an
> end, and
> when your life is filled with bitterness.
> Let there be no time—
> when your heart is burdened with grief, and
> when you are vanquished by swarms of despair;
> when you are reduced to quicksilver by hordes of
> anguish;

---

[19]Coppola, *Urdu Poetry*, p. 342

when your loveliness is diminished to be just a
dream, and
when your beauty's pride is humbled.
Let there be no time—
when in the middle of long nights you thirst for
tranquility,
your eyes search for someone to comfort you
just like autumn-damaged longing gasps for
spring, and
no forehead is lowered at your doorsteps
to please you with deceitful humility and fidelity.
And to test your faith by false promises of tomorrow.
Please God—
do not bring back the time when you remember
a heart that is still restless for you,
and an eye that is still waiting for you.

'Khuda Voh Vaqt Na Laaye'
khuda voh vaqt n laaye k sogvaar ho tu
sukuun ki niind tujhe bhi haraam ho jaae
teri musarrat-e paiham tamaam ho jaae
teri hayaat tujhe talkh jaam ho jaae
ghamon se aaiina-e dil gudaaz ho tera
hujuum-e yaas se betaab ho ke rah jaae
vufuur-e dard se siimaab ho ke rah jaae
tera shabaab faqat khwaab ho ke rah jaae
ghurur-e husn saraapa nayaaz ho tera
taviil raaton mein tu bhi qaraar ko tarse
teri nigaah kisi gham-gusaar ko tarse
khazaan-rasiida tamanna bahaar ko tarse
koi jabiin na tere sang-a astaan p jhuke
k jins-e a'jaz o a'qiidat se tujh ko shaad kare
fareb-e vaa'da-e farda p i'timaad kare

khuda voh vaqt n laaye k tujh ko yaad aae
voh dil k tere liye beqaraar ab bhi hai
voh aankh jis ko tera intizaar ab bhi hai

'ख़ुदा वो वक़्त न लाए'
ख़ुदा वो वक़्त न लाए कि सोगवार हो तू
सुकूँ की नींद तुझे भी हराम हो जाए
तेरी मुसर्रत-ए पैहम तमाम हो जाए
तेरी हयात तुझे तल्ख़ जाम हो जाए
ग़मों से आईना-ए दिल गुदाज़ हो तेरा
हुजूम-ए यास से बेताब हो के रह जाए
वुफ़ूर-ए दर्द से सीमाब हो के रह जाए
तेरा शबाब फ़क़त ख़्वाब हो के रह जाए
ग़ुरूर-ए हुस्न सरापा नियाज़ हो तेरा
तवील रातों में तू भी क़रार को तरसे
तेरी निगाह किसी ग़म-गुसार को तरसे
ख़िज़ाँ-रसीदा तमन्ना बहार को तरसे
कोई जबीं न तेरे संग-ए आस्ताँ पे झुके
कि जिंस-ए इज़्ज़ ओ अक़ीदत से तुझ को शाद करे
फ़रेब-ए वादा-ए फ़र्दा पे एतेमाद करे
ख़ुदा वो वक़्त न लाए कि तुझ को याद आए
वो दिल कि तेरे लिए बेक़रार अब भी है
वो आँख जिस को तेरा इंतिज़ार अब भी है

◆

GHAZAL

Ghalib Ahmed, in an essay published in *Adab-e Latif,* mentioned that Faiz went through three phases in his ghazal-writing endeavours. In the first phase, he experimented with purely romantic themes, presumably because of the influence of poets like Akhtar Shirani. In the second phase, he got hold of progressive themes and, as a result, some of his ghazals read like hidden poems. In the third and final phase, he put a distinctive stamp on ghazal writing which was comparable to Ghalib in terms of style and lyricism.[20] The following ghazal is a good example of early romanticism.

Love is not falling on its knees
in supplication to tranquility.
Beauty owes nothing
to the act of a lover's wait.

The limits of your hostility
are well known.
There is no count
of my unfulfilled desires.

Outspread your power
of seeing and observing.
Wine's intoxication
is beyond any measure.

The smile of my friend
is now below the lips.
It is not like spring's
disorderly splendour.

I'm completing
my circle of growth.
This has nothing to do
with loving you.

Who can soothe
the pain of waiting?
Your indifference
is not firmly grounded.

---

[20]Begum, ed., *Adab-e Latif,* p. 169.

Faiz, I want her to live;
her well-being is essential.
How does it matter
that she is not loyal or sincere?

'I'shq Minnat Kash-e Qaraar Nahien'

ish'q minnat kash-e qaraar nahien
husn majbuur-e intizaar nahien

teri ranjish ki intiha maa'luum
hasraton ka meri shumaar nahien

apni nazrein bakher de saaqi
mai b andaazah-e khumaar nahien

zer-e lab hai abhi tabassum-e dost
muntashar-e jalvah-e bahaar nahien

apni takmiil kar raha huun main
varna tujh se to mujh ko pyaar nahien

chaara-e intizaar kaun kare
teri nafrat bhi ustavaar nahien

'Faiz' zinda rahein voh hain to sahi
kya hua gar vafa sh'iaar nahien

'इश्क़ मिन्नत कश-ए क़रार नहीं'

इश्क़ मिन्नत कश-ए क़रार नहीं
हुस्न मजबूर-ए इंतिज़ार नहीं

तेरी रंजिश की इंतिहा मालूम
हसरतों का मेरी शुमार नहीं

अपनी नज़रें बिखेर दे साक़ी
मय ब-अंदाज़ा-ए खुमार नहीं

ज़ेर-ए लब है अभी तबस्सुम-ए दोस्त
मुंतशिर जल्वा-ए बहार नहीं

अपनी तकमील कर रहा हूँ मैं
वर्ना तुझ से तो मुझ को प्यार नहीं

चारा-ए इंतिजार कौन करे
तेरी नफ़रत भी उस्तुवार नहीं

'फ़ैज़' ज़िंदा रहें वो हैं तो सही
क्या हुआ गर वफ़ा-शिआर नहीं

◆

'THE LAST LETTER'

Faiz wrote this poem, and the next one called 'Hasiina-e Khayal Se' (as also another poem titled 'Anjaam', which is not included in this book) because he fell in love when he was a student. This is what he told Amrita Pritam, renowned Punjabi poet and writer, in an interview:

> I fell in love, as happens to everyone at that age. I was 17 or 18, and I fell in love with an Afghan girl who was my playmate when I was a child. Her family had moved from Afghanistan at about the same time as my father. They lived in a village near Lyallpur, and my sister was married in that same village, so I would go there often to see her. One morning, I awoke and saw a beautiful girl feeding her parrot. One look and I was smitten. We would look at each other and eventually progressed to holding hands in secret, but it never went beyond that. Her parents married her off to a rich zamindar. It was a great blow and depressed me for quite a while.[21]

---

[21]Hashmi, *Love and Revolution*, p. 51.

That time, my dear, is not far away
when the pain will block all pathways of life
and the inner sorrow will cross all limits.
My yearning and abortive eyes will get tired.
My tears and my sighs will be snatched away from
me.
My worthless youth will be taken away from me.

Perhaps you will remember a lot about lost love.
You will make your innocent heart unhappy.
You will come to my grave to shed tears.
To offer beautiful flowers from the adolescent springs.

Perhaps you will reject me and walk away from my
tomb.
Perhaps you will laugh at my useless fidelity.
You may not even respect the code of kindness.
You will not care about what goes on inside a
broken heart.

In short, you may laugh at my unrequited love.
You can cry or complain.
Whether you regret the past or be happy about it,
the one who loved you will stay quiet and asleep.

'Aakhri Khatt'

voh vaqt meri jaan bahut duur nahien hai
jab dard se ruk jaaeingi sab ziist ki raahein
aur hadd se guzar jaayega andoh-e nihaani
thak jaaeingi tarsi hui nakaam nigaahein
chhin jaaeinge mujhse mere aansu meri aahein
chhin jaayegi mujhse meri bekaar javaani

shaayad meri ulfat ko bahut yaad karogi
apne dil-e maa'suum ko na-shaad karogi

aaogi meri gor pe tum ashk bahaane
nau-khez bahaaron ke hasien phuul charahne

shaayad meri turbat ko bhi thukra ke chalogi
shaayad meri besuud vafaaon pe hansogi
is vaz'a-e karam ka bhi tumhein ehsaas n hoga
lekin dil-e nakaam ka ehsaas n hoga

alqissa maa'l-e gham-e ulfat pe hanso tum
ya ashk bahaati raho faryaad karo tum
maazi pe nadaamat ho tumhein ya k mussarrat
khaamosh pada soega vaamaandah-e ulfat

'आख़िरी ख़त'

वो वक़्त मेरी जान बहुत दूर नहीं है
जब दर्द से रुक जाएँगी सब ज़ीस्त की राहें
और हद से गुज़र जाएगा अंदोह-ए निहानी
थक जाएँगी तरसी हुई नाकाम निगाहें
छिन जाएँगे मुझसे मेरे आँसू मेरी आहें
छिन जाएगी मुझसे मेरी बेकार जवानी

शायद मेरी उल्फ़त को बहुत याद करोगी
अपने दिल-ए मासूम को नाशाद करोगी
आओगी मेरी गोर पे तुम अश्क बहाने
नौ-ख़ेज़ बहारों के हसीं फूल चढ़ाने

शायद मेरी तुर्बत को भी ठुकरा के चलोगी
शायद मेरी बेसूद वफाओं पे हँसोगी
इस वज़्न-ए करम का भी तुम्हें पास न होगा
लेकिन दिल-ए नाकाम को एहसास न होगा

अल-क़िस्सा मआल-ए ग़म-ए उल्फ़त पे हँसो तुम
या अश्क बहाती रहो फरियाद करो तुम
माज़ी पे नदामत हो तुम्हें या कि मसर्रत
ख़ामोश पड़ा सोएगा वामांदा-ए उल्फ़त

✦

GHAZAL

What did Faiz think of the ghazal as a medium of poetic expression? Here is a comment from one of his essays that gives us a clue. He wrote:

> Of all forms of traditional expression, the *ghazal* is in some ways the most facile and the easiest to manipulate... At the same time, it has a fairly rigid verbal and formal framework which permits little deviation. And then it so easily lends itself to music, and music is so easily integrated into other media like the film or television. All these factors account for the ghazal's popularity among the literary elite. It hobnobs with the former for the same reasons that it repels the latter—it transcends class barriers and, thus, comes to symbolize the 'poetic personality' of an age and is held accountable for all the failings of this age.[22]

Let each dimension of reality
validate itself.
Please allow the infidels
to perform their prayers.

Let the heart be open
to each longing.
Let each moment of helplessness
be highly inventive.

---

[22]Majeed, *Culture and Identity*, pp. 214–15.

Who needs a healer
if pain itself
is offering life?

Love, when hidden,
becomes the talk of the town.
When it comes to the lips,
it becomes a mystery.

I'm looking for a good time
to roll in.
Let the tyranny exceed limits
of good grace.

Faiz, I'm spending my life
and not achieving any wholeness.
Let the secret of what is
and what is not be revealed.

'Har Haqiiqat Majaaz Ho Jaaye'

har haqiiqat majaaz ho jaaye
kaafron ki namaaz ho jaaye

dil rahiin-e niyaaz ho jaaye
be-kasi kaarsaaz ho jaaye

minnat-e chaarah-saaz kaun kare
dard jab jaan-navaaz ho jaaye

i'shq dil mein rahe to rusva ho
lab p aaye to raaz ho jaaye

lutf ka intizaar karta huun
jaur taahadd-e naaz ho jaaye

u'mr be-suud kat rahi hai Faiz
kaash afshaaye raaz ho jaaye

'हर हक़ीक़त मजाज़ हो जाए'

हर हक़ीक़त मजाज़ हो जाए
काफ़िरों की नमाज़ हो जाए

दिल रहीन-ए नियाज़ हो जाए
बेकसी कारसाज़ हो जाए

मिन्नत-ए चारा-साज़ कौन करे
दर्द जब जाँ-नवाज़ हो जाए

इश्क़ दिल में रहे तो रुस्वा हो
लब पे आए तो राज़ हो जाए

लुत्फ़ का इंतिज़ार करता हूँ
जौर ता हद्द-ए नाज़ हो जाए

उम्र बेसूद कट रही है 'फ़ैज़'
काश इफ़शा-ए राज़ हो जाए

◆

'FOR THE BEAUTY OF MY FASCINATION'

As mentioned previously, this poem celebrates the beauty of Faiz's first love. In writing this poem, he was also influenced by a poem by Robert Browning, the famous English poet (1812–1889), on whom he had written a thesis for his MA English examination. Notice the last line: '*mujhe voh ik nazar ik jaavdaani si nazar de de*' (Give me that awareness, that eternal gaze, something that lasts forever). Why is the eye so important for lovers? This is what Joseph Campbell, American mythologist, had to say about it:

> So through the eyes love attains the heart, for the eyes are the scouts of the heart … And when they are in full accord and form… in one resolve, at that time perfect

love is born from what the eyes have made welcome
to the heart. For as all true lovers know, love is perfect
kindness, which is born, there is no doubt, from the
heart and the eyes.[23]

Please give it to me.
Honeyed lips, impeccable forehead,
alluring eyes.
So that once again,
I lose myself
in the embellishments of life.
So that your eyes can take
my whole being in its lap.
Forever, I find comfort within this snare.
From the radiance of beauty
I should never return
to the darkness of this world.

My heart should cleanse itself
from the marks of old yearnings.
I should free myself from the worries of
the incoming grief.
I want my past and future to mesh
into each other, completely.
Give me that awareness,
that eternal gaze,
something that lasts forever.

'Hasiina-e Khayaal Se'

mujhe de de
rasiile hont maa'suumaana peshaani hasiin aankhein

---

[23]Bill Moyers and Joseph Campbell, *The Power of Myth*, New York: Doubleday, 1988.

k main ik baar phir rangiinion mein gharq ho jaauun
meri hasti ko teri ik nazar aaghosh mein le le
hamesha ke liye is daam mein mahfuuz ho jaauun
zia-e husn se zulmaat-e duniya mein n phir aauun
guzushta hasraton ke daagh mere dil se dhul jaaein
main aane vaale gham ki fikr se aazaad ho jaauun
mere maazi o mustaqabil sara-sar mehv ho jaaein
mujhe voh ik nazar ik jaavdaani si nazar de de

'हसीना-ए ख़याल से'

मुझे दे दे
रसीले होंट मा'सूमाना पेशानी हसीं आँखें
कि मैं इक बार फिर रंगीनियों में ग़र्क़ हो जाऊँ
मेरी हस्ती को तेरी इक नज़र आग़ोश में ले ले
हमेशा के लिए इस दाम में महफ़ूज़ हो जाऊँ
ज़िया-ए हुस्न से ज़ुल्मात-ए दुनिया में न फिर आऊँ
गुज़िश्ता हसरतों के दाग़ मेरे दिल से धुल जाएँ
मैं आने वाले ग़म की फ़िक्र से आज़ाद हो जाऊँ
मेरे माज़ी ओ मुस्तक़बिल सरासर महव हो जाएँ
मुझे वो इक नज़र इक जावेदानी सी नज़र दे दे

◆

'MY LOVE, RETURN YOUR BEAUTY TO ME'

The first part of *Naqsh-e Faryadi* (the nearly two dozen poems before 'Mujh Se Pehli Si Mohabbat Meri Mahbuub N Maang') consists of poems and ghazals written by Faiz during his student years. These are romantic compositions, which, according to N.M. Rashed, 'have no relationship with life' or the realities of life in the late 1920s and early 1930s. There is no social or political message in these poems, but they were written with a lot of feelings and interesting word combinations.

My love, even now,
you can return your beauty to me.
My heart still carries the light
of your love's freshness and luminosity.
Your splendour makes the circle
of my life, a slice of paradise.
I feel your presence during my
moments of solitude
in the inner core of my being.
Every little thread of my psyche
still yearns for you.
Every colourless moment
awaits your arrival.
My eyes are fixed
on the path that you take
which is still embellished
for your visit.
How long will
my melancholy-filled existence
suffer one shock after another?
How long will
my life be afflicted
with your lack of kindness?
With sweetness taking a nap
in the depths of your voice,
I will not be able to enter
the sadness of my solitude.
My hazy eyes bearing the impact
of my abundant tears
will not be able to capture
the majesty of your beauty,
and when they call you,
my lips will not get any pleasure.

The melodies of my yearning
will dry up in my throat.
God forbid, they might become
part of my memories.
These old stories can get lost
in the tide of sorrow.
In the layers of my heart,
your visage,
after it is spruced up,
can move away.
The bright illumination
of the house of my heart
can get doused.
God forbid,
the darkness of the strange world
surround you.
My love, even now,
you can return your beauty to me.

'Meri Jaan Ab Bhi Apna Husn Vaapis Pher De Mujh Ko'

meri jaan ab bhi apna husn vaapis pher de mujh ko
abhi tak dil mein tere i'shq ki qandiil raushan hai
tere jalvohn se bazm-e zindagi jannat-b-daaman hai
meri ruuh ab bhi tanhaaii mein tujh ko yaad karti hai
har ik taar-e nafas mein aarzu bedaar hai ab bhi
har ik berang saa'it muntazir hai teri aamad ki
nigaahein bichh rahi hain raasta zarkaar hai ab bhi
magar jaan-e haziin sadme sahegi aakhrish kab tak
teri bemeharion p jaan de gi aakhrish kab tak
teri aavaaz mein soii hui shiiriiniaan aakhir
mere dil ki fasurda khalvaton mein ja n paayeingi
y ashkon ki faraavaani se dhundhlaaii hui aankhein
teri raa'naaiion ki tamkanat ko bhuul jaaeingi

pukaareinge tujhe to lab koi lazzat n paaeinge
gulu mein teri ulfat ke taraane suukh jaaeinge
mubaada yaad-haa-e a'hd-e maazi mehv ho jaaein
y paariin afasaane mauj-haa-e gham mein kho jaaein
mere dil ki tahaon se teri suurat dhull ke beh jaaye
hariim-e i'shq ki sham'a-e darakhshaan bujh ke rah
jaaye
mubaada ajnabi duniya ki zulmat gher le tujh ko
meri jaan ab bhi apna husn vaapis pher de mujh ko

'मेरी जाँ अब भी अपना हुस्न वापस फेर दे मुझ को'

मेरी जाँ अब भी अपना हुस्न वापस फेर दे मुझ को
अभी तक दिल में तेरे इ'श्क़ की क़िंदील रौशन है
तेरे जल्वों से बज़्म-ए ज़िंदगी जन्नत-ब-दामन है
मेरी रूह अब भी तन्हाई में तुझ को याद करती है
हर इक तार-ए नफ़स में आरज़ू बेदार है अब भी
हर इक बेरंग साअत मुंतज़िर है तेरी आमद की
निगाहें बिछ रही हैं रास्ता ज़र-कार है अब भी
मगर जान-ए हज़ीं सदमे सहेगी आख़िरश कब तक
तेरी बेमेहरियों पर जान देगी आख़िरश कब तक
तेरी आवाज़ में सोई हुई शीरीनियाँ आख़िर
मेरे दिल की फ़ुसुर्दा ख़ल्वतों में जा न पाएँगी
ये अश्कों की फ़रावानी से धुँदलाई हुई आँखें
तेरी रानाइयों की तमकनत को भूल जाएँगी
पुकारेंगे तुझे तो लब कोई लज्ज़त न पाएँगे
गुलू में तेरी उल्फ़त के तराने सूख जाएँगे
मबादा याद-हा-ए अहद-ए माज़ी महव हो जाएँ
ये पारीना फ़साने मौज-हा-ए ग़म में खो जाएँ
मेरे दिल की तहों से तेरी सूरत धुल के बह जाए
हरीम-ए इश्क़ की शम-ए दरख़्शाँ बुझ के रह जाए
मबादा अजनबी दुनिया की ज़ुल्मत घेर ले तुझ को
मेरी जाँ अब भी अपना हुस्न वापस फेर दे मुझ को

◆

'THE NIGHT MUSIC'

Naqsh-e Faryadi contains two poems with the same title 'Surud-e Shabaana', but the second poem (reproduced below) is considered to be a better composition. It is one of those poems where we get to know the poet as a recorder of the inner states of a human being and as an artist who paints a picture with his words. The person behind the words is not identified, but maybe he is the poet himself. Whoever he is, the person is in a sombre and depressed mood and that is the same mood which nature is also projecting. So, the person's inner and outer experiences are not very different. There is despair and listlessness and a 'waterfall of silence'. If the poem had ended here, it would have been considered an ordinary poem. What made it extraordinary was the fact that the poet decided to use three powerful metaphors for the purpose of personification or reification. First, there is the 'tired voice of moonlight' that is 'sleeping on dense trees'; second, the Milky Way is saying 'something with half-opened eyes'; third, 'the heart's instrument by its silent strings is filtering blissful intoxication'. The last line brings everything together: longing, dreams and the beautiful face of the beloved! Coppola[24] mentions an important point. Faiz, he thinks, is employing here a psychoanalytic technique called 'synaesthesia', which means that by stimulating one sense organ we can stimulate another, thus forming a chain of responses. In this case, the first metaphor is visual, that leads to the second, which is vocal, which leads to the third, which is feeling or emotion.

Midnight, moon, oblivion.
The gathering of existence

---

[24]Coppola, *Urdu Poetry*, p. 344.

is bleak and dismal.
The silence looks like
an image of invocation.
The assembly of stars
seems to be despairing and listless.
There is a waterfall of silence.
And it is flowing.
On all four sides,
there is a loss of consciousness.
Life is just like a dream.
The world is nothing but a mirage.
It is sleeping on dense trees.
The tired voice of the moonlight.
The Milky Way is saying something
with half-opened eyes.
It is telling stories of love, of sacrifice.
The heart's instrument,
by its silent strings,
is filtering blissful intoxication.
There is longing, and there are dreams,
 and there is your beautiful face!

'Surud-e Shabaana'

niim-shab chaand khud-faraamoshi
mahfil-e hast o buud viiraan hai
paikar-e iltijaa hai khaamoshi
bazm-e anjum fasurda saamaan hai
aabshaar-e sukuut jaari hai
chaar suu bekhudi si taari hai
zindagi juzv-e khwaab hai goya
saari duniya saraab hai goya
so rahi hai ghane darakhton par
chaandni ki thaki hui aavaaz

kahkashaan niimva nigaahon se
kah rahi hai hadiis-e shauq-e niyaaz
saaz-e dil ke khaamosh taaron se
chhan raha hai khumaar-e kaif aagiin
aarzu khwaab tera ruu-e hasiin

'सुरुद-ए शबाना'

नीम-शब चाँद ख़ुद-फ़रामोशी
महफ़िल-ए हस्त ओ बूद वीराँ है
पैकर-ए इल्तिजा है ख़ामोशी
बज़्म-ए अंजुम फ़ुसुर्दा-सामाँ है
आबशार-ए सुकूत जारी है
चार-सू बेख़ुदी सी तारी है
ज़िंदगी जुज़्व-ए ख़्वाब है गोया
सारी दुनिया सराब है गोया
सो रही है घने दरख़्तों पर
चाँदनी की थकी हुई आवाज़
कहकशाँ नीम-वा निगाहों से
कह रही है हदीस-ए शौक़-ए नियाज़
साज़-ए दिल के ख़ामोश तारों से
छन रहा है ख़ुमार-ए कैफ़-आगीं
आरज़ू ख़्वाब तेरा रू-ए हसीं

◆

QAT'A

Often I'm overcome by despair.
My heart likes to stay sad and unhappy.
You give grief and then forget about it.
For me, beneficence is important.

vaqf-e hirmaan o yaas rehta hai
dil hai aksar udaas rahta hai

tum to gham de ke bhuul jaate ho
mujhko ehsaan ka paas rahta hai

वक़्फ़-ए हिरमान ओ यास रहता है
दिल है अक्सर उदास रहता है
तुम तो ग़म दे के भूल जाते हो
मुझको एहसाँ का पास रहता है

◆

QAT'A

My heart's domain is covered with sadness.
Melancholia is now reaching my soul.
The deception of life reveals nature's plan.
In this awareness, the days of my youth are
passing away.

faza-e dil p udaasi bikharti jaati hai
fasurdgi hai k jaan tak utarti jaati hai
fareb-e ziist se kudrat ka mudd'aa maa'luum
y hosh hai k javaani guzarti jaati hai

फ़जा-ए दिल पे उदासी बिखरती जाती है
फ़सुर्दगी है कि जाँ तक उतरती जाती है
फ़रेब-ए ज़ीस्त से क़ुदरत का मुद्दा मालूम
ये होश है कि जवानी गुज़रती जाती है

◆

'THE WAIT'

Who has not waited for the loved one to arrive at some
point in one's life? If you say that it has happened to you,
then this poem conveys an experience that you might
find familiar: '*y aazmaaish-e sabr-e gurezpaa kab tak /* *qasam*
tumhaari bahut gham utha chukka huun main' (Please come

for my tranquility and for my restlessness, I'm really tired).

Days come and go,
but there is no news
about your coming.
The garden of life
is still troubled by spring.
The world of my thoughts
is still in the grip of sorrows.
The unfulfilled desires
which are pledged
to the grief of your separation, my love—
they still live in my serenity.
The long night, my love is still very long.
My sad eyes are thirsty and
are eagerly looking forward to
seeing you.
How long the spring of beauty
can be forbidden
by the lack of constancy?
How long my patience will continue
to be put to the test?
I can swear by your name,
and I can't tell you
how much I have already suffered.
My assertion of patience was wrong.
Please come for my tranquility
and my restlessness,
I'm really drained.

'Intizaar'

guzar rahe hain shab o roz tum nahien aatiin
riyaaz-e ziist hai aazurdah-e bahaar abhi

mere khayaal ki duniya hai sogvaar abhi
jo hasratein tere gham ki kaphail hain pyaari
abhi talak meri tanhaaiion mein basti hain
taviil raatein abhi tak taviil hain pyaari
udaas aankhein teri diid ko tarasti hain
bahar-e husn p paabandi-e jafa kab tak
y aazmaaish-e sabr-e gurezpaa kab tak
qasam tumhaari bahut gham utha chuka huun main
ghalat tha daa'va-e sabr o shakeb aa jaao
qaraar-e khaatar-e be-taab thak gaya huun main

'इंतिज़ार'

गुज़र रहे हैं शब ओ रोज़ तुम नहीं आतीं
रियाज़-ए ज़ीस्त है आज़ुरदा-ए बहार अभी
मेरे ख़याल की दुनिया है सोगवार अभी
जो हसरतें तेरे ग़म की कफैल हैं प्यारी
अभी तलक मेरी तन्हाइयों में बस्ती हैं
तवील रातें अभी तक तवील हैं प्यारी
उदास आँखें तेरी दीद को तरसती हैं
बहार-ए हुस्न पे पाबंदी-ए जफ़ा कब तक
ये आज़माइश-ए सब्र-ए गुरेज़-पा कब तक
क़सम तुम्हारी बहुत ग़म उठा चुका हूँ मैं
ग़लत था दावा-ए सब्र ओ शकेब आ जाओ
क़रार-ए ख़ातिर-ए बेताब थक गया हूँ मैं

◆

'BEAUTY AND DEATH'

Everything dies, that is the law of life, but that is not what
the poet is saying here. His concern is about the selective
push by the angel of death to take away, first and foremost,
which is most beautiful, which is most loved, which is most
promising. Death is not just a killer; it is a selective killer:

'ajal ki aankh faqat ek ko tarasti hai / kaaii dilon ki ummidon ka jo sahaara ho' (The eye of death thirsts for the only one/that is the anchor and hope of many hearts).

If there is a flower in the garden
that eclipses everything around it,
that adds light to the colourful ambience,
that has not experienced
the oppressive blows of autumn,
that the blood of spring's heart has nourished,
that is the flower, that is the only thing,
which quickly catches the flowerpicker's glimpse.

Although the garden of existence
is jam-packed with thousands of flowers,
the eye of death thirsts for the only one
that is the anchor and hope of many hearts,
that is free from the foulness of the world,
that is very much in the world
but not part of its contamination,
that has neither seen the lack of happiness
nor the unsavory profusion of sorrow;
that flower sleeps in the lap of what is pure and true
while in the silence of the night angels sing elegies;
the spring-like morning weaves circles around it,
and the gentle breeze brings flowers
from paradise as an act of oblation.

'Husn Aur Maut'

*jo phuul saare gulistaan mein sab se achha ho
farogh-e nuur ho jis se faza-e rangiin mein
khizaan ke jor o sitam ko n jis ne dekha ho*

bahaar ne jise khuun-e jigar se paala ho
voh ek phuul samaata hai chashm-e gulchiin mein

hazaar phuulon se aabaad baagh-e hasti hai
ajal ki aankh faqat ek ko tarasti hai
kaaii dilon ki ummidon ka jo sahaara ho
faza-e dahr ki aaluudgi se baala ho
jahaan mein aa ke abhi jis ne kuchh n dekha ho
n qaht-e aa'ish o mussarrat n gham ki arzaani
kanaar-e rahmat-e haq mein use sulaati hai
sakuut-e shab mein farishton ki marsia-khwaani
tavaaf karne ko sub-h-e bahaar aati hai
saba charahne ko jannat ke phuul laati hai

'हुस्न और मौत'

जो फूल सारे गुलिस्ताँ में सब से अच्छा हो
फ़रोग़-ए नूर हो जिस से फ़ज़ा-ए रंगीं में
ख़िज़ाँ के जौर ओ सितम को न जिस ने देखा हो
बहार ने जिसे ख़ून-ए जिगर से पाला हो
वो एक फूल समाता है चश्म-ए गुलचीं में

हज़ार फूलों से आबाद बाग़-ए हस्ती है
अजल की आँख फ़क़त एक को तरसती है
कई दिलों की उमीदों का जो सहारा हो
फ़ज़ा-ए दहर की आलूदगी से बाला हो
जहाँ में आ के अभी जिस ने कुछ न देखा हो
न क़हत-ए ऐश ओ मसर्रत न ग़म की अर्ज़ानी
कनार-ए रहमत-ए हक़ में उसे सुलाती है
सुकूत-ए शब में फ़रिश्तों की मर्सिया-ख़्वानी
तवाफ़ करने को सुब्ह-ए बहार आती है
सबा चढ़ाने को जन्नत के फूल लाती है

✦

'THE PANORAMA OF LOVE'

This is an unusual poem, written by a young poet who is still trying to find a place for himself under the sun. We can call it a love story in three acts. What exactly does the lover imagine before he comes face to face with the beloved? The meeting which is going to take place is a dream of pleasure that continuously repeats itself. Then, the lovers meet. The intensity of this experience brings '*kuchh uljhi hui baatein kuchh bahke hue naghme*' (Some tangled talking points,/some impaired melodies). Then comes the most painful part: the separation, the departure: '*voh kya dukh tha teri sehmi hui khaamosh aahon mein*' (What was that suffering/in those scary, silent sighs?). One feels ripples of sadness rising in one's heart as the poem comes to a quick conclusion.

Imagination

Some naughtiness
in the agitated glance
of an intoxicated eye.
Dream-like pleasures
in the colour of rouge
on her cheeks.
Smiles on red lips
luminous,
like jasmine flowers
drowning
in the pomegranate
flower wine.

Encounter

Eyes looking, sifting the world
of feelings and emotions.

Sleeplessness, stories, moon, desires.
Some tangled talking points,
some impaired melodies.
Some tears that fall from the eyes
without any reason.

Departure

The lips of a sad face
make an offering of silence.
The smile was fatigued,
white hands quivered.
What was that helplessness
in those graceful eyes?
What was that suffering
in those scary, silent sighs?

'Teen Manzar'

tassavvar

shokhiaan muztar nigaah-e diidah-e sarshaar mein
i'shratein khwabiidah ghaazaa-e rukhsaar mein
surkh honton par tabassum ki ziyaaein jis tarah
yaasaman ke phuul duube hon mai-e gulnaar mein

saamna

chhinti hui nazron se jazbaat ki duniya-ein
bekhwabiaan afsaane mahtaab tamanna-ein
kuchh uljhi hui baatein kuchh behke hue naghme
kuchh ashk jo aankhon se bevajah chhalak jaayein

rukhsat

fasurda rukh labon par ik niyaaz aamez khaamoshi
tabassum muzmahil tha marmariin haathon mein larzish thi

voh kaisi bekasi thi teri pur-tamkiin nigaahon mein
voh kya dukh tha teri sehmi hui khaamosh aahon mein

'तीन मंज़र'

तसव्वुर

शोख़ियाँ मुज़्तर-निगाह-ए दीदा-ए सरशार में
इशरतें ख़्वाबीदा रंग-ए ग़ाज़ा-ए रुख़सार में
सुर्ख़ होंटों पर तबस्सुम की ज़िथाएँ जिस तरह
यासमन के फूल डूबे हों मय-ए गुलनार में

सामना

छनती हुई नज़रों से जज़्बात की दुनियाएँ
बेख़्वाबियाँ अफ़्साने महताब तमन्नाएँ
कुछ उलझी हुई बातें कुछ बहके हुए नग़्मे
कुछ अश्क जो आँखों से बेवजह छलक जाएँ

रुख़्सत

फ़सुर्दा रुख़ लबों पर इक नियाज़ आमेज़ ख़ामोशी
तबस्सुम मुज़्महिल था मरमरीं हाथों में लर्ज़िश थी
वो कैसी बेकसी थी तेरी पुर-तम्कीं निगाहों में
वो क्या दुख था तेरी सहमी हुई ख़ामोश आहों में

◆

'A MELODY'

This is a ghazal-poem with a message of hope. There are things that we do not control. Yet the will to live, the will to conquer adversity is essential. When the big boat is sinking, taking the lifeboat and going to the shore (one's home) is the real key to survival. As long as there is home, the soul has a place to be. As long as there is home, there is a way to prevent melancholy and darkness from entering our lives.

There is nothing that I own.
Neither death, nor effort, nor living.
In the commotion of the world,
I have lost my sense of balance.

My saviour is far away,
the wind is blistery,
and the crocs are closing in.
There is little time left.
So hurry up.
Where is the lifeboat?

The vicissitudes of life
are not sparing my dreams.
It's time to keep the fire burning
in my chest.

No time to worry, Saqi,
the gathering will come back to life.
We shall prolong the time
that we spend drinking.

The sorrows of love
are precious possessions.
Don't give away your treasure
to melancholic darkness.

'Surud'

maut apni n a'mal apna n jiina apna
kho gaya shorish-e giiti mein qariina apna

na-khuda duur hava tez, qariin kaam-e nahang
vaqt hai phenk de lahron mein safiina apna

a'rsa-e dahr ke hangaame tah-e khwaab sahi
garam rakh aatish-e paikaar se siina apna

saaqiya ranj n kar jaag uthe gi mahfil
aur kuchh der utha rakhte hain piina apna

beshqiimat hain y gham-haa-e mohabbat mat bhuul
zulmat-e yaas ko mat saunp khaziina apna

'सुरूद'

मौत अपनी न अमल अपना न जीना अपना
खो गया शोरिश-ए गीती में क़रीना अपना

नाख़ुदा दूर हवा तेज़ क़रीं काम-ए नहंग
वक़्त है फेंक दे लहरों में सफ़ीना अपना

अरसा-ए दहर के हंगामे तह-ए ख़ाब सही
गर्म रख आतिश-ए पैकार से सीना अपना

साक़िया रंज न कर जाग उठेगी महफिल
और कुछ देर उठा रखते हैं पीना अपना

बेशक़ीमत हैं ये ग़म-हा-ए मुहब्बत मत भूल
ज़ुल्मत-ए यास को मत सौंप ख़ज़ीना अपना

◆

'DESPAIR'

This poem is a manifesto of hopelessness and it hits you hard. You feel the pinch. Just as Robert Frost once said: 'The reader of a good poem can tell the moment it strikes him that he has taken a mortal wound—that he will never get over it',[25] Faiz insists, '*kaavash-e be-hasuul rahne de*' (Leave aside all effort because it serves no purpose): it is dark inside the tunnel. It is a poem for that moment of darkness

[25]Roger Housden, *10 Poems to Last a Lifetime,* New York: Harmony Books, 2004, p. 15.

where every effort to find hope becomes futile.

> Strings of the lute of the heart are broken.
> Palaces of tranquility that kissed the ground
> on which they were built are nowhere to be
> found.
> They left behind stories of worrisome actions.
> Wine glasses of the gathering of existence are
> broken.
> Lost is the relaxation one received from the rivers
> and fountains of paradise.
> There is no use lamenting and crying.
> The complaints about the lack of good fortune,
> and the failure to reach the journey's end is
> fruitless.
> The descent of blessings has come to an end.
> The door of acceptance has been shut for a long
> time.
> No prayer works for any merciful God.
> The candle of yearning for beauty has been
> doused.
> Only memories remain of invalid arguments.
> Put aside futile efforts.
> I'm looking for those who preserve secrets of love.
> Those who are groaning with grief.
> Leave aside all effort because it serves no purpose.

'Yaas'

barbat-e dil ke taar tuut gaye
hain zamiin bos raahton ke mahal
mit gaaye qissa haa-e fikr o a'mal
bazm-e hasti ke jaam chhuut gaye
chhin gaya kaif-e kausar o tasniim

zahmat-e girya o buka besuud
shikvah-e bakht-e naa-rasa besuud
ho chuka khatm rahmaton ka nazuul
band hai muddaton se baab-e qabuul
beniyaaz-e d'ua hai rabb-e kariim
bujh gaaii sham'a-e aarzu-e jamiil
yaad baaqi hai bekasi ki daliil
intzaar-e fazuul rahne de
raaz-e ulfat nibhaane vaale
baar-e gham se karaahne vaale
kaavash-e behasuul rahne de

'यास'

बरबत-ए दिल के तार टूट गए
हैं ज़मीं-बोस राहतों के महल
मिट गए क़िस्सा-हा-ए फ़िक्र ओ अ'मल
बज़्म-ए हस्ती के जाम फूट गए
छिन गया कैफ़-ए कौसर ओ तसनीम
ज़हमत-ए गिर्या ओ बुका बेसूद
शिकवा-ए बख़्त-ए ना-रसा बेसूद
हो चुका ख़त्म रहमतों का नुज़ूल
बंद है मुद्दतों से बाब-ए क़ुबूल
बेनियाज़-ए दुआ है रब्ब-ए करीम
बुझ गई शम्-ए आरज़ू-ए जमील
याद बाक़ी है बेकसी की दलील
इन्तिज़ार-ए फ़ुज़ूल रहने दे
राज़-ए उल्फ़त निभाने वाले
बार-ए ग़म से कराहने वाले
काविश-ए बेहुसूल रहने दे

◆

'TONIGHT'

This is another nocturnal melody, short and meaningful. The poet wants to bring all the attention to the 'night' because it is a link between the painful past and an uncertain future. There is certainty about one thing: that the days of misery are over. But there is a lot of uncertainty about tomorrow, whether we shall ever see dawn. What can we do in such a situation? The poet is very cautious. He says, 'Don't touch the chords of sorrow.' This means that something that caused suffering is no longer there, but he does not make any promises about the future.

This poem was written many years before Independence, but it is a perfect fit for the night of 14 August 1947. It reminds us of the words that Prime Minister Nehru spoke on the eve of Independence, 'A moment comes, which comes but rarely in history, when we step out from the old to the new, when an age ends, and when the soul of a nation, long suppressed, finds utterance.'[26]

> Tonight—
> Do not touch the chords of sorrow.
> The days of misery are over.
> Who knows what will happen tomorrow?
> What separated the last night from its tomorrow
> has been wiped out.
> Whether dawn will come is a question mark.
> Life is… just this night.
> This night offers the possibility of eternity.

---

[26]Salman Rushdie and Elizabeth West, eds, *Mirrorwork: 50 Years of Indian Writing 1947–1997,* New York: Henry Holt and Company, 1997, p. 3.

Tonight—
Do not touch the chords of sorrow.
Do not repeat the story of your anguish.
Do not grieve over things past.
Make your heart free of all thoughts of tomorrow.
The past has not earned your tears.
Don't ask about the tale of your lamentations.
Don't express any regrets.

Tonight—
Do not touch the chords of sorrow.

'Aaj Ki Raat'

aaj ki raat saaz-e dard n chher
dukh se bharpuur din tamaam hue
aur kal ki khabar kise maa'luum
dosh o farda ki mit chuki hain haduud
ho n ho ab sahar kise maa'luum
zindagi hech lekin aaj ki raat
ezdiyyat hai mumkin aaj ki raat
aaj ki raat saaz-e dard n chher
ab n dohra afasaana haae alam
apni qismat p sogvaar n ho
fikr-e farada utaar de dil se
u'mr-e rafta p ashkbaar n ho
a'hd-e gham ki hikaayatein mat puuchh
ho chukien sab shikaayatein mat puuchh
aaj ki raat saaz-e dard n chher

'आज की रात'

आज की रात साज़-ए दर्द न छेड़
दुख से भरपूर दिन तमाम हुए
और कल की ख़बर किसे मालूम

दोश ओ फ़र्दा की मिट चुकी हैं हुदूद
हो न हो अब सहर किसे मालूम
ज़िंदगी हेच! लेकिन आज की रात
एज़दियत है मुमकिन आज की रात
आज की रात साज़-ए-दर्द न छेड़
अब न दोहरा फ़साना-हा-ए अलम
अपनी क़िस्मत पे सोगवार न हो
फ़िक्र-ए फ़र्दा उतार दे दिल से
उम्र-ए रफ़्ता पे अश्क-बार न हो
अहद-ए ग़म की हिकायतें मत पूछ
हो चुकीं सब शिकायतें मत पूछ
आज की रात साज़-ए दर्द न छेड़

◆

GHAZAL

I don't have the audacity
to request a favour.
Yet I lack the courage
of self-control.

I was restrained
from seeing you.
Otherwise, everything is well
with the world.

Don't cease your routine
of oppressing me.
I am there.
My love is there too.

Your discerning eyes
be blessed.
You can't see any complaint
in my heart.

The time of union and disunion
has come to an end.
There is no spice left in life.

'Himmat-e Iltija Nahien Baaqi'

himmat-e iltija nahien baaqi
zabt ka hausla nahien baaqi

ik teri diid chhin gaaii mujh se
varna duniya mein kya nahien baaqi

apni mashq-e sitam se haath n kheench
main nahien ya vafa nahien baaqi

teri chashm-e alam navaaz ki khair
dil mein koi gila nahien baaqi

ho chuka khatm a'hd-e hijr o vasaal
zindagi mein maza nahien baaqi

'हिम्मत-ए इल्तिजा नहीं बाक़ी'

हिम्मत-ए इल्तिजा नहीं बाक़ी
ज़ब्त का हौसला नहीं बाक़ी

इक तेरी दीद छिन गई मुझ से
वर्ना दुनिया में क्या नहीं बाक़ी

अपनी मश्क़-ए सितम से हाथ न खींच
मैं नहीं या वफ़ा नहीं बाक़ी

तेरी चश्म-ए अलम-नवाज़ की ख़ैर
दिल में कोई गिला नहीं बाक़ी

हो चुका ख़त्म अहद-ए हिज्र ओ विसाल
ज़िंदगी में मज़ा नहीं बाक़ी

◆

'ON A PATHWAY'

This poem is a grand celebration of the beauty of the beloved. A pathway (rahguzar) is a fixed entity somewhere. People use the pathway to go from one place to another, but the poet makes a pleasant discovery. The beloved had used this pathway 'once upon a time'. That was enough to make this pathway special: '*gharaz voh husn ab is rah ka juzv-e manzar hai/niyaaz-e i'shq ko ik sajdah gah mayyusar hai*' (In short, that beauty is now a part of the vista of this pathway. /For a desiring lover, this is a place of reverence and worship). This is a heart-rending idea wrapped in somewhat mellow poetic language.

> In whose sight
> there are a million delights hidden.
> That beauty in whose yearning
> there are heavenly kingdoms concealed.
> Thousands of graces
> are sitting under her feet.
> Her each glance is coloured
> by the intoxication of youth.
> Whose primal youth sends flashes
> of lightning to my imagination.
> Her playfulness thirsts for
> the pride of her friendship.
> On the style of tremors of her feet,
> doomsdays can be sacrificed.
> On the verse-book of her visage sunrises
> of many mornings can be sacrificed.
> Under her black curls,
> there is a crowd of star constellations—
> a bunch of comforts of romantic, long nights.
> Eyes on whose maquillage even

the creator puts on airs.
One feels shy about praising
her style of poetic recitation.
The colours of spring march in
as a gift of her lips.
Fountains and rivers of paradise—
her delicate body that lends honour
to the dress she wears.
Her height receives salutations
from the cypress trees.
In short, a beauty that is not beholden
to anything else.
A beauty whose vision is beyond
the capacity of ordinary words.
That beauty passed through
this pathway once upon a time—
with grace and honour, she strolled this way.
And since then, this pathway has stayed delightful
and pleasant.
In its dust resides
the exhilaration of wine and verse.
In its air, there are flows
of stylishness and speed.
In its ambiance, there are echoes
of the softness of discourses.
In short, that beauty is now an integral part
of the vista of this pathway.
For a desiring lover, this is a place
of reverence and worship.

'Ek Rahguzar Par'

voh jiski diid mein laakhon mussarratein pinhaan
voh husn jis ki tamanna mein jannatein pinhaan

hazaar fitne tah-e paa-e naaz khaak nashiin
har ik nigaah khumaar-e shabaab se rangiin
shabaab jis se takhiiul p bijliaan barsein
vaqaar jis ki rafaaqat ko shokhiaan tarsein
adaa-e laghzash-e paa par qiyamatein qurbaan
biyaaz-e rukh p sahar ki sabahatein qurbaan
siyaah zulfon mein vaarafta nakhaton ka hajuum
taviil raaton ki khwaabiida raahton ka hajuum
voh aankh jis ke banao p khaaliq itraaye
zabaan-e sh'er ko taa'riif karte sharm aaye
voh hont faiz se jin ke bahaar laala farosh
bahisht o kausar o tasniim o salsbiil badosh
gudaaz jism qaba jis p sajke naaz kare
daraaz qad jise sarv-e sahi namaaz kare
gharaz voh husn jo mahtaaj-e vasf o naam nahien
voh husn jis ka tassavvur bashar ka kaam nahien
kisi zamaane mein is rahguzar se guzra tha
basad gharuur o tajjamul idhar se guzra tha
aur ab y rahguzar bhi hai dil fareb o hasiin
hai is ki khaak mein kaif-e sharaab o sh'er makiin
hava mein shokhi-e raftaar ki adaayein hain
faza mein narmi-e guftaar ki sadaayein hain
gharaz voh husn ab is rah ka juzv-e manzar hai
niyaaz-e i'shq ko ik sajdah gah mayyusar hai

'एक रहगुज़र पर'

वो जिस की दीद में लाखों मसर्तें पिन्हाँ
वो हुस्न जिस की तमन्ना में जन्नतें पिन्हाँ
हज़ार फ़ित्ने तह-ए पा-ए नाज़ ख़ाक-नशीं
हर इक निगाह ख़ुमार-ए शबाब से रंगीं
शबाब जिस से तख़य्युल पे बिजलियाँ बरसें
वक़ार जिस की रफ़ाक़त को शोख़ियाँ तरसें
अदा-ए लग़्ज़िश-ए पा पर क़यामतें क़ुर्बां

बयाज़-रुख़ पे सहर की सबाहतें क़ुर्बां
सियाह ज़ुल्फ़ों में वा रफ़्ता निकहतों का हुजूम
तवील रातों की ख़्वाबीदा राहतों का हुजूम
वो आँख जिस के बनाव प ख़ालिक इतराए
ज़बान-ए शेर को तारीफ़ करते शर्म आए
वो होंट फ़ैज़ से जिन के बहार लाला-फ़रोश
बहिश्त ओ कौसर ओ तसनीम ओ सलसबील बदोश
गुदाज़ जिस्म क़बा जिरा पे राज के नाज़ करे
दराज़ क़द जिसे सर्व-ए सही नमाज़ करे
ग़रज़ वो हुस्न जो मोहताज-ए वस्फ़ ओ नाम नहीं
वो हुस्न जिस का तसव्वुर बशर का काम नहीं
किसी ज़माने में इस रह-गुज़र से गुज़रा था
बसद ग़ुरूर ओ तजम्मुल इधर से गुज़रा था
और अब ये राह-गुज़र भी है दिल-फ़रेब ओ हसीं
है इस की ख़ाक में कैफ़-ए शराब ओ शे'र मकीं
हवा में शोख़ी-ए रफ़्तार की अदाएँ हैं
फ़ज़ा में नर्मी-ए गुफ़्तार की सदाएँ हैं
ग़रज़ वो हुस्न अब इस रह का जुज़्व-ए मंज़र है
नियाज़-ए इश्क़ को इक सज्दा-गह मयस्सर है

◆

GHAZAL

By giving me your wine-like eyes,
you will make the hand of nature
ineffective.

My heart is running
fast and hard.
Saqi, please stiffen the wine
you serve today.

Something is lacking.
How should I show

my passion for frenzy?
Rip up my collar to the point
where my heart is.

The one who is quietly playing
with my destiny,
please make me oblivious
to what fate has in store for me.

My offering is going to waste.
I want her
to pay attention.

Faiz, I know how my wishes
will come to fruition.
I will be happy and satisfied
even if things end the way, they are.

'Chashm-e Maiguun Zara Idhar Kar De'

chashm-e maiguun zara idhar kar de
dast-e qudrat ko beasar kar de

tez hai aaj dard-e dil saaqi
talkhi-e mai ko tez tar kar de

josh-e vahshat hai tishna-kaam abhi
chaak-e daaman ko taa jigar kar de

meri qismat se khelne vaale
mujh ko qismat se bekhabar kar de

lutt rahi hai meri mata'a-e niyaaz
kaash voh is taraf nazar kar de

Faiz tak-miil-e aarzu maa'luum
ho sake to yuunhi basar kar de

'चश्म-ए मयगूँ ज़रा इधर कर दे'

चश्म-ए मयगूँ ज़रा इधर कर दे
दस्त-ए क़ुदरत को बेअसर कर दे

तेज़ है आज दर्द-ए दिल साक़ी
तल्ख़ी-ए मय को तेज़-तर कर दे

जोश-ए वहशत है तिश्ना-काम अभी
चाक-ए दामन को ता जिगर कर दे

मेरी क़िस्मत से खेलने वाले
मुझ को क़िस्मत से बेख़बर कर दे

लुट रही है मेरी मता-ए नियाज़
काश वो इस तरफ़ नज़र कर दे

'फ़ैज़' तकमील-ए आरज़ू मालूम
हो सके तो यूँही बसर कर दे

◆

Most of the poems and ghazals presented up to this point
are descriptive. There is ample use of similes, but no
real depth. Young Faiz is describing beauty as a romantic
poet named Akhtar Shirani did at that time. There is
no connection between poetry and real life, except
through adolescent romance. But even romance is static:
it has no place to go; it is not evolving. There is some
undercurrent of tension, but it is subdued. Metaphors,
as we know, usher in multilayered thoughts, ambiguity
and unimaginable depth. They pave the way for theme-
based creativity. The reason we have included these early
Naqsh-e Fariyadi compositions in this book is to show that
no poet achieves greatness at the very start of their poetic
journey. Young Faiz has his appeal, but for the broader
purpose, it is a small milestone. As we proceed further,

we shall witness a significant transformation both in his style and substance.

'A VIEW'

The poet is looking at something, presumably at night, outside his window. The whole thing is enveloped in complete silence, as if the world had gone to sleep. What we read, we can see, and more importantly, we can feel it. The poem has a subtext of deep subjective pain, sadness and loneliness as well as a touch of mystery. There must be a reason that the poet captures the mood in a language that is hauntingly beautiful. It is easy to express any noise in words, but silence is always deceptive. It is filled with meaning, but at the surface level, there is nothing there. Silence does things that we can't even imagine. The poet complains about his physical reality being crushed by the weight of silence. There is no voice, but there is the heaviness, which is destructive. As the roof is damaged, there is an opening for the tide of despair to flow in from the skies. Even the moon is despondent. The song of life is heard in the darkness around, but it is more like a dirge, a different chant because life is taking a turn. This poem is an indication of the change that is happening. Faiz, the young romantic, is trying to claim a new ground, something new for the world of Urdu poetry.

> This is my roof.
> This is my door.
> Both are under the crushing weight of silence.
> A tide of despair is flowing in from the skies.
> There is a moon, and its story of light,
> sadness mixed with the dust of pathways.

In the dreamy bedrooms,
there is partial darkness.
On nature's harp, a song of life
and a strain of extinction.
Faint, very faint harmonics—
nothing but wailing and moaning.

'Ek Manzar'
baam o dar khaamushi ke bojh se chuur
aasmaanon se juu-e dard ravaan
chaand ka dukhbhara fasaana-e nuur
shaah raahon ki khaak mein ghaltaan
khwaab gaahon mein niim taariiki
muzmahil lai rubaab-e hasti ki
halke halke suron mein nauha-kunaan

'एक मंज़र'

बाम ओ दर ख़ामुशी के बोझ से चूर
आसमानों से जू-ए दर्द रवाँ
चाँद का दुख-भरा फ़साना-ए नूर
शाह-राहों की ख़ाक में ग़लताँ
ख़्वाब-गाहों में नीम तारीकी
मुज़्महिल लय रुबाब-ए हस्ती की
हल्के हल्के सुरों में नौहा-कुनाँ

◆

'MY FRIEND'

This poem is hard to put in a single box. Is it about friendship? Is it about fond remembrance? Is it about loss? Is it about love or loss of love? In fact, it is about all of this and more. We can forget everything about this poem, except its ending: *'chalo ke chal ke charaaghaan karein diyaar-e habiib/hain intizaar mein agli mohabbaton ke mazaar/ mohabbatein jo fana ho gaaii hain mere nadiim'* (Let us go and light up lamps in our beloved's place. /The tombs of future love are waiting to be assembled. /Those loves that died, my friend!).

> That which enriched
> the world of imagination and verse,
> the climate of thought and action
> was like plants whose flowers
> were purple-coloured,
> and with whose light
> moon and stars bloomed.
> The courage of the madness of love
> was at its youthful peak because of it.
> Where have those yearnings
> gone to sleep, my friend?
> Those impatient eyes and
> those pathways in wait.
> Those sighs that were suppressed
> because of self-control.
> Those nights of separation and expectation,
> very long and dark.
> Those half-dreamy chambers and velvety arms.
> Those were stories,
> and they were lost, my friend.
> Sulking in the veins of life
> is the blood of life.
> Getting enmeshed are soul's filaments
> with old wounds.
> Let us go and light up lamps
> in our beloved's place.
> The tombs of future love

are waiting to be assembled.
Those loves that died, my friend!

'Mere Nadiim'

khayal o sh'er ki duniya mein jaan thi jin se
faza-e fikr o a'mal arghuvaan thi jin se
voh jinke nuur se shaadaab the mah o anjum
junuun-e i'shq ki himmat javaan thi jin se
voh aarzuuein kahaan so gaii hain mere nadiim
voh nasabuur nigaahein voh muntazar raahein
voh paas-e zabt se dil mein dabi hui aahein
voh intizaar ki raatein taviil tiirah o taar
voh niim khwaab shabistaan voh makhmaliin baahein
kahaaniaan thi kahien kho gaaii hain mere nadiim
machal raha hai rag-e zindagi mein khuun-e bahaar
ulajh rahe hain puraane ghamon se ruuh ke taar
chalo k chal ke charaaghaan karein diyaar-e habiib
hain intizaar mein agli mohabbaton ke mazaar
mohabbatein jo fana ho gaaii hain mere nadiim

'मेरे नदीम'

ख़याल ओ शे'र की दुनिया में जान थी जिन से
फ़ज़ा-ए फ़िक्र ओ अ'मल अर्ग़वान थी जिन से
वो जिनके नूर से शादाब थे मह ओ अंजुम
जुनून-ए इ'श्क़ हिम्मत जवान थी जिन से
वो आरज़ुएँ कहाँ सो गई हैं मेरे नदीम
वो ना-सुबूर निगाहें वो मुंतज़िर राहें
वो पास-ए ज़ब्त से दिल में दबी हुई आहें
वो इंतिज़ार की रातें तवील तीरा ओ तार
वो नीम-ख़्वाब शबिस्ताँ वो मख़मलीं बाहें
कहानियाँ थीं कहीं खो गई हैं मेरे नदीम
मचल रहा है रग-ए ज़िंदगी में ख़ून-ए बहार
उलझ रहे हैं पुराने ग़मों से रूह के तार

चलो कि चल के चराग़ाँ करें दयार-ए हबीब
हैं इंतिज़ार में अगली मोहब्बतों के मजार
मोहब्बतें जो फ़ना हो गई हैं मेरे नदीम

◆

'NOT THAT OLD LOVE'

This poem represents a turning point in young Faiz's evolution as a poet: we witness the end of his early romanticism and the start of a new journey where the personal and interpersonal merge and become one. This is the junction where two loves—love of the beloved and loving appreciation of the downtrodden, as also the love of the land—meet for the first time and create tension. From a purely romantic poet, Faiz makes a huge transition to being a poet who has not forgotten how to celebrate the beauty of the beloved. In addition to that, he is committing himself to the cause of social and political change and freedom. The poem, best known for its lyricism and captivating beauty, shows the poet torn between these two loves. But in the end, there is no tension: love metaphorically binds everything and brings everything together.

My dearest—
don't ask for the love we once had.

When you were mine, life was shining.
The pain of separation from you
made everything else seem less painful.
Springtime lasted forever
as an affirmation of your beauty.
There was nothing else so precious,
I thought, other than your alluring eyes.

If I won your affection,
it would make fate bow before me.
This is not what happened.

I had only wished that
it should have happened this way.
There are miseries other than
the affliction of being in love.
There are pleasures other than
the joy of union.

The curse of countless centuries and
savagery is woven into silk, satin and brocade,
human flesh is for sale in the alleys and bazaars,
covered with blood, rinsed in blood.
Bodies that emerged from kilns of affliction.
Secretions are flowing from the rotting blisters.
My eyes turn back to witness these sad scenes.
Your beauty is delightfully attractive,
but what should I do?

There are miseries other than
the agony of being in love.
There are pleasures other than
the rapture of union.

My dearest—
don't ask for that love again.

'Mujh Se Pehli Si Mohabbat Meri Mahbuub N Maang'

mujh se pehli si mohabbat meri mahbuub n maang

main ne samjha tha k tu hai to darakhshaan hai hayaat
tera gham hai to gham-e dahr ka jhagra kya hai
teri suurat se hai a'alam mein bahaaron ko sabaat

teri aankhon ke siva duniya mein rakha kya hai
tu jo mil jaaye to taqdiir niguun ho jaaye
yuun n tha main ne faqat chaaha tha yuun ho jaaye
aur bhi dukh hain zamaane mein mohabbat ke siva
raahatein aur bhi hain vasl ki raahat ke siva
an-ginat sadiyon ke taariik bahemaana tilism
reshm o atlas o kam khwaab mein bunvaae hue
ja-b-ja bikte hue kuucha o bazaar mein jism
khaak mein lithre hue khuun mein nahlaae hue
jism nikle hue amraaz ke tannuoron se
piip behti hui ghalte hue naa-suuron se

laut jaati hai udhar ko bhi nazar kya kiije
ab bhi dilkash hai tera husn magar kya kiije

aur bhi dukh hain zamaane mein mohabbat ke siva
raahatein aur bhi hain vasl ki raahat ke siva
mujh se pehli si mohabbat meri mahbuub n maang

'मुझ से पहली सी मोहब्बत मेरी महबूब न माँग'

मुझ से पहली सी मोहब्बत मेरी महबूब न माँग
मैंने समझा था कि तू है तो दरख़्शाँ है हयात
तेरा ग़म है तो ग़म-ए दहर का झगड़ा क्या है
तेरी सूरत से है आ'लम में बहारों को सबात
तेरी आँखों के सिवा दुनिया में रखा क्या है
तू जो मिल जाए तो तक़दीर निगूँ हो जाए
यूँ न था मैं ने फ़क़त चाहा था यूँ हो जाए
और भी दुख हैं ज़माने में मोहब्बत के सिवा
राहतें और भी हैं वस्ल की राहत के सिवा
अन-गिनत सदियों के तारीक बहीमाना तिलिस्म
रेशम ओ अतलस ओ कमख़ाब में बुनवाए हुए
जा-ब-जा बिकते हुए कूचा ओ बाज़ार में जिस्म
ख़ाक में लिथड़े हुए खून में नहलाए हुए
जिस्म निकले हुए अमराज़ के तन्नूरों से

पीप बहती हुई गलते हुए नासूरों से

लौट जाती है उधर को भी नज़र क्या कीजे
अब भी दिलकश है तेरा हुस्न मगर क्या कीजे

और भी दुख हैं ज़माने में मोहब्बत के सिवा
राहतें और भी हैं वस्ल की राहत के सिवा
मुझ से पहली सी मोहब्बत मेरी महबूब न माँग

◆

GHAZAL

The one who bet
both of his realms on your love,
he is going away
after spending a night of grief.

The tavern is desolate,
each cup of wine is doleful.
When you left,
the days of spring left too.

Permission to be sinful
and that too, just for a few days.
Makes Almighty look like
a poor risk-taker to me.

The struggles of the daily grind
sometimes made me forget you.
The worries of making a living
are even more heart-enticing
than being in love.

Unwittingly, she did smile today, Faiz.
Don't ask me how my smashed heart responded,
showing its desperate yearning.

'Donon Jahaan Teri Mohabbat Mein Haar Ke'

donon jahaan teri mohabbat mein haar ke
voh ja raha hai koi shab-e gham guzaar ke

viiraan hai maikadah khum o saaghar udaas hain
tum kya gaye k ruuth gaye din bahaar ke

ik fursat-e gunaah mili voh bhi chaar din
dekhe hain ham ne hausle par vardgaar ke

duniya ne teri yaad se be-gaana kar diya
tujh se bhi dil fareb hain gham rozgaar ke

bhuule se muskara to diye the voh aaj Faiz
mat puuchh valvale dil-e na-kardah kaar ke

'दोनों जहान तेरी मोहब्बत में हार के'

दोनों जहान तेरी मोहब्बत में हार के
वो जा रहा है कोई शब-ए ग़म गुज़ार के

वीराँ है मयकदा खुम ओ साग़र उदास हैं
तुम क्या गए कि रूठ गए दिन बहार के

इक फ़ुर्सत-ए गुनाह मिली वो भी चार दिन
देखे हैं हम ने हौसले पर्वरदिगार के

दुनिया ने तेरी याद से बेगाना कर दिया
तुझ से भी दिल-फ़रेब हैं ग़म रोज़गार के

भूले से मुस्कुरा तो दिए थे वो आज 'फ़ैज़'
मत पूछ वलवले दिल-ए ना-कर्दा-कार के

◆

GHAZAL

I didn't commit myself to fulfil
this promise or the other one,

she was annoyed with me
but not so much.

I don't know
why I am expecting something
while I am sitting on the pathway
which is not even the pathway
that you usually take.

The glance of passionate love
should not be unveiled
at the peak of the gathering.
She is not mindful of the risks,
but it is hard to believe
that she is entirely unaware.

What is the purpose of this resolve
to end this love affair?
There is no peace of mind
here or there.

'Vafaa-e Vaa'da Nahien Vaa'da-e Digar Bhi Nahien'

vafaa-e vaa'da nahien vaa'da-e digar bhi nahien
voh mujh se ruuthe to the lekin is qadar bhi nahien

n jaane kis liye ummid vaar baitha huun
ik aisi raah p jo teri rahguzar bhi nahien

nigaah-e shauq sar-e bazm behijaaab n ho
voh bekhabar hi sahi itne bekhabar bhi nahien

ye a'hd-e tark-e mohabbat hai kis liye aakhir
sukuun-e qalb idhar bhi nahien udhar bhi nahien

'वफ़ा-ए वादा नहीं वादा-ए दिगर भी नहीं'

वफ़ा-ए वादा नहीं वादा-ए दिगर भी नहीं

वो मुझ से रूठे तो थे लेकिन इस क़दर भी नहीं

न जाने किस लिए उम्मीद-वार बैठा हूँ
इक ऐसी राह पे जो तेरी रहगुज़र भी नहीं

निगाह-ए शौक़ सर-ए बज़्म बेहिजाब न हो
वो बेख़बर ही सही इतने बेख़बर भी नहीं

ये अहद-ए तर्क-ए मोहब्बत है किस लिए आख़िर
सुकून-ए क़ल्ब उधर भी नहीं इधर भी नहीं

◆

'DEAR RIVAL'

This poem is not very different from 'Mujh Se Pehli Si Mohabbat Meri Mahbuub N Maang', but it is different in terms of the context. According to Firaq Gorakhpuri, 'It is not a poem; it is the unified evening ... of heaven and hell. Shakespeare, Goethe, Kalidas and Sa'adi; even they could not have said anything better to the rival.'[27] As an accepted principle established in traditional Urdu poetry, no conversation with the raqiib (rival) is desirable because of the doubt about his intention to impede the lover. How can you talk to a person who wants to destroy the most important relationship that you cherish? But the poet finds one common link: there is a beauty with whom both of them are in love, and that shared interest could be used to build a bond between the antagonists. The first five stanzas of the poem are nothing but praise of the beloved's beauty, what joys and pleasure her presence provides, the gifts of her drunken youth, how others praise her charms, how the breeze carries the fragrance of her dress around, the allure

---

[27]Hashmi, *Love and Revolution*, pp. 105–6.

of her cheeks and lips, the anguish of love and what she has taught the contenders in a very subtle and indirect way. Then suddenly, the tone of the poem changes: it is no longer a love poem. It becomes a commentary on the world the poet lives in. It is all about suffering, pain and the agony of the poor. Such is the intensity of the condition in which the poor of the land live and how they are exploited, that the poet can't control himself. This makes him forget the beauty, the charms and the allurements of the beloved. Thus we reach a point where the poet loses common ground with the raqiib. The poem seems to be incomplete in the end, but what is not said is more important than what is said.

> Come closer—
> when I see you, I remember the beauty
> whose memories are associated with you.
> She was the one who made my heart a fairyland.
> For whose love I had given up everything.
> I made the world a parody of the real world.
>
> These pathways are familiar to you
> as your feet touch them,
> you know that this is the gift
> of her drunken youth.
> Caravans have passed praising her charms
> while they adorned her eyes.
>
> Some gusts of breezes have played with you
> and they have carried the fading fragrance of her
> dress.
> You have benefitted from the rainfall
> that fell on your roof and contained the moon's
> light,
> that had the pain of the nights past.

You have seen that forehead, those cheeks, those lips.
I have squandered my life in their pursuit.
She has looked at you with her magical but
somewhat wandering eyes.
Now you know why and what for
I have spent my whole life.

We share the gift of the anguish of love.
So many that I can hardly count.
What have I lost and what have I learned
in this labour of love?
If I try to explain this to anyone other than you
I would fail.

I have learned compassion,
I have learned how to support the poor.
I have learned the meaning of despair and
suffering from pain and agony.
I have understood the helplessness of the helpless—
of those with chilled sighs and bruised faces.

When those who are powerless
get together and cry,
their tears get sleepy before they fall.
The food of these frail humans
is snatched by eagle-like birds
as they come down, spreading their wings.

When a poor worker's flesh is sold in the market,
the weak blood flows in the streets.
A fire in the centre of the heart flares and mounts
up.
Precisely at that moment, I can't control myself.

'Raqiib Se'

aa k vaabasta hain us husn ki yaadein tujh se
jis ne is dil ko pari-khaana bana rakha tha
jiski ulfat mein bhula rakhii thi duniya ham ne
dahr ko dahr ka afsaana bana rakha tha

aashna hain tere qadmon se voh raahein jin par
uski madhosh javaani ne i'naayat ki hai
kuarvaan guzre hain jin se usi raa'naaii ke
jiski in aankhon ne besuud i'baadat ki hai

tujh se kheli hain voh mahbuub havaaein jin mein
uske malbuus ki afsurda mahak baaqi hai
tujh p bhi barsa hai us baam se mahtaab ka nuur
jis mein biiti hui raaton ki kasak baaqi hai

tu ne dekhi hai voh peshaani voh rukhsaar voh hont
zindagi jinke tasavvur mein luta di ham ne
tujh p utthi hain voh khoii hui saahir aankhein
tujh ko maa'luum hai kyon u'mr ganva di ham ne

ham p mushtarka hain ihsaan gham-e ulfat ke
itne ihsaan k ginvaauun to ginvaan n sakuun
ham ne is i'shq mein kya khoya hai kya siikha hai
juz tere aur ko samjhaauun to samjha n sakuun

aa'jzii siikhi ghariibon ki himaayat siikhi
yaas o hirmaan ke dukh dard ke maa'ni siikhe
zer daston ke masaaib ko samajhna siikha
sard aahon ke rukh-e zard ke maa'ni siikhe

jab kahin baith ke rote hain voh be-kas jinke
ashk aankhon mein bilakte hue so jaate hain
na-tavaanon ke nivaalon p jhapat-te hain u'qaab
baazu tole hue mandlaate hue aate hain

jab kabhi bikta hai bazaar mein mazduur ka gosht
shaahraahon p ghariibon ka lahu behta hai
aag si siine mein rah rah ke ubalti hai n puuchh
apne dil par mujhe qaabu hi nahien rahta hai

'रक़ीब से'

आ कि वाबस्ता हैं उस हुस्न की यादें तुझ से
जिस ने इस दिल को परी-ख़ाना बना रखा था
जिस की उल्फ़त में भुला रखी थी दुनिया हम ने
दहर को दहर का अफ़साना बना रखा था

आश्ना हैं तेरे क़दमों से वो राहें जिन पर
उस की मदहोश जवानी ने इ'नायत की है
कारवाँ गुज़रे हैं जिन से उसी रा'नाई के
जिस की इन आँखों ने बेसूद इ'बादत की है

तुझ से खेली हैं वो महबूब हवाएँ जिन में
उस के मल्बूस की अफ़्सुर्दा महक बाक़ी है
तुझ पे बरसा है उसी बाम से महताब का नूर
जिस में बीती हुई रातों की कसक बाक़ी है

तू ने देखी है वो पेशानी वो रुख़्सार वो होंट
ज़िंदगी जिन के तसव्वुर में लुटा दी हम ने
तुझ पे उट्ठी हैं वो खोई हुई साहिर आँखें
तुझ को मा'लूम है क्यूँ उम्र गँवा दी हम ने

हम पे मुश्तरका हैं एहसान ग़म-ए उल्फ़त के
इतने एहसान कि गिनवाऊँ तो गिनवा न सकूँ
हमने इस इ'श्क़ में क्या खोया है क्या सीखा है
जुज़ तेरे और को समझाऊँ तो समझा न सकूँ

आजिज़ी सीखी ग़रीबों की हिमायत सीखी
यास ओ हिरमान के दुख-दर्द के मअ'नी सीखे
ज़ेर-दस्तों के मसाइब को समझना सीखा
सर्द आहों के रुख़-ए ज़र्द के मअ'नी सीखे

जब कहीं बैठ के रोते हैं वो बेकस जिनके
अश्क आँखों में बिलकते हुए सो जाते हैं
ना-तवानों के निवालों पे झपटते हैं उ'क़ाब
बाजू तोले हुए मंडलाते हुए आते हैं

जब कभी बिकता है बाज़ार में मज़दूर का गोश्त
शाह-राहों पे ग़रीबों का लहू बहता है
आग सी सीने में रह रह के उबलती है न पूछ
अपने दिल पर मुझे क़ाबू ही नहीं रहता है

◆

'LONELINESS'

This short poem is considered Faiz's greatest creation by many literary critics, notably N.M. Rashed. There are only nine lines, but they are written in a language that is highly evocative. It does not talk about anything significant. The only description is of a scene with no human presence: a vista as night is dwindling. It is cloudy, though the clouds are splintering. There are lamps, but they are sleepy and glimmering. There are blurred images of footsteps, but it is not clear whether anyone is coming or going. There is a command towards the end—snuff the candles, take away the wine cups, fasten the bolts and bars: no one will come here. Even before you are fully aware of the situation being presented in the poem, it is all over.

Because the poem is highly ambiguous, it lends itself to many interpretations. Is it just a mood poem where the poet is describing a night scene without implying anything concrete? If it is merely a word picture, we can leave it there, but the progressives tend to see the poem as an indictment of British rule, of how everything is falling apart, how the party is almost over. That is why you can take away the wine cups and flagons. A somewhat silly interpretation hinted by

Rashed himself was that the narrator of the poem was 'a prostitute waiting for a customer' who was not showing up for the night. This interpretation is silly, so to speak.

The metaphorical structure and ambiguity of the poem is its greatest asset. There is something enigmatic, like Mona Lisa's smile, prompting hundreds of guesses, but no guess is better than the others. According to Vasilieva,

> On the surface, the poem describes the apex of loneliness with no reward for waiting, but on closer inspection, the entire atmosphere of the poem is suffused with life. Take the language. How many verses contain verbs which signify movement, itself a symbol of life and action. Someone's coming or not coming, a traveler is going somewhere else, the night is declining, the stars' cloud scattering, the lamps flickering, the highways sleeping … and when the night is ending, obviously daybreak is near with its promise of new hope and yet another wait.[28]

In the end, we have to accept this poem as a great work of art. We can read it; we can look at it. Not to say anything more is possibly the best response.

> Someone came.
> O, sad heart!
> No, no one.
> Maybe a wanderer!
> He will find somewhere else to go.
> The night is dwindling.
> The mass of stars is splintering.
> The sleepy lamps in the far away hallways

---

[28]Ibid. 106–7.

have started to glimmer.
Every pathway has gone to sleep
waiting for someone
to come visiting.
The strange dust blurred
images of vague footsteps.
Now douse these candles,
take away wine cups and decanters.
Fasten the bolts, bars,
and locks of your dreamless doors.
No one, no one, will come here!

'Tanhaaii'

phir koi aaya dil-e zaar nahien koi nahien
rah-rau ho ga kahien aur chala jaayega
dhal chuki raat bikharne laga taaron ka ghubaar
larkharaane lage aivaanon mein khwaabiida charaagh
so gaaii raasta tak tak ke har ek raah guzaar
ajnabi khaak ne dhundhla diye qadmon ke suraagh
gul karo sham'aein barha do mai o miina o ayaagh
apne bekhwaab kivaaron ko muqaffal kar lo
ab yahaan koi nahien koi nahien aaega

'तनहाई'

फिर कोई आया दिल-ए-ज़ार नहीं कोई नहीं
राह-रौ होगा कहीं और चला जाएगा
ढल चुकी रात बिखरने लगा तारों का ग़ुबार
लड़खड़ाने लगे ऐवानों में ख़्वाबीदा चराग़
सो गई रास्ता तक तक के हर इक राहगुज़ार
अजनबी ख़ाक ने धुँदला दिए क़दमों के सुराग़
गुल करो शमएँ बढ़ा दो मय ओ मीना ओ अयाग़
अपने बेख़्वाब किवाड़ों को मुक़फ़्फ़ल कर लो
अब यहाँ कोई नहीं कोई नहीं आएगा

◆

GHAZAL

I tried to hide the secret of love,
but to little or no avail.
I put my heart on fire
with no success or benefit.

There is no desire to see
anything more.
I fell in love with you.
That was more than enough.

She did not mesh well,
even when she was in love with me.
I enjoyed that feeling of belonging,
but it was to no avail at the end.

Today, I saw something
very special in her eyes.
Surreptitiously, very secretively,
unknown to others.

Faiz, I never reached
the limits of grief;
even after falling in love.

'Raaz-e Ulfat Chhupa Ke Dekh Liya'

raaz-e ulfat chhupa ke dekh liya
dil bahut kuchh jalake dekh liya

aur kya dekhne ko baaqi hai
aap se dil laga ke dekh liya

voh mere ho ke bhi mere n hue
un ko apna bana ke dekh liya

aaj un ki nazar mein kuchh ham ne
sab ki nazrein bacha ke dekh liya

Faiz takmiil-e gham bhi ho n saki
i'shq ko aazma ke dekh liya

'राज़-ए उल्फ़त छुपा के देख लिया'

राज़-ए उल्फ़त छुपा के देख लिया
दिल बहुत कुछ जला के देख लिया

और क्या देखने को बाक़ी है
आप से दिल लगा के देख लिया

वो मेरे हो के भी मेरे न हुए
उनको अपना बना के देख लिया

आज उन की नज़र में कुछ हम ने
सब की नज़रें बचा के देख लिया

'फ़ैज़' तकमील-ए ग़म भी हो न सकी
इ'श्क़ को आज़मा के देख लिया

◆

GHAZAL

Once again,
I tried to be spring's rival.
I don't know how many people,
I mourned.

I know it was a waste,
but not that much.
Today, I lost something
in the game of life.

I got close to your threshold,
but then returned.

The dignity of love
was badly dishonoured.

He will pull back
from the rest of the world,
anyone close to you.

I tried but failed to repair
your aloofness.
Bit by bit, little by little,
I lost my longing for you.

Faiz, let the world mind its business.
You should sit calmly
and continue to write your verse.

'Phir Hariif-e Bahaar Ho Baithe'

phir hariif-e bahaar ho baithe
jaane kis kis ko aaj ro baithe

thi magar itni raaegaan bhi n thi
aaj kuchh zindagi se kho baithe

tere dar tak pahunch ke laut aaye
ishq ki aabru dabo baithe

saari duniya se duur ho jaaye
jo zara tere paas ho baithe

n gaaii teri be-rukhi n gaaii
ham teri aarzu bhi kho baithe

Faiz hota rahe jo hota hai
she'r likhte raha karo baithe

'फिर हरीफ़-ए बहार हो बैठे'
फिर हरीफ़-ए बहार हो बैठे

जाने किस किस को आज रो बैठे

थी मगर इतनी राएगाँ भी न थी
आज कुछ ज़िंदगी से खो बैठे

तेरे दर तक पहुँच के लौट आए
इ'श्क़ की आबरू डुबो बैठे

सारी दुनिया से दूर हो जाए
जो ज़रा तेरे पास हो बैठे

न गई तेरी बेरुख़ी न गई
हम तेरी आरज़ू भी खो बैठे

'फ़ैज़' होता रहे जो होना है
शेर लिखते रहा करो बैठे

◆

'FEW MORE DAYS, MY LOVE!'

This poem was written a few days after the start of the
Second World War in September 1939. Faiz also wrote
a poem in which he pleaded with Gandhi to end the
Quit India campaign and come to the aid of the Soviet
Union against Nazi Germany. He joined the Indian Army
because he felt it was essential to defeat the fascists. In this
poem, Faiz is visualizing the end of the British Rule. The
expression 'chandroz' is significant because it highlights
beautifully how close we were, in the poet's thinking, to
attaining our goal of a free India.

A few more days, my love,
just a few more days.
We are condemned to breathe
in the shadow of oppression

and we should suffer a little more,
the aches and cries.
For what our forefathers endowed.
We are helpless, and our bodies are in prison,
our emotions are chained.
Our thoughts are held captive,
and our speech is being censored.
Bravo, we continue to live.
Is life a mendicant's apparel
that is mended by each moment by our agony?
The days of tyranny
are now coming to an end.
Be patient.
The days of the complainant
are coming to an end.
In this time of scorched desert,
we have to live, but not like this.
The nameless persecution
by the foreign hands
we have to bear today,
but not for long.
Your beauty is captive
to the dust of tribulations,
counting the days of its suffering,
the unwanted cruelty
of the full moon nights,
meaningless agony of the heart,
of the body's despairing cry.
Few more days, my love,
just a few more days!

'Chandroz Aur Meri Jaan!'
chandroz aur meri jaan faqat chand hi roz

zulm ki chhaaon mein dam lene pe majbuur hain ham
aur kuchh der sitam sahlein tarap lein ro lein
apne ajdaad ki miraas hai maa'zuur hain ham
jism par qaid hai jazbaat pe zanjiirein hain
fikr mahbuus hai guftaar par taa'ziirein hain
apni himmat hai k ham phir bhi jiye jaate hain
zindagi kya kisi muflis ki qaba hai jis mein
har ghari dard ke paivand lage jaate hain
lekin ab zulm ki mii'aad ke din thore hain
ek zara sabr k faryaad ke din thore hain
a'rsa-e dahr ki jhulsi hui viiraani mein
ham ko rehna hai pe yuun hi to nahien rehna hai
ajnabi haathon ka benaam giraanbaar sitam
aaj sehna hai hamesha to nahien sehna hai
ye tere husn se lipti hui aalaam ki gard
apni do roza javaani ki shikaston ka shumaar
chaandni raaton ka be-kaar dahakta hua dard
dil ki besuud tarap jism ki maayuus pukaar
chand roz aur meri jaan faqat chand hi roz

'चंदरोज़ और मेरी जान!'

चंदरोज़ और मेरी जान! फ़क़त चंद ही रोज़
ज़ुल्म की छाँव में दम लेने पे मजबूर हैं हम
और कुछ देर सितम सह लें तड़प लें रो लें
अपने अज्दाद की मीरास है माजूर हैं हम
जिस्म पर क़ैद है जज़्बात पे ज़ंजीरें हैं
फ़िक्र महबूस है गुफ़्तार पर ताज़ीरें हैं
अपनी हिम्मत है कि हम फिर भी जिए जाते हैं
ज़िंदगी क्या किसी मुफ़लिस की क़बा है जिस में
हर घड़ी दर्द के पैवंद लगे जाते हैं
लेकिन अब ज़ुल्म की मी'याद के दिन थोड़े हैं
इक ज़रा सब्र कि फ़रियाद के दिन थोड़े हैं
अरसा-ए दहर की झुलसी हुई वीरानी में

हम को रहना है पे यूँही तो नहीं रहना है
अजनबी हाथों का बेनाम गिराँ-बार सितम
आज सहना है हमेशा तो नहीं सहना है
ये तेरे हुस्न से लिपटी हुई आलाम की गर्द
अपनी दो रोज़ा जवानी की शिकस्तों का शुमार
चाँदनी रातों का बेकार दहकता हुआ दर्द
दिल की बेसूद तड़प जिस्म की मायूस पुकार
चंद रोज़ और मेरी जान फ़क़त चंद ही रोज़

◆

'SPEAK UP'

This short poem is different from others in *Naqsh-e Faryadi*
in terms of its total, uninhibited directness. It is not a
balancing act between various alternatives; instead it is all
about expressing what is within, what is suppressed, what
stays hidden in the dark corridors of one's being, that if
spoken in words could land a person in prison. The lips
are free now, but there is no guarantee that they will be
open tomorrow. There is little time, the poet says, before
the body and the tongue will become extinct. More
than a poem, it is a declaration of free expression amid
all kinds of challenges and constraints. Silence and silent
suffering is not an option any longer. The poem makes its
impact through its creative brevity, truth and sincerity of
the message. There is only one thing one has to do at the
moment: speak up.

Speak up—your lips are free now.
Speak up—you have a tongue
that is your possession.

This stout body belongs to you.
Speak up—you still control

your breathing.

Look, in the iron forger's shop—
flames are high, and the iron is red hot.

Locks with a pivotal hook
are opening their jaws.
Every chain's edges
are spread far and wide.

Speak up, and this little time is enough.
Before your body and tongue become extinct.
Speak up, that truth is still alive.
Speak up, whatever you have to say,
Now is the time.
Say it!

'Bol'

bol k lab aazaad hain tere
bol zabaan ab tak teri hai

tera sutvaan jism hai tera
bol k jaan ab tak teri hai

dekh k aahan-gar ki dukaan mein
tund hain sh'ole surkh hai aahan

khulne lage quflon ke dahaaane
phaila har zanjiir ka daaman

bol ye thora vaqt bahut hai
jism o zabaan ki maut se pehle

bol k sach zinda hai ab tak
bol jo kuchh kehna hai keh le

'बोल'

बोल कि लब आज़ाद हैं तेरे
बोल ज़बाँ अब तक तेरी है

तेरा सुत्वाँ जिस्म है तेरा
बोल कि जाँ अब तक तेरी है

देख कि आहन–गर की दुकाँ में
तुंद हैं शोले सुर्ख़ है आहन

खुलने लगे क़ुफ़्लों के दहाने
फैला हर ज़ंजीर का दामन

बोल ये थोड़ा वक़्त बहुत है
जिस्म ओ ज़बाँ की मौत से पहले

बोल कि सच ज़िंदा है अब तक
बोल जो कुछ कहना है कह ले

◆

GHAZAL

How many times
have I filled its apparel's knot
with the beauty of two worlds,
but my heart's tendency to self-destruct
never changes.

For its sake, countless times I have
tried to pierce the core of particles,
but this eye of wonderment
never loses its capacity to astonish
and it has not changed.

Since the day my lazy eye
gained power of inner sight,

my ability to recognize known faces
has diminished.

*'Kaii Baar Is Ka Daaman Bhar Diya Husn-E Do
Aa'lam Se'*

*kaii baar is ka daaman bhar diya husn-e do aa'lam se
magar dil hai k is ki khaana-viiraaani nahien jaati*

*kaii baar is ki khaatir zarre zarre ka jigar chiira
magar y chashm-e hairaan jis ki hairaani nahien jaati*

*meri chashm-e tan aasaan ko basiirat mil gaii jab se
bahut jaani hui surat bhi pehchaani nahien jaati*

'कई बार इस का दामन भर दिया हुस्न-ए दो आलम से'

कई बार इस का दामन भर दिया हुस्न-ए दो आलम से
मगर दिल है कि इस की ख़ाना-वीरानी नहीं जाती

कई बार इस की ख़ातिर ज़रें ज़रें का जिगर चीरा
मगर ये चश्म-ए हैराँ जिस की हैरानी नहीं जाती

मेरी चश्म-ए तन आसाँ को बसीरत मिल गई जब से
बहुत जानी हुई सूरत भी पहचानी नहीं जाती

◆

'THIS IS WHAT MY VERSE IS ALL ABOUT'

The importance of this poem, titled 'Mauzo-e-Sukhan',
cannot be overstated. This is among the two or three
poems of Faiz where he tried to explain the essence of his
creativity. Most poets would not be talking about this and
leave it to the reader to figure out what the poet was writing
about, but Faiz could not resist the impulse to talk about
this because, during the early years, he faced an internal
struggle: 'Should I follow what has gone before me (keep

the focus on the beloved), or should I create something unique about myself and the world I live in?' Following the past was an easy option, but it didn't suit his temperament. He didn't want to be a traditional revolutionary poet because revolutionary poetry, by definition, is momentary, loud and prescriptive. One passion, which is deeply personal, drove him inward (his inner pull, his love, his life), the other revealed to him the purposefulness of life, to speak for the deprived—exploitation of labor by capital and, above all a foreign rule that had to use oppression as a means of sustaining itself. The way Faiz resolved this dilemma was not by making an either-or choice but by choosing both. Look at the first four stanzas of the poem. They are all about the beloved, about her charms and her allurements, thinking about her, missing her in his solitude and hoping for some magical revelation. The poet even reaches a conclusion: 'This is the world of my thought and my verse ... this is the essence of who I am.' He could have ended the poem at that point, but he did not. He goes on to talk about the suffering of the multitudes, life battling death each day, fields that grow hunger and slaughterhouses of dreams. This is the reality which the poet with a social conscience can't run away from. He thinks about all this, but then he says, 'Just think about the slowly opening lips of that beauty.' The circle is thus completed. The two passions mingle and blend; they become one, and in their oneness lies the greatness of Faiz's aesthetic creativity. Further, this poem is also the basic structure on which the poet later builds the superstructure of a vision of universal love, freedom and social justice, as we will elaborate by analysing the text.

It is dimming moment by moment,
slowly smoldering sad evening.
It will emerge, after a bath,
from where the moon's spring flows.
And the eyes that wanted answers
will get a chance.
And these thirsting hands
will meet those hands.

Is this the border of her veil?
Is this the fleeting sight of her face?
Or is this her simmering mantle?
There is something
that is making the valance colourful.
We don't know
whether under the dark shade
of her tresses
the earring still has the same
shiny twinkling sound.

Today once again
the beauty will reveal itself
in its fullest loveliness.
There will be half-sleepy eyes and
a captivating curved line of kohl.
Placed on the natural colour of the cheeks
there is a slight dusting of powder.
Sandalwood-like hands
have a faded trace of henna.

This is the world of my thoughts
and my verse.
This is the essence of what poetry is.
This is what I mean.

How much the offspring of Adam and Eve
suffered under the shadow
of red and black centuries?
Life and death fight a battle each day.
How much have we suffered?
How much our ancestors have suffered?

Multitudes who live in these glowing cities.
Why do they live
with the desire to die one day?
These bountiful fields
which are on the verge of losing their foliage,
why do they always grow hunger?

These walls that surround us
are strong and secretive.
They have doused lamps of youth
numbering thousands.
Every little place here
contains slaughterhouses of dreams.
The radiance of these places brightens
thoughtful minds.

These are, and there might be
many more subjects.
But think about the slowly opening
lips of that beauty.
And lo and behold, the faint outlines
of her alluring figure.
Tell me where else
will you find that kind of magic?

This is what the subject of my verse is.
This is what the poet's native land is.
It is nowhere else, but here.

'Mauzo-e Sukhan'

gul hui jaati hai afsurda sulagati hui shaam
dhul ke niklegi abhi chashma-e mahtaab se raat
aur mushtaaq nigaahon ki suni jaae gi
aur un haathon se mas honge ye tarse hue haath

unka aanchal hai k rukhsaar k pairaahan hai
kuchh to hai jis se hui jaati hai chilman rangiin
jaane us zulf ki mauhuum ghani chhaaon mein
timtimaata hai voh aveza abhi tak k nahien

aaj phir husn-e dil aara ki vohi dhaj ho gi
vohi khwaabiida si aankhein vohi kaajal ki lakiir
rang rukhsaar pe halka sa voh ghaaze ka ghubaar
sandali haath pe dhundhli si hina ki tahriir

apne afkaar ki ash'aar ki duniya hai yahi
jaan-e mazmuun hai yahi shaahid-e maa'ni hai yahi

aaj tak surkh o siya sadiyon ke saae ke tale
aadam o havva ki aulaad pe kya guzari hai?
maut aur ziist ki rozaana saf-aaraaii mein
ham pe kya guzregi ajdaad pe kya guzri hai?

in damakte hue shahron ki faraavaan makhluuq
kyon faqat marne ki hasrat mein jiya karti hai
ye hasiin khet phata parta hai joban jin ka
kis liye un mein faqat bhuuk ugaa karti hai

ye har ik simt pur-asraar kari diivaarein
jal-bujhe jin mein hazaroon ki javaani ke charaagh
ye har ek gaam p un khwaabon ki maqtal gaahein
jin ke partau se charaaghaan hain hazaaron ke dimaagh

ye bhi hain aise kaii aur bhi mazmuun honge
lekin us shokh ke ahista se khulte hue hont

haae us jism ke kambakht dil aavez khutuut
aap hi kahiye kahien aise bhi afsuun hon ge

apna mauzo-e sukhan in ke siva aur nahien
tab'e shaa'yir ka vatan in ke siva aur nahien

'मौजू-ए सुख़न'

गुल हुई जाती है अफ़्सुर्दा सुलगती हुई शाम
धुल के निकलेगी अभी चश्मा-ए महताब से रात
और मुश्ताक़ निगाहों की सुनी जाएगी
और उन हाथों से मस होंगे ये तरसे हुए हाथ

उन का आँचल है कि रुख़्सार कि पैराहन है
कुछ तो है जिस से हुई जाती है चिलमन रंगीं
जाने उस ज़ुल्फ़ की मौहूम घनी छाँव में
टिमटिमाता है वो आवेज़ा अभी तक कि नहीं

आज फिर हुस्न-ए दिल-आरा की वही धज होगी
वही ख़्वाबीदा सी आँखें वही काजल की लकीर
रंग-ए रुख़्सार पे हल्का सा वो ग़ाज़े का गुबार
संदली हाथ पे धुंदली सी हिना की तहरीर

अपने अफ़्कार की अश'आर की दुनिया है यही
जान-ए मज़मूँ है यही शाहिद-ए मअ'नी है यही

आज तक सुख़ ओ सियह सदियों के साए के तले
आदम ओ हव्वा की औलाद पे क्या गुज़री है?
मौत और ज़ीस्त की रोज़ाना सफ़-आराई में
हम पे क्या गुज़रेगी अज्दाद पे क्या गुज़री है?

इन दमकते हुए शहरों की फ़रावाँ मख़्लूक़
क्यूँ फ़क़त मरने की हसरत में जिया करती है
ये हसीं खेत फटा पड़ता है जौबन जिन का!
किस लिए इन में फ़क़त भूक उगा करती है

ये हर इक सम्त पुर-असरार कड़ी दीवारें
जल-बुझे जिन में हज़ारों की जवानी के चराग़
ये हर इक गाम पे उन ख़्वाबों की मक़्तल-गाहें
जिन के परतव से चरागाँ हैं हज़ारों के दिमाग़

ये भी हैं ऐसे कई और भी मज़मूँ होंगे
लेकिन उस शोख़ के आहिस्ता से खुलते हुए होंट
हाए उस जिस्म के कम्बख़्त दिल-आवेज़ ख़तूत
आप ही कहिए कहीं ऐसे भी अफ़्सूँ होंगे

अपना मौज़ू-ए सुख़न उन के सिवा और नहीं
तब्अ-ए शा'इर का वतन उन के सिवा और नहीं

◆

'WE THE PEOPLE'

This is a political poem. Its tone is depressing in the midst
of dense metaphors, making it somewhat hard to read. It
ends on two related metaphors—'*dasht o zindaan ki havas*'
and '*chaak-e gariibaan ki talaash*'—both evoking an imagery
of defiance and struggle. The poet finds that things are
drifting. There is a lack of authentic leadership. Tearing
one's collar is the ultimate act of mutual division and lack
of unity. The title 'Ham Log' implies that we are all in the
same boat. As a mood poem, it depicts the mood of the
entire nation at a certain point in time.

A row of extinguished candles
in the vestibules of the inner space.
Afraid and tired of the sun's bright light.
Just like the molten beauty of the beloved.
Not letting go of our darkness.

Questions of gain and loss,
how did this start and where will it end.

The same old inquests, the same old queries.
Frustrated by the colourlessness of today's import.
Sadness is tied to what happened in the past.
I'm crippled by the thought of what tomorrow
might bring.

Thoughts lacking any unifying purpose provide no
comfort.
Burning tears that eyes can't bear.
Unbearable pain that does not transform itself
into a song.
Pain that is stuck in the dark corners of the heart.
And our search for a twisted and perplexing
remedy.
A lust for the wilderness and the cell of a jailhouse.
A search for a remedy and tearing of clothes.

'Ham Log'

dil ke aivaan mein liye gul-shuda sham'aon ki qataar
nuur-e khurshiid se sahme hue uktaae hue
husn-e mahbuub ke saiyaal tasavvar ki tarah
apni taariiki ko bhiinche hue liptaa-e hue

ghaayat-e suud o ziyaan suurat-e aaghaaz o m'aal
vohi besuud tajassus vohi bekaar savaal
muzmhil saa'at-e imroze ki berangi se
yaad-e-maazi se ghamiin dahshat-e farda se nidhaal

tishna afkaar jo taskiin nahien paate hain
sokhta ashk jo aankhon mein nahien aate hain
ik karaa dard k jo giit mein dhalta hi nahien
dil ki taariik shigaafon se nikalta hi nahien
aur ek uljhi hue mauhuum se darbaan ki talaash
dasht o zindaan ki havas chaak-e giribaan ki talaash

'हम लोग'

दिल के ऐवाँ में लिए गुल-शुदा शम्ओं की क़तार
नूर-ए ख़ुर्शीद से सहमे हुए उकताए हुए
हुस्न-ए महबूब के सय्याल तसव्वुर की तरह
अपनी तारीकी को भेंचे हुए लिपटाए हुए

ग़ायत-ए सूद ओ ज़ियाँ सूरत-ए आगाज़ ओ म'आल
वही बेसूद-ए तजस्सुस वही बेकार सवाल
मुज़्महिल सा'इत-ए इमरोज़ की बेरंगी से
याद-ए-माज़ी से ग़र्मीं दहशत-ए फ़र्दा से निढाल

तिश्ना अफ़्कार जो तस्कीन नहीं पाते हैं
सोख़्ता अश्क जो आँखों में नहीं आते हैं
इक कड़ा दर्द कि जो गीत में ढलता ही नहीं
दिल के तारीक शिगाफ़ों से निकलता ही नहीं
और इक उलझी हुई मौहूम सी दरबाँ की तलाश
दश्त ओ ज़िंदाँ की हवस चाक-ए गिरेबाँ की तलाश

◆

GHAZAL

The days when my luck
will be tested are near.
The days when I get a chance
to be close to her
are coming.

Whatever I told my heart;
whatever my heart said to me.
The days to share that news
are coming.

Leave your heart and soul
at a high point on the road.

The days for being looted
are coming.

Her eyes revealed her
half-drunken state.
The days to keep eyes veiled
are coming.

The gentle breeze is once again making
inquiries about us.
The days to adorn the garden
are coming.

'Nasiib Aazmaane Ke Din Aa Rahe Hain'

nasiib aazmaane ke din aa rahe hain
qariib un ke aane ke din aa rahe hain

jo dil se kaha hai jo dil se suna hai
sab un ko sunaane ke din aa rahe hain

abhi se dil o jaan sar-e raah rakh do
k lutne lutaane ke din aa rahe hain

tapakne lagi un nigaahon se masti
nigaahein churaane ke din aa rahe hain

saba phir hamein puuchhti phir rahi hai
chaman ko sajaane ke din aa rahe hain

'नसीब आज़माने के दिन आ रहे हैं'

नसीब आज़माने के दिन आ रहे हैं
क़रीब उन के आने के दिन आ रहे हैं

जो दिल से कहा है जो दिल से सुना है
सब उन को सुनाने के दिन आ रहे हैं

अभी से दिल ओ जाँ सर-ए राह रख दो
कि लुटने लुटाने के दिन आ रहे हैं

टपकने लगी उन निगाहों से मस्ती
निगाहें चुराने के दिन आ-रहे हैं

सबा फिर हमें पूछती फिर रही है
चमन को सजाने के दिन आ रहे हैं

two

A BLEMISHED SUNRISE

My two books subsequent to *Naqsh-e Faryadi*, namely, *Dast-e Saba* (1952) and *Zindaan Nama* (1956) are souvenirs of my four year stay in prison. Although basically these writings are related to the mental impressions and thought processes which started with 'Mujh se pehli si mohabbat meri mahbuub n maang', prison itself, nevertheless, is a fundamental experience in which a new window of thought and vision opens itself. Thus prison is first like another adolescence when all sensations again become sharp and one experiences once again that same original astonishment at feeling the dawn breeze, at seeing the shadows of evening, the blue of the sky and feeling the passing breeze.

—Faiz on his period of incarceration[29]

THE INDIAN ARMY

While in Faiz's personal life things were looking up following his marriage with Alys and the early success of *Naqsh-e Faryadi*, the world at large was facing the spectre of Nazi Germany's brutal aggression. When Stalin signed a

---

[29]Hameed, ed., *Daybreak*, p. 79.

pact with Hitler, the progressives began to look upon the conflict as a war of imperialists seeking global domination. Therefore, they were neither for the war nor against it. But when Germany attacked the Soviet Union, their outlook changed overnight. The imperialists' war became the peoples' war and the sentiment became favourable towards the British and the Allies. Objective observers saw the hypocrisy of the leftists and progressives in this sudden change of heart about who were the bad guys in this conflict. For Faiz personally, while the Nazi invasion of the Soviet Union was a concern, he was equally bothered by the Japanese attack on India. This is what he said about it:

> We did not care much about the war. We thought this was something concerned with the British and the Germans, but in 1941, the Japanese entered the war. On the one hand, the Japanese came to the borders of India and on the other hand, the Nazis and the Fascists came to the doorsteps of Moscow and Leningrad. We felt it was time to go and join the fight, so we joined the army.[30]

Faiz joined the Public Relations Department of the Indian Army as a captain in 1942 and moved to Delhi. His main work related to the monitoring of communications concerning developments in various theatres of war and summarizing them for use by the Army personnel. This turned out to be an influential role, given the fact that information on a daily basis was the most valued commodity. Recognition came quickly—a year later, Faiz was promoted to major and after another year, he became a lieutenant colonel. His main contribution to the war effort

---

[30]Majeed, *Culture and Identity*, pp. 9–10.

was a team-oriented approach to sharing news among the troops and motivating them to fight for their motherland (India) and not for Britain or the Soviet Union. As the war came to an end in 1946, Faiz got another honour: an MBE (Member of the British Empire) in recognition of his meritorious service.

As his tenure with the army was coming to an end, Faiz was looking for new job opportunities. It was then that an old friend came to him with a job offer. The person who made the offer was Mian Iftikharuddin, whom Faiz had known as the publisher of *Adab-e-Latif*. Mian was starting a new daily newspaper called *Pakistan Times* and he wanted Faiz to be its editor-in-chief. Faiz had some reservations because he had never managed a daily newspaper in his life and also 'Pakistan' was still a possibility but not a reality. After consulting his friends and some personal reflection, Faiz agreed to take up this job and in early 1947, he moved back to Lahore. Success came early, as *Pakistan Times* and its sister publication *Imroze* became the most popular newspapers in Lahore within months of their launch.

15 AUGUST 1947

By mid-July 1947, following the passage of the Indian Independence Act by the British Parliament, it was quite certain that while India would earn its long-awaited freedom soon, the country itself would be divided into two independent countries. In early August, Alys had taken their two daughters (Salima born in Delhi in 1942 and Moneeza born in Shimla in 1946) for a summer vacation with Dr Taseer's family in Srinagar. Faiz was troubled by the impending storm that would destroy millions of homes and families as the date of Partition drew closer. He had started working on a poem called 'Sub-h-e Aazaadi' and he shared it with his close friends when he visited Srinagar. The poem, when published, created quite a stir because people both on the right and the left had expected to hear a different kind of poem. But Faiz was never someone who wrote to meet others' expectations. He responded only to his inner voice. The editorial that Faiz wrote for the paper also provides a peek into his inner thinking. He wrote:

> It is 15 August today. The dawn that brought this day into the world also restored to our people their long-lost freedom. Through many bleak decades of political serfdom, millions of us have waited and hoped for this dawn. It has arrived at last and yet, for us in Punjab, it is not bright with laughter and buoyant with a song. It is black with sorrow and red with blood. The reality of freedom, compared to the reality of the death and suffering around us, appears insubstantial and far away.[31]

THE CONSPIRACY

Alys woke up early on the morning of 9 March 1951, sensing some activity outside their home. Very soon, they found out that the police had come to take Faiz with them, with no adequate explanation other than 'we have our orders'. Later, Prime Minister Liaquat Ali Khan announced on the radio that a conspiracy had been discovered involving several military officers, the most prominent among them being Major General Akbar Khan, and a

---

[31] Hashmi, *Love and Revolution*, p. 127.

few civilians, that included Faiz as chief editor of *Pakistan Times*. The government needed a legal shield to prosecute the 'conspirators' and, therefore, the legislative assembly quickly passed the Rawalpindi Conspiracy Act. This is how Faiz explained his role in the whole thing:

> At the end of 1950, I met an old friend of mine from the army who had been appointed Chief of General Staff, General Akbar Khan ... I met him by chance in Murree ... and he said to me, 'Look, we people in the army ... are very disgruntled because this country is going to the dogs. We have made no constitution for four years, there is so much corruption, there is so much nepotism, no elections are being held ... and there is no hope and we want to do something.' I said, 'Do what?' He said, 'Overthrow the government, and we want to have a non-party government and have elections and a constitution ... and this that and the other.' I said, 'All right!' He said, 'Well, we want your advice.' I said, 'This is an army exercise, I can't give you any advice.' He said, 'Anyway, you come to our meeting and listen to our plan.'[32]

Faiz went to the meeting along with two of his civilian friends, and that was all.

After his arrest, Faiz was kept in solitary confinement for four months; his family didn't know for three months whether he was dead or alive. All the conspirators got jail sentences for varying lengths of time; Faiz got four years. While the separation from Alys and the family was painful, Faiz took advantage of the free time in jail to write poetry. It is worth mentioning that while he was a newspaper

---

[32]Majeed, *Culture and Identity*, p. 12.

editor and became involved in trade union activities, he had virtually stopped writing poetry. In jail, time was not a constraint. Faiz finished two books of poetry, *Dast-e Saba* (published when he was still in jail) and *Zindaan Nama* (published after his release).

Faiz suffered a great personal loss while he was still in prison. After the sudden death of his father when Faiz had been a student, his elder brother, Tufail, had proved to be a pillar of strength for the family. Faiz loved and respected him. Even in the conspiracy case, Tufail was the one who took care of the legal support that Faiz needed. It was, therefore, natural for Faiz to be extremely happy to hear that Tufail was coming to see him in jail. But the good news suddenly turned into tragedy as Tufail died of a heart attack on 17 July 1952. Faiz expressed his feelings a day later in an elegy titled 'Noha'.

> I have a complaint, my brother, that while going
> away
> you carried with you the book of my past life.
> That book contained many precious snapshots.
> It contained my childhood and the time of my youth.
> As a replacement, you gave me, while going,
> a shining blood-coloured rose of grief.
> What should I do with it, brother?
> How should I wear this robe of honour?
> You can take account of all my torn shirts.
> This is the last time.
> Please answer this question.
> You have never disappointed me by not giving me
> an answer.
> Come, and take away your shining gift of a rose.
> And give back to me the book of my past life.

'Noha'

mujh ko shikvah hai mere bhaai k tum jaate hue
le gaye saath meri u'mr-e guzishta ki kitaab
is mein to meri bahut qiimti tasviirein thien
is mein bachpan tha mera aur mera a'hd-e shabaab
is ke badle mujhe tum de gaaye jaate jaate
apne gham ka ye damakta hua khuun rang gulaab
kya karuun bhaai ye e'zaaz main kyon kar pahnuun
mujh se le lo meri sab chaak qamiizon ka hisaab
aakhri baar hai lo maan lo ik ye bhi savaal
aaj tak tum se main lauta nahien maayuus-e javaab
aa ke le jaao tum apna ye damakta hua phuul
mujh ko lauta do meri u'mr-e guzushta ki kitab

'नोहा'

मुझ को शिकवा है मेरे भाई कि तुम जाते हुए
ले गए साथ मेरी उम्र-ए गुज़िश्ता की किताब
इस में तो मेरी बहुत क़ीमती तस्वीरें थीं
इस में बचपन था मेरा और मेरा अहद-ए शबाब
इस के बदले मुझे तुम दे गए जाते जाते
अपने ग़म का ये दमकता हुआ खूँ-रंग गुलाब
क्या करूँ भाई ये एज़ाज़ में क्यूँ-कर पहनूँ
मुझ से ले लो मेरी सब चाक क़मीज़ों का हिसाब
आख़िरी बार है लो मान लो इक ये भी सवाल
आज तक तुम से मैं लौटा नहीं मायूस-ए जवाब
आ के ले जाओ तुम अपना ये दमकता हुआ फूल
मुझ को लौटा दो मेरी उम्र-ए गुज़िश्ता की किताब

Dast-e Saba, dedicated to 'Kulsoom' (Alys's Muslim name), was published in November 1952 (Faiz was in Hyderabad jail at that time). There was a book launch function in which leading literary figures of the time participated. Book launching, as an activity, was still a novelty, but the fact that so many people gathered to honour the book and the author, was uplifting news for the family. There was some celebration in the jail as well. Faiz was finally released from prison on 20 April 1955 and the new legislative assembly voided the remaining sentences of all the accused.

This chapter contains selections from the first set of poems that were written in prison.[33] Selections from the other set, that were published as *Zindaan Nama*, will be taken up in the next chapter.

QAT'A

Sadly, my tablet and my pen have been seized.
But I have dipped my fingers into my heart's
blood.
If my lips are sealed, it doesn't matter,
I have lodged a tongue into every ring of my
chain.

mat'a-e lauh o qalam chhin gaaii to kya gham hai
k khuun-e dil mein dabo li hain ungliyaan maine
zaban p mohr lagi hai to kya k rakh di hai
har ek halqa-e zanjiir mein zaban main ne

मता-ए लौह ओ क़लम छिन गई तो क्या ग़म है
कि ख़ून-ए दिल में डुबो ली हैं उँगलियाँ मैंने
ज़बाँ पे मोहर लगी है तो क्या कि रख दी है
हर एक हल्क़ा-ए ज़ंजीर में ज़बाँ मैंने

◆

---

[33]This chapter also includes some compositions written between 1941 and 1950, before the poet was imprisoned.

'STAY PUT MY RESTLESS HEART'

This poem represents a composite of two different moods. The tyranny of the foreign regime is at its peak, which is quite disheartening: '*tiirgi hai k umandati hi chali jaati hai/ shabki rag rag se lahu phuut raha ho jaise/chal rahi hai kuchh is andaaz se nabz-e hasti/donon aa'lam ka nasha tuut raha ho jaise*' (Darkness is expanding/and the blood is spurting; / it is gushing from every vein/that night seems to possess/ The rhythm of life is stretching as if the allure of this world/ and the next one is breaking down). But on the bright side, there are signs that dawn is just around the corner, waiting to break: '*sub-h hone hi ko hai ae dil-e betaab thahar*' (The sun will rise soon, /stay put my restless heart). The poem, as a whole, is a delicate balancing act.

> Darkness is expanding,
> and the blood is spurting;
> it is gushing from every vein
> that night seems to possess.
> The rhythm of life is stretching
> as if the allure of this world
> and the next one is breaking down.
> Let the night's toasty blood flow freely.
> This darkness is the facial coating of dawn.
> The sun will rise soon,
> stay put my restless heart.
> A chain is jangling behind the valance of music.
> The powers that be are still in the process
> of getting their act together.
> The wine-cup of life is letting the tears escape.
> Drunken feet are custom bound and unsteady.
> Mad lovers are not yet insane enough.

Taverns are not yet welcoming
the ones who are thirsty.
The structures of domination
are withering, though slowly.
The customs that weigh us down
are reaching their tipping point;
the rattling of chains would, however,
be heard for sometime to come.

'Ae Dil-e Betaab Thahar'

tiirgi hai k umandati hi chali jaati hai
shab ki rag rag se lahu phuut raha ho jaise
chal rahi hai kuchh is andaaz se nabz-e hasti
donon aa'lam ka nasha tuut raha ho jaise
raat ka garm lahu aur bhi bah jaane do
yahi taariiki to hai ghaaza-e rukhsaar-e sahar
sub-h hone hi ko hai ae dil-e betaab thahar
abhi zanjiir chhanakti hai pas-e parda-e saaz
mutlaq ul hukm hai shiraaza-e asbaab abhi
saaghar-e naab mein aansu bhi dhalak jaate hain
laghzish-e paa mein hai paabandi-e aadaab abhi
apne diivaano ko diivaaana to ban lene do
apne maikhaanon ko maikhaana to ban lene do
jald ye satvat-e asbaab bhi uth jaaegi
ye giraanbaari-e aadaab bhi uth jaaegi
khvah zanjiir chhankati hi chhanakti hi rahe

'ऐ दिल-ए बेताब ठहर'

तीरगी है कि उमंडती ही चली आती है
शब की रग रग से लहू फूट रहा हो जैसे
चल रही है कुछ इस अंदाज़ से नब्ज़-ए हस्ती
दोनों आ'लम का नशा टूट रहा हो जैसे
रात का गर्म लहू और भी बह जाने दो

यही तारीकी तो है ग़ाज़ा-ए रुख़सार-ए सहर
सुब्ह होने ही को है ऐ दिल-ए बेताब ठहर
अभी ज़ंजीर छनकती है पस-ए पर्दा-ए साज़
मुतलक़-उल-हुक्म है शीराज़ा-ए अस्बाब अभी
साग़र-ए नाब में आँसू भी ढलक जाते हैं
लग़्ज़िश-ए पा में है पाबंदी-ए आदाब अभी
अपने दीवानों को दीवाना तो बन लेने दो
अपने मयख़ानों को मयख़ाना तो बन लेने दो
जल्द ये सतवत-ए अस्बाब भी उठ जाएगी
ये गिराँ-बारी-ए आदाब भी उठ जाएगी
ख़्वाह ज़ंजीर छनकती ही छनकती ही रहे

◆

GHAZAL

Sometimes faint images of the past
appear in my memory.
A test of the heart and sight—
those intimacies, those withdrawals.

Sometimes caravans stop
in the desert of yearning.
All that talk about love,
and manifestations of the union.

No comfort for my eyes and the heart;
joy and grief are not less either.
Whenever she has met me,
it seems our love affair started afresh.

The lonesome pleasure is a burden,
though light and bearable.
But there is a hidden pain—
the reason why this world
befriended me.

Tell me, the difference today evening
between a drunk and the morality chief?
One has come and taken a seat, in this tavern
and the other has appeared after visiting another
one.

*'Kabhi Kabhi Yaad Mein Ubharte Hain Naqsh-E Maazi
Mite Mite Se'*

*kabhi kabhi yaad mein ubharte hain naqsh-e maazi mite
mite se*
*voh aazmaaish dil o nazar ki voh qurbatein si voh
faasle se*

*kabhi kabhi aarzu ke sehra mein aa ke rukte hain
qaafle se*
*voh saari baatein lagaav ki si voh saare u'nvaan
visaal ke se*

*nigaah o dil ko qaraar kaisa nishaat o gham mein
kami kahaan ki*
*voh jab mile hain to un se har baar ki hai ulfat naye
sire se*

*bahut giraan hai ye a'ish-e tanha kahien subuk tar
kahien guvaara*
*voh dard-e pinhaan k saari duniya rafiiq thi jiske
vaaste se*

*tumhein kaho rind o mohatsib mein hai aaj shab kaun
farq aisa*
*ye aa ke baithe hain maikade mein voh uthke aaye hain
maikade se*

'कभी कभी याद में उभरते हैं नक़्श-ए माज़ी मिटे मिटे से'

कभी कभी याद में उभरते हैं नक़्श-ए माज़ी मिटे मिटे से

वो आज़माइश दिल ओ नज़र की वो क़ुर्बतें सी वो फ़ासले से

कभी कभी आरज़ू के सहरा में आ के रुकते हैं क़ाफ़िले से
वो सारी बातें लगाव की सी वो सारे उनवाँ विसाल के से

निगाह ओ दिल को क़रार कैसा नशात ओ ग़म में कमी कहाँ की
वो जब मिले हैं तो उन से हर बार की है उल्फ़त नए सिरे से

बहुत गिराँ है ये ऐश-ए तन्हा कहीं सुबुक-तर कहीं गवारा
वो दर्द-ए पिन्हाँ कि सारी दुनिया रफ़ीक़ थी जिस के वास्ते से

तुम्हीं कहो रिंद ओ मोहतसिब में है आज शब कौन फ़र्क़ ऐसा
ये आ के बैठे हैं मयकदे में वो उठ के आए हैं मयकदे से

◆

'MY CONFIDANTE, MY FRIEND'

This poem gives the appearance of a monologue, but it is a conversation between the poet and the people. What the poet is saying is manifest, but what the people are saying is hidden behind a veil of silence. The tyranny of the corrupt regime has taken away the people's voice. There is a hint about the ruling class and the religious establishment coming together to act as a wall between the people and the revolution. There is no remedy, unless people decide to fight this injustice: '*tere aazaar ka chaarah nahien nishtar ke siva / aur ye saffaak masiiha mere qabze mein nahien*' (There is no cure for what ails you without a lancet. / And this hard remedy is not within my reach).

If I were sure, my confidante, my friend.
If I were convinced that your heart's extreme tiredness,
the sadness of your eyes,
the fire that burns in the centre of your being

would lessen by my empathy and the expression
of my love.
If my word of commiseration is the cure that
would awaken
your desolate brain that has lost its radiance.
If this makes the stains of ignominy leave your
brow
and your frail youthfulness is healed.
If I were sure, my confidante, my friend.
I would charm and amuse you every day and night,
evening and daybreak, I would sing songs for you,
sweet and gentle.
Songs of waterfalls, of springtime, of flower-laden
gardens,
of morning's arrival, of moon-lit nights and of
starry heavens.
I would tell you stories of beauty and love,
how ice-like cold frames of self-respecting beauties
melt with just a touch of warm hands,
how the distinctive features of a known face
change in a matter of minutes,
how the beloved's cheeks, shiny and translucent,
start to glow with just a sip of red wine,
how the branches of a rose bush bend for the
flower-picker,
how the night's assembly starts to smell sweet,
if I continue to sing for you, and you only,
weaving songs while sitting idly, just for you,
but sadly, my songs will not lessen your pain.
A song can't do the job of a surgeon,
though it would console and comfort;
it is not a surgical instrument, though it might
help.

There is no cure for what ails you without cutting
and slitting.
And this hard remedy is not within my reach,
not within the range of any living and breathing
being,
other than you, other than you, other than you.

'Mere Hamdam Mere Dost'

gar mujhe is ka yaqiin ho mere hamdam mere dost
gar mujhe is ka yaqiin ho k tere dil ki thakan
teri aankhon ki udaasi tere siine ki jalan
meri dil-joii mere pyar se mit jayegi
gar mera harf-e tassalli voh dava ho jis se
ji uthe phir tera ujra hua benuur damaagh
teri peshaani se dhull jayein y tazliil ke daagh
teri biimaar javaani ko shafa ho jaaye
gar mujhe is ka yaqiin ho mere hamdam mere dost
roz o shab shaam o sahar main tujhe bahlaata rahuun
main tujhe giit sunaata rahuun halke shiriin
aab shaaron ke bahaaron ke chaman zaaron ke giit
aamad-e sub-h ke sayyaaron ke giit
tujh se main husn o mohabbat ki hikaayaat kahuun
kaise maghruur hasiinaayon ke barfaab se jism
garam hathon ki haraarat mein pighal jaate hain
kaise ik chehre ke thahre hue maanuus naquush
dekhte dekhte yak lakht badal jaate hain
kis tarah aariz-e mahbuub ka shaffaaf bilaur
yak b yak baadah-e ahmar se dahak jaata hai
kaise gulchiin ke liye jhukti hai khud shaakh-e gulaab
kis tarah raat ka aivaan mahek jaata hai
yuun hi gaata rahuun gaata rahuun teri khaatir
giit bunta rahuun baitha rahuun teri khaatir
par mere giit tere dukh ka mudaava hi nahien

naghma jarrah nahien muunis o ghamkhwaar sahi
giit nishtar to nahien marham-e aazaar sahi
tere aazaar ka chaarah nahien nishtar ke siva
aur y saffaak masiiha mere qabze mein nahien
is jahaan ke kisi zii-ruuh ke qabze mein nahien
haan magar tere siva tere siva tere siva

'मेरे हमदम मेरे दोस्त'

गर मुझे इस का यक़ीं हो मेरे हमदम मेरे दोस्त
गर मुझे इस का यक़ीं हो कि तेरे दिल की थकन
तेरी आँखों की उदासी तेरे सीने की जलन
मेरी दिल-जूई मेरे प्यार से मिट जाएगी
गर मेरा हर्फ़-ए तसल्ली वो दवा हो जिससे
जी उठे फिर तेरा उजड़ा हुआ बेनूर दिमाग़
तेरी पेशानी से ढल जाएँ ये तजलील के दाग़
तेरी बीमार जवानी को शिफ़ा हो जाए
गर मुझे इस का यक़ीं हो मेरे हमदम मरे दोस्त
रोज़ ओ शब शाम ओ सहर मैं तुझे बहलाता रहूँ
मैं तुझे गीत सुनाता रहूँ हल्के शीरीं
आबशारों के बहारों के चमन-ज़ारों के गीत
आमद-ए सुब्ह के महताब के सय्यारों के गीत
तुझ से मैं हुस्न ओ मोहब्बत की हिकायात कहूँ
कैसे मग़रूर हसीनाओं के बरफ़ाब से जिस्म
गर्म हाथों की हरारत में पिघल जाते हैं
कैसे इक चेहरे के ठहरे हुए मानूस नुक़ूश
देखते देखते यक-लख़्त बदल जाते हैं
किस तरह आरिज़-ए महबूब का शफ़्फ़ाफ़ बिलोर
यक-ब-यक बादा-ए अहमर से दहक जाता है
कैसे गुलचीं के लिए झुकती है ख़ुद शाख़-ए गुलाब
किस तरह रात का ऐवान महक जाता है
यूँही गाता रहूँ गाता रहूँ तेरी ख़ातिर
गीत बुनता रहूँ बैठा रहूँ तेरी ख़ातिर
पर मेरे गीत तेरे दुख का मुदावा ही नहीं

नग़मा जरॉह नहीं मूनिस ओ ग़मख़्वार सही
गीत नश्तर तो नहीं मरहम-ए आज़ार सही
तेरे आज़ार का चारा नहीं नश्तर के सिवा
और ये सफ़्फ़ाक मसीहा मेरे क़ब्ज़े में नहीं
इस जहाँ के किसी ज़ी-रूह के क़ब्ज़े में नहीं
हाँ मगर तेरे सिवा तेरे सिवा तेरे सिवा

◆

'THE DAWN OF FREEDOM—AUGUST 1947'

Faiz was already living in Lahore and editing *Pakistan Times* when Partition was announced. His mental state was somewhere between happy and sad. He started writing a poem, but he completed it in Srinagar, where he joined Alys, who had gone on a brief vacation with Dr Taseer and his family. The poem, which is beautifully written, became his most controversial poem. People on the right and the left were unhappy, and they raised objections, especially about the opening line '*ye daagh daagh ujaala, ye shab-gaziida sahar*' (This blemished sunrise, this daybreak of a night—mangled and mutilated). People on the right were upset that the poem did not celebrate the creation of Pakistan, which was their dream. Those on the left felt that the poem was too vague. If you overlooked the title of the poem, it did not read like a poem about Independence. Why is freedom from colonialism not a manzil (destination)? Poet Ali Sardar Jafri, who believed in strictly following the party line, remarked that such a poem could have been written by a Muslim Leaguer or an RSS member.

All these critics forgot that Faiz was a secular humanist. For him, the idea that Hindus and Muslims had to live in two separate countries because they worshipped different gods was ludicrous. Secularism was such a deeply held belief for him that he was not willing to compromise on it. However, the Communist Party of India had, only six months earlier, accepted the division of the country into two parts known as India and Pakistan. He was upset about the loss of lives and bloodshed on a devastating scale because of this division. The day of freedom should have been a day of joy and celebration for all and not a day when innocents are butchered in the name of the religion they were born into. This outcome was acceptable to many poets and politicians, but for Faiz, the last line best summed up his mental state: '*chale chalo k voh manzil abhi nahien aaii*' (Keep moving, we haven't reached the goal yet). Faiz's words were good predictors: the country he loved the most has remained under direct or indirect control of the army. While some people have enriched themselves, the masses lack a good health and education system, there is rampant hunger and poverty, and the religious establishment has grabbed immense power without any accountability. People reach their goal only when there is progress for all.[34]

> This blemished sunrise, this daybreak of a night—
> mangled and mutilated.
> What we were waiting for, this is not the dawn.
> This is not the dawn in whose expectation friends
> set out

---

[34]The partition of India was a tragedy of epic proportions during which millions of lives were lost to communal violence. Many people ask why Faiz did not write a poem about this. His daughter Salima posed the same question to her father. His reply was: 'Because it was too big.' Rakshanda Jalil, *Liking Progress, Loving Change: A Literary History of the Progressive Writers' Movement in Urdu*, New Delhi: Oxford University Press. 2014, p. 276.

in search of a journey's end, finding it somewhere—
in the wasteland of the sky where stars reach their
goal.
I was hoping to find a shoreline somewhere of
the night's slow-moving tide.
Somewhere it will find an anchor for this vessel of
heart's grief.

Driven by the youthful blood on mysterious pathways,
when the friends started the journey, how many
hands touched them.
From the restless sleeping bowers of beauty's dwellings
arms kept howling, bodies kept bellowing.
But very precious was the passion to see the face
of dawn.
Very close to the mantles of sparkling beauties.
Lightly soaring longings, faintly fatigued.

Rumours say—
darkness has been separated from the light.

Rumors say—
marching steps have reached their goal.
There are new norms set in place by the new
guardians of suffering.
The joys of the union are lawful, but the agony of
separation is not.
The liver's blaze, the clamour of the eye, slow
flaming of the heart.
The cure for the pain of separation doesn't work
anymore.
From where did this honeyed morning breeze
come and
where did it go?

The light on the streets knows nothing about it.
The night's burden has not lessened.
The time when the eye and the heart
find some solace has not yet arrived.
Keep moving.
We haven't reached the goal yet.

'Sub-h-e Aazaadi'

ye duugh daagh ujaala ye shab-gaziida sahar
voh intizaar tha jis ka ye voh sahar to nahien
ye voh sahar to nahien jis ki aarzu le kar
chale the yaar k mil jaayegi kahien n kahien
falak ke dasht mein taaron ki aakhri manzil
kahien to ho ga shab-e sust mauj ka saahil
kahien to ja ke ruke ga safiina-e gham-e dil

javaan lahu ki pur-israar shaah raahon se
chale jo yaar to daaman pe kitne haath pare
dayaar-e husn ki besabr khwaab gaahon se
pukarti rahiin baahein badan bulaate rahe
bahut aziiz thi lekin rukh-e sahar ki lagan
bahut qariin tha husiinaan-e nuur ka daaman
subuk subuk thi tamanna dabi dabi thi thakan

suna hai ho bhi chuka hai firaaq-e zulmat o nuur
suna hai ho bhi chuka hai visaal-e manzil o gaam
badal chuka hai bahut ahl-e dard ka dastuur
nashaat-e vasl halaal o a'zaab-e hijr haram
jigar ki aag nazar ki umang dil ki jalan
kisi pe chaarah-e hijraan ka kuchh asar hi nahien
kahaan se aaii nigaar-e saba kidhar ko gaaii

abhi charaagh-e sar-e rah ko kuchh khabar hi nahien
abhi giraani-e shab mein kami nahien aaii

najaat-e diidaah o dil ki ghari nahien aaii
chale chalo k voh manzil abhi nahien aaii

'सुब्ह-ए आज़ादी'

ये दाग़ दाग़ उजाला ये शब-गज़ीदा सहर
वो इंतिज़ार था जिस का ये वो सहर तो नहीं
ये वो सहर तो नहीं जिस की आरज़ू ले कर
चले थे यार कि मिल जाएगी कहीं न कहीं
फ़लक के दश्त में तारों की आख़िरी मंज़िल
कहीं तो होगा शब-ए सुस्त-मौज का साहिल
कहीं तो जा के रुकेगा सफ़ीना-ए ग़म-ए दिल

जवाँ लहू की पुर-असरार शाह-राहों से
चले जो यार तो दामन पे कितने हाथ पड़े
दयार-ए हुस्न की बेसब्र ख़्वाब-गाहों से
पुकारती रहीं बाहें बदन बुलाते रहे
बहुत अज़ीज़ थी लेकिन रुख़-ए सहर की लगन
बहुत क़रीं था हसीनान-ए नूर का दामन
सुबुक सुबुक थी तमन्ना दबी दबी थी थकन

सुना है हो भी चुका है फ़िराक़-ए ज़ुल्मत ओ नूर
सुना है हो भी चुका है विसाल-ए मंज़िल ओ गाम
बदल चुका है बहुत अहल-ए दर्द का दस्तूर
नशात-ए वस्ल हलाल ओ अज़ाब-ए हिज़्र हराम
जिगर की आग नज़र की उमंग दिल की जलन
किसी पे चारा-ए हिज़्राँ का कुछ असर ही नहीं
कहाँ से आई निगार-ए सबा किधर को गई

अभी चराग़-ए सर-ए रह को कुछ ख़बर ही नहीं
अभी गिरानी-ए शब में कमी नहीं आई
नजात-ए दीदा ओ दिल की घड़ी नहीं आई
चले-चलो कि वो मंज़िल अभी नहीं आई

◆

'TABLET AND PEN'

This poem is a testament to Faiz's ability to make strong political statements that show great determination, yet the words chosen by him are not loud or noisy. Also, for Faiz, there is nothing that is purely political; there has to be a little blending of taghazzul and beauty. Notice the sheer elegance of the following two lines: '*baaqi hai lahu dil mein to har ashk se paida / rang-e lab o rukhsaar-e sanam karte raheinge*' (If the blood remains in the heart, / every tear of ours shall produce colour / for the lips and cheeks of the one we love). This poem was an unperturbed reply, written in highly appealing lyrical verse, to those who had raised a storm against 'Sub-h-e Aazaadi'.

While we foster the tablet and the pen,
no one can stop us from scripting
what is happening all around;
sharing what love's grief is doing to us,
and showing kindness to the time's wasteland.
This is what we shall continue doing.
Yes, times will get tighter.
Yes, the tyrants will find new ways
to abuse and maltreat us.
We accept this bitterness and this oppression.
As long as there is breath,
we shall do something to lessen the pain.
If the tavern is safe,
then with the help of wine of love
we shall beautify the doors and walls
of the places of worship.
If the blood remains in the heart,
every tear of ours shall produce colour

for the lips and cheeks of the one we love.
Those who are indifferent
let them celebrate their detachment.
This is an expression of our heart's desire,
and we shall continue to manifest it.

'Lauh o Qalam'

ham parvarish-e lauh o qalam karte raheinge
jo dil pe guzarti hai raqam karte raheinge
asbaab-e gham-e i'shq baham karte raheinge
viraani-e dauraan pe karam karte raheinge
haan talkhi-e ayyaam abhi aur barhegi
haan ahl-e sitam mashq-e sitam karte raheinge
manzuur ye talkhi ye sitam ham ko gavaara
dam hai to mudaava-e alam karte raheinge
maikhaana salaamat hai to ham surkhi-e mai se
taz'iin-e dar o baam-e haram karte raheinge
baaqi hai lahu dil mein to har ashk se paida
rang-e lab o rukhsaar-e sanam karte raheinge
ik tarz-e taghaaful hai so voh unko mubarak
ik arz-e tamanna hai so ham karte raheinge

'लौह ओ क़लम'

हम परवरिश-ए लौह ओ क़लम करते रहेंगे
जो दिल पे गुज़रती है रक़म करते रहेंगे
असबाब-ए ग़म-ए इश्क़ बहम करते रहेंगे
वीरानी-ए दौराँ पे करम करते रहेंगे
हाँ तल्ख़ी-ए अय्याम अभी और बढ़ेगी
हाँ अहल-ए सितम मश्क़-ए सितम करते रहेंगे
मंज़ूर ये तल्ख़ी ये सितम हम को गवारा
दम है तो मुदावा-ए अलम करते रहेंगे
मयख़ाना सलामत है तो हम सुर्ख़ी-ए मय से
तज़ईन-ए दर ओ बाम-ए हरम करते रहेंगे

बाक़ी है लहू दिल में तो हर अश्क से पैदा
रंग-ए लब ओ रुख़्सार-ए सनम करते रहेंगे
इक तर्ज-ए तग़ाफ़ुल है सो वो उन को मुबारक
इक अर्ज़-ए तमन्ना है सो हम करते रहेंगे

◆

QAT'A

Please don't ask me how long has been my wait.
Or about the time I didn't yearn for you.
I see your reflection in the beautiful springs,
reminding me of your lips, your arms
and your embrace.

n puuchh jab se tera intizaar kitna hai
k jin dinon se mujhe tera intizaar nahien
tera hi a'ks hai in ajnabi bahaaron mein
jo tere lab tere baazu tera kanaar nahien

न पूछ जब से तेरा इंतिज़ार कितना है
कि जिन दिनों से मुझे तेरा इंतिज़ार नहीं
तेरा ही अ'क्स है इन अजनबी बहारों में
जो तेरे लब तेरे बाज़ू तेरा कनार नहीं

◆

QAT'A

The morning breeze hides the softness of her
hands.
Stop-and-go, my heart gets a lingering feeling;
those hands are searching in the meeting place
where wounds of heart lie, where pain hurts the
most.

saba ke haath mein narmi hai un ke haathon ki
thahar thahar ke ye hota hai aaj dil ko gumaan
voh haath dhuundh rahe hain bisaat-e mahfil mein
k dil ke daagh kahaan hain nishast-e dard kahaan

सबा के हाथ में नर्मी है उन के हाथों की
ठहर ठहर के ये होता है आज दिल को गुमाँ
वो हाथ ढूँड रहे हैं बिसात-ए महफ़िल में
कि दिल के दाग़ कहाँ हैं नशिस्त-ए दर्द कहाँ

◆

'THE COMMOTION OF HARP AND FLUTE'

Poems like this one are rare in Urdu. Even when they are written, they are considered to be experimental. Faiz used this style primarily as a way of showing different perspectives, but he employed this technique in many other cases as well. Each voice represents a worldview. The first voice is that of defeatism, signalling the end of idealism. You can't get stars and moons; the stories we tell are all false dreams. Our desire is not satisfied by the sweetness of the beloved's lips or the fragrance of her face. In short, there is no cure for life's illnesses. Dying, therefore, is the only option. The second voice's response is about the dynamism of life. There is boundless richness in existence. The assembly is always illuminated, although there might be darkness in some corners. For every sunset, there is a sunrise. None of this is good enough to change the thinking behind the first voice. The second voice comes back, this time more forcefully, talking about the freedom to act, the power of human speech, and how the boundless energy of human spirit prevails in all circumstances.

First Voice

No more trying—
the discourse about flying away
has come to an end.
Nooses thrown at the stars were futile,
bloody attacks in the night
that targeted the moon are over.
What future promises can we make for these eyes?
What can we do to console the heart
while we tell stories of false dreams?
The sweetness of her lips,
the fragrance of her face—
these are no longer the headlines of desire.
I can't find a cure for my life's illnesses
in the freshness of my heart
and in the delight of my eyes.
Let us not visit stories about living.
What are we going to gain
by embroiling ourselves in these fictions?
Dying is the only choice before us.
We shall deal with it whenever we are ready.
This is your cloak. That is my cloak.
This is my grave. That is your grave.

Second Voice

The boundless riches of existence are
neither your estate nor mine.
In this meeting place,
it doesn't matter if the light of one's heart
is wounded, or it is shining bright.
This meeting place is always illuminated.

If one tiny corner is desolate,
how does it matter?
Your days may be lacklustre,
but if dusk and dawn follow their routine,
if the steps of the season of roses have not been
halted,
if the sun and moon are spreading their
splendour as usual,
if the valley of cheeks and lips continues to
bloom,
if there is freshness and loveliness wherever the
eye wanders,
if there is awareness of the pleasure that arises
from the heart's pain,
if there is the blessing of the moist eyes,
then give your thanks to the teary eyes.
Give your thanks to the delight of what is seen.
Give your thanks to dusk and dawn, sun and
moon.

First Voice

If this is how the sun and moon function,
what good can come out of them?
What is the use of the charms of the night?
Or how dawn unfolds its allure?
When the blood of the heart has turned into ice,
when eyes reveal a coating of iron,
what will happen to the teary eyes?
Or just the pure delight of seeing?
When domes of verse turn into ashes,
and threads of melodies are broken,
musical instruments will not produce any music.

What will happen to this pen of pearls?
When the cage itself becomes the dwelling,
when the pouch and collar become a rope,
it doesn't matter
whether the season of flowers would come or not,
or what would happen to the heart's grief?

Second Voice

As long as these hands are alive
and the blood is running warm,
as long as truth is hidden in the heart,
as long as there is strength in our speech and
voice,
we shall teach the yoke and chains
the commotion of harp and flute,
that tumult before which
Caesar's and Khusrau's drums sound weak.
We are free, and also free are our thoughts and
actions,
our hearts are filled with courage,
in each moment we live a lifetime,
each tomorrow is our today.
This dusk and this dawn.
This sun and this moon.
These starry constellations too belong to us.
This tablet and pen, this drum and signal, these
riches.
These are all ours.

'Shorish-e Barbat o Nai'

pehli aavaaz

ab sa'ii ka imkaan aur nahien parvaaz ka mazmuun
ho bhi chuka
taaron pe kamandein phaink chuke mahtaab pe shab
khuun ho bhi chuka
ab aur kisi farda ke liye in aankhon se kya paimaan kiije
kis khwaab ke jhuute afsuun se taskiin-e dil-e nadaan kiije
shiiriini-e lab khushbuu-e dahan ab shauq ka u'nvaan
koi nahien
shaadaabi-e dil tafriih-e nazar ab ziist ka darmaan koi
nahien
jiine ke fasaane rahne do ab un mein ulajh kar kya
lein ge
ik maut ka dhanda baaqi hai jab chaaheinge nipta lein ge
ye tera kafan voh mera kafan ye meri lahad voh teri hai

duusri aavaaz

hasti ki mat'a-e bepaayaan jaagiir teri hai n meri hai
is bazm mein apni mash'al-e dil bismal hai to kya
rakhshaan hai to kya
ye bazm charaaghaan rahti hai ik taaq agar viiraan
hai to kya
afsurdah hain gar ayyaam tere badla nahien maslak-e
shaam o sahar
thahre nahien mausam-e gul ke qadam qaaim hai
jamal-e shams o qamar
aabaad hai vaadi-e kaakul o lab shaadaab o hasiin
gulgasht-e nazar
maqsuum hai lazzat-e dard-e jigar maujuud hai
n'emat-e diida-e tar
is diida-e tar ka shukr karo is zauq-e nazar ka shukr karo

is shaam o sahar ka shukr karo in shams o qamar ka
shukr karo

pehli aavaaz

gar hai yahi maslak-e shams o qamar in shams o
qamar ka kya ho ga
ra'naaii-e shab ka kya ho ga andaaz-e sahar ka kya ho ga
jab khuun-e jigar barfaab bana jab aankhein aahan
posh huein
is diidah-e tar ka kya ho ga is zauq-e nazar ka kya ho ga
jab sh'er ke khaime raakh hue nagmon ki tanaabein
tuut gaaiin
ye saaz kahaan sar phoreinge is kilk-e guhar ka kya ho ga
jab kunj-e qafas maskan thahra aur jaib o garibaan
tauq o rasan
aaye k n aaye mausam-e gul is dard-e jigar ka kya ho ga

duusri aavaaz

ye haath salaamat hain jab tak is khuun mein
haraarat hai jab tak
is dil mein sadaaqat hai jab tak is nutq mein taaqat
hai jab tak
is tauq o salaasal ko ham tum sikhlaeinge shorish-e
barbat o nai
voh shorish jis ke aage zabuun hangaama-e tabl-e kaisar
o kai
aazaad hain apne fikro o a'mal bharpuur khaziina
himmat ka
ik u'mr hai apni har saa'at imroze hai apna har farda
ye shaam o sahar ye shams o qamar ye akhtar o kau
kab apne hain
ye lauh o qalam ye tibl o a'lam ye maal o hasham sab
apne hain

'शोरिश-ए बर्बत ओ नै'

पहली आवाज़

अब स'ई का इम्काँ और नहीं पर्वाज़ का मज़मूँ हो भी चुका
तारों पे कमंदें फेंक चुके महताब पे शब-ख़ूँ हो भी चुका
अब और किसी फ़र्दा के लिए उन आँखों से क्या पैमाँ कीजे
किस ख़्वाब के झूटे अफ़्सूँ से तस्कीन-ए दिल-ए नादाँ कीजे
शीरीनी-ए लब ख़ुशबू-ए दहन अब शौक़ का उ'न्वां कोई नहीं
शादाबी-ए दिल तफ़रीह-ए नज़र अब ज़ीस्त का दरमाँ कोई नहीं
जीने के फ़साने रहने दो अब इन में उलझ कर क्या लेंगे
इक मौत का धंदा बाक़ी है जब चाहें गे निप्टा लेंगे
ये तेरा कफ़न वो मेरा कफ़न ये मेरी लहद वो तेरी है

दूसरी आवाज़

हस्ती की मता-ए बे-पायाँ जागीर तेरी है न मेरी है
इस बज़्म में अपनी मिशअल-ए दिल बिस्मिल है तो क्या रख़्शाँ है तो
क्या
ये बज़्म चराग़ाँ रहती है इक ताक़ अगर वीराँ है तो क्या
अफ़्सुर्दा हैं गर अय्याम तेरे बदला नहीं मस्लक-ए शाम ओ सहर
ठहरे नहीं मौसम-ए गुल के क़दम क़ाएम है जमाल-ए शम्स ओ क़मर
आबाद है वादी-ए काकुल ओ लब शादाब ओ हसीं गुल गश्त-ए नज़र
मक़्सूम है लज़्ज़त-ए दर्द-ए जिगर मौजूद है नेमत-ए दीदा-ए तर
इस दीदा-ए तर का शुक्र करो इस ज़ौक़-ए नज़र का शुक्र करो
इस शाम ओ सहर का शुक्र करो इन शम्स ओ क़मर का शुक्र करो

पहली आवाज़

गर है यही मस्लक-ए शम्स ओ क़मर इन शम्स ओ क़मर का क्या
होगा
रा'नाई-ए शब का क्या होगा अंदाज़-ए सहर का क्या होगा
जब ख़ून-ए जिगर बर्फ़ाब बना जब आँखें आहन-पोश हुईं
इस दीदा-ए तर का क्या होगा इस ज़ौक़-ए नज़र का क्या होगा
जब शे'र के ख़ेमे राख हुए नग़्मों की तनाबें टूट गईं
ये साज़ कहाँ सर फोड़ेंगे इस क्लिक-ए गुहर का क्या होगा

जब कुंज-ए क़फ़स मस्कन ठहरा और जैब ओ गरेबाँ तौक़ ओ रसन
आए कि न आए मौसम-ए गुल इस दर्द-ए जिगर का क्या होगा

दूसरी आवाज़

ये हाथ सलामत हैं जब तक इस ख़ूँ में हरारत है जब तक
इस दिल में सदाक़त है जब तक इस नुत्क़ में ताक़त है जब तक
इन तौक़ ओ सलासिल को हम तुम सिखलाएँ गे शोरिश-ए बरबत ओ
नय
वो शोरिश जिस के आगे ज़ुबूँ हँगामा-ए तब्ल-ए क़ैसर ओ कै
आज़ाद हैं अपने फ़िक्र ओ अ'मल भरपूर ख़ज़ीना हिम्मत का
इक उम्र है अपनी हर सा'इत इमरोज़ है अपना हर फ़र्दा
ये शाम ओ सहर ये शम्स ओ क़मर ये अख़्तर ओ कौकब अपने हैं
ये लौह ओ क़लम ये तब्ल ओ अलम ये माल ओ हशम सब अपने हैं

◆

QAT'A

In the house of passion, it is doomsday again.
Hon. Justices are seated, while sinners stand
facing them.
Let us see who is found guilty of fidelity.
All the sinners are standing at the chopping
block.

phir hashr ke saamaan hue aivaan-e havas mein
baithe hain zavil-a'dal gunaahgaar khare hain
haan jurm-e vafa diikhiiye kis kis p hai saabit
voh saare khata kaar sar-e daar khare hain

फिर हश्र के सामाँ हुए ऐवान-ए हवस में
बैठे हैं ज़विल-अद्ल गुनाहगार खड़े हैं
हाँ जुर्म-ए वफ़ा देखिए किस किस पे है साबित
वो सारे ख़ताकार सर-ए दार खड़े हैं

◆

'THE SEASON OF SHACKLE AND THE HANGING POST'

This is a revolutionary poem unlike most revolutionary poems. For everything that is said, there is much more that is left unsaid. The poet uses the dynamic metaphor of mausam (season) to convey his message. For nature, at the surface, things appear to be different, but deep down, there is grief, and hope that sustains itself. Spring brings fresh flowers and glad tidings. Autumn is fallen leaves and barren landscapes. But, for human beings, things are different in every season. The poet talks about a time of struggle and sacrifice, separation from the beloved, frenzy and madness and shackle and the hanging post. The message is harsh, but because of the beauty of the presentation, the inherent lyricism and the choice of brilliant words, there is no noisy clarion call. Everything flows smoothly; the message goes straight to the heart.

> Pathways in the garden
> remind one of the seasons of waiting.
> Nothing looks here like spring.
> The weight burdens the heart
> of distressing daily routines—
> a season when the beauty is put to the test.
> Bless the view that brings to sight
> the spectacle of the friend's cheeks.
> Bless the season when the restless heart gets
> to the point of calmness and restfulness.
> No cup of wine and the cup-bearer.
> A season when the clouds float
> over highlands and the mountains.
> What should one do without the company,
> dear friends?

A season when shadows dance
over oak and maple trees.
The scars of the heart were always painful,
but not too much.
This time, it is different—
the season of separation from the beloved.
This is the season of frenzy and madness,
shackle, and the hanging post.
This is the season of coercion and making a
choice.
Prison is under your control;
it is not under your control.
In the garden, it is the season of flaming red roses,
their grace and elegance.
Morning breeze's tipsy morning walk is
not under a noose of rope.
No net can catch the season of spring.
Sadly, I have not seen it, but others will see.
The season of blooming of the garden
where you hear one thousand notes
that the nightingale sings celebrating
the bursting of the spring.

'Taoq o Daar Ka Mausam'

ravish ravish hai voh iintizaar ka mausam
nahien hai koi bhi mausam bahaar ka mausam
giraan hai dil p gham-e rozgaar ka mausam
hai aazmaaish-e husn-e nigaar ka mausam
khusha nazzaara-e rukhsaar-e yaar ki saa'at
khusha qaraar dil-e beqaraar ka mausam
hadiis-e baadah o saaqi nahien to kis masraf
khiraam-e abr-e sar-e kohsaar ka mausam
nasiib sohbat-e yaaraan nahien to kya kiije

ye raqs saaya-e sarv o chinar ka mausam
ye dil ke daagh to dukhte the yuun bhi par kam kam
kuchh ab ke aur hai hijraan-e yaar ka mausam
yahi junuun ka yahi taoq o daar ka mausam
yahi hai jabr yahi ikhtiaar ka mausam
qafas hai bas mein tumhaare tumhaare bas mein nahien
chaman mein aatish-e gul ke nikhaar ka mausam
saba ki mast khiraami tah-e kamand nahien
asiir-e daam nahien hai bahaar ka mausam
bala se ham ne n dekha to aur dekheinge
furogh-e gulshan o saut-e hazaar ka mausam

'तौक़ ओ दार का मौसम'

रविश-रविश है वही इंतिजार का मौसम
नहीं है कोई भी मौसम बहार का मौसम
गिराँ है दिल पे ग़म-ए रोज़गार का मौसम
है आज़माइश-ए हुस्न-ए निगार का मौसम
ख़ुशा नज़्ज़ारा-ए रुख़्सार-ए यार की सा'इत
ख़ुशा क़रार-ए दिल-ए बेक़रार का मौसम
हदीस-ए बादा ओ साक़ी नहीं तो किस मसरफ़
ख़िराम-ए अब्र-ए सर-ए कोहसार का मौसम
नसीब-ए सोहबत-ए याराँ नहीं तो क्या कीजे
ये रक़्स-ए साया-ए सर्व ओ चिनार का मौसम
ये दिल के दाग़ तो दुखते थे यूँ भी पर कम कम
कुछ अब के और है हिज्रान-ए यार का मौसम
यही जुनूँ का यही तौक़ ओ दार का मौसम
यही है जब्र यही इख़्तियार का मौसम
क़फ़स है बस में तुम्हारे तुम्हारे बस में नहीं
चमन में आतिश-ए गुल के निखार का मौसम
सबा की मस्त-ख़िरामी तह-ए कमंद नहीं
असीर-ए दाम नहीं है बहार का मौसम
बला से हम ने न देखा तो और देखेंगे
फ़रोग़-ए गुलशन ओ सौत-ए हज़ार का मौसम

◆

QAT'A

Sitting with the vision of your comeliness in my eyes
makes the space around me glow like your apparel.
The gentle breeze has just returned from your quarters.
My dawn has the fragrance of your immaculate body.

tera jamaal nigaahon mein le ke uttha huun
nikhar gaaii hai faza tere pairahan ki si
nasiim tere shabistaan se ho ke aaii hai
meri sahar mein mehak hai tere badan ki si

तिरा जमाल निगाहों में ले के उट्ठा हूँ
निखर गई है फ़ज़ा तेरे पैरहन की सी
नसीम तेरे शबिस्ताँ से हो के आई है
मेरी सहर में महक है तेरे बदन की सी

◆

GHAZAL

In a comment about writing a modern ghazal, Faiz said:

One advantage in the form of the ghazal is that you can write the old themes in old vocabulary and similes and yet be describing a contemporary reality. The traditional struggle between the mystic and the sermonizing priest, between the authority and the ordinary man, is also a contemporary theme.[35]

---

[35]Hameed, ed., *Daybreak*, pp. 354–5.

This ghazal is an excellent example of how a poet can say a lot while hiding his real intent in traditional usage; what he wants to convey is wrapped in a classical metaphoric structure. Is the poet addressing the beloved or something else? Is he searching for something else, but what is it precisely? When he talks about the madness of love, what kind of love is that? Faiz talks about his 'two loves' in his verse, but are they not two separate entities? There is a point where they merge and become one, and this ghazal is an excellent example of that fusion. Professor Gopi Chand Narang provides the historical context,

> This memorable ghazal was written in prison when the poet was waiting for daybreak, which is metaphorically the verdict, gallows or the dawn of freedom. This was the time when much else was happening in the country. The prime minister of the country was assassinated in a public meeting. His killer, too was killed. Because of the tragic events, the country took a turn that changed the course of its history. This event is not mentioned by the poet, but a mood of melancholy and yearning runs through the deep structure with an undercurrent of longing and hope that the much-awaited dawn, that is, the glowing face of the beloved, could not be stopped from showing herself.[36]

Neither have you come,
nor the long night of waiting has ended.
Dawn was in search, and it has edged,
time and again.

My engagement during the days

---

[36]Narang, *The Urdu Ghazal*, p. 297.

of my madness of love
had great purpose,
though my heart suffered badly
in the process.

The evening that I spent
listening to the honourable preacher,
has certainly ended with my wandering
in the alley of love.

Imagine something that was not
mentioned in the story!
Sadly that very matter
has hurt the authority the most.

Neither flowers blossomed,
nor was there a meeting with the beloved.
What a strange way to spend the spring!

I don't know what terrible things
the flower-picker did to the garden,
the gentle breeze was so restless
when it passed by my cell in the jailhouse.

'Tum Aae Ho N Shab-e Intizaar Guzri Hai'

tum aae ho n shab-e intizaar guzri hai
talaash mein hai sahar baar baar guzri hai

junuun mein jitni bhi guzri bakaar guzri hai
agarche dil pe kharaabi hazaar guzri hai

hui hai hazrat-e naaseh se guftugu jis shab
voh shab zaruur sar-e kuu-e yaar guzri hai

voh baat saare fasaane mein jis ka zikr na tha
voh baat un ko bahut nagavaar guzri hai

na gul khile hain n un se mile n mai pi hai
a'jiib rang mein ab ke bahaar guzri hai

chaman pe ghaarat-e gul chiin se jaane kya guzri
qafas se aaj saba beqaraar guzri hai

'तुम आए हो न शब-ए इंतिज़ार गुज़री है'

तुम आए हो न शब-ए इंतिज़ार गुज़री है
तलाश में है सहर बार बार गुज़री है

जुनूँ में जितनी भी गुज़री ब-कार गुज़री है
अगरचे दिल पे ख़राबी हज़ार गुज़री है

हुई है हज़रत-ए नासेह से गुफ़्तुगू जिस शब
वो शब ज़रूर सर-ए कू-ए यार गुज़री है

वो बात सारे फ़साने में जिस का ज़िक्र न था
वो बात उन को बहुत नागवार गुज़री है

न गुल खिले हैं न उन से मिले न मय पी है
अजीब रंग में अब के बहार गुज़री है

चमन पे गारत-ए गुल-चीं से जाने क्या गुज़री
क़फ़स से आज सबा बेक़रार गुज़री है

◆

GHAZAL

When the wounds of separation
begin to heal,
I find some excuse
to remember you once again.

When the headlines of the story
about my friend gain traction,
tresses of every beloved

in homes near and far
are elaborately coiffed.

Every stranger comes across
as a friend and a confidante;
anyone who makes it a habit
to pass through your alley.

Those who find themselves
in foreign lands
talk with the gentle breeze
about their homes,
and eyes of the dawn
are suddenly filled with tears.

As tongues are tied up
and the power of speech is taken away,
the air is filled to the brim
with more voices and melodies.

As the door to the jailhouse
is sealed with darkness,
Faiz finds stars
that rise up in his heart.

'Tumhaari Yaad K Jab Zakhm Bharne Lagte Hain'

tumhaari yaad ke jab zakhm bharne lagte hain
kisi bahaane tumhein yaad karne lagte hain

hadiis-e yaar ke u'nvaan nikharne lagte hain
to har hariim mein geso sanvarne lagte hain

har ajnabi hamein mahram dikhaaii deta hai
jo ab bhi teri gali se guzarne lagte hain

saba se karte hain ghurbat nasiib zikre vatan

to chashme sub-h mein aansuu bharne lagte hain

voh jab bhi karte hain us nutq ki bakhiagiri
faza mein aur bhi naghme bikharne lagte hain

dar-e qafas pe andhere ki muhr lagti hai
to Faiz dil mein sitaarey utarne lagte hain

'तुम्हारी याद के जब ज़ख़्म भरने लगते हैं'

तुम्हारी याद के जब ज़ख़्म भरने लगते हैं
किसी बहाने तुम्हें याद करने लगते हैं

हदीस-ए यार के उनवाँ निखरने लगते हैं
तो हर हरीम में गेसू सँवरने लगते हैं

हर अजनबी हमें महरम दिखाई देता है
जो अब भी तेरी गली से गुज़रने लगते हैं

सबा से करते हैं गुर्बत-नसीब ज़िक्र-ए वतन
तो चश्म-ए सुब्ह में आँसू उभरने लगते हैं

वो जब भी करते हैं इस नुत्क़ ओ लब की बख़िया-गरी
फ़ज़ा में और भी नग़्मे बिखरने लगते हैं

दर-ए क़फस पे अँधेरे की मोहर लगती है
तो 'फ़ैज़' दिल में सितारे उतरने लगते हैं

◆

QAT'A

This is a remarkable qat'a that encapsulates harsh reality: how ordinary people, who are the real source of power in any society, end up being the victims of aggression of the powerful folks who themselves lack legitimacy.

There is a commotion in the alley of ecstasy even today

about the Sheikh's garb and the royal crown.
We are the ones who carry the legends of Mansur
and Qais
and the love of flowers and the curved turban.

hamaare dam se hai kuu-e junuun mein ab bhi khajil
a'ba-e sheikh o qaba-e amiir o taaj-e shahi
hamien se sunnat-e mansuur o qais zinda hai
hamien se baaqi hai gul-damani o kaj-kulaahi

हमारे दम से है कू-ए जुनूँ में अब भी ख़जिल
अबा-ए शैख़ ओ क़बा-ए अमीर ओ ताज-ए शाही
हमीं से सुन्नत-ए मनसूर ओ कैस ज़िंदा है
हमीं से बाक़ी है गुल-दमनी ओ कज-कुलाही

♦

GHAZAL

An evening star got burnt
and was reduced to ashes in the twilight.
The locks of the night of separation
made waves in the darkness of dusk.

Someone should howl.
It has been a long time
since the sky halted the caravan
of day and night.

My nostalgic wine-measuring friends
insist that no moon should rise at night,
and no cloud should appear during the day.

Breeze once again knocked
at the doors of the jailhouse.
Dawn is close.
Tell the heart not to panic.

'Shafaq Ki Raakh Mein Jal Bujh Gaya Sitaara-e Shaam'

shafaq ki raakh mein jal bujh gaya sitaara-e shaam
shab-e firaaq ke gesu faza mein lahraae

koi pukaaro k ik u'mr hone aaii hai
falak ko qaaflaa-e roz o shaam thahraae

ye zid hai yaad-e hariifaan-e badaah-paima ki
k shab ko chaand n nikle n din ko abr aaye

saba ne phir dar-e zindaan pe aa ke di dastak
sahar qariib hai dil se kaho n ghabraae

'शफ़क़ की राख में जल बुझ गया सितारा-ए शाम'

शफ़क़ की राख में जल बुझ गया सितारा-ए शाम
शब-ए फ़िराक़ के गेसू फ़ज़ा में लहराए

कोई पुकारो कि इक उम्र होने आई है
फ़लक को क़ाफ़िला-ए रोज़ ओ शाम ठहराए

ये ज़िद है याद हरीफ़ान-ए बादा-पैमा की
कि शब को चाँद न निकले न दिन को अब्र आए

सबा ने फिर दर-ए ज़िंदाँ पे आ के दी दस्तक
सहर क़रीब है दिल से कहो न घबराए

♦

'FOR YOUR BEAUTY AND GRACE'

This poem was a gift to Alys on her birthday from Faiz,
while he was in prison. As we read the poem, we find that
the poet is praising the beauty of the person for whom
the poem was written. But is this beauty all about physical
appearance? Faiz tried to answer this question in a short
essay titled 'The Concept of Beauty' in which he went

beyond the form or presence of a person at a particular time. He wrote,

> It [beauty] is both the tranquility of harmony and the turbulence of 'some other proportion'; it is as tangible as reality, and as elusive as a ghost, it is ecstasy, torment, experience and memory all rolled into 'infinite variety', it acquires an emotional and perceptual permanence which age does not wither, nor custom stale.

The reference to 'some other proportion' was drawn from Bacon's saying, 'No excellent beauty hath not some strangeness in the proportion.'[37]

> The poet writes his salutation
> in the name of your beauty!
> When the colours of your apparel
> become visible from your rooftop,
> they freshen up your morning, your noon,
> and evening sometime.
> And when you wear any long dress,
> cypresses and pines in the garden
> sense they are embellished.
> When I start to write my ghazal
> it is like my heart gets tipsy
> in the shadow of your lips and cheeks.
>
> The poet writes his salutation
> in the name of your beauty!
>
> As long as there is shine
> of henna on your hands,

---

[37]Majeed, *Culture and Identity*, p. 128.

as long as there is love
for the bride of melody in this world,
your beauty will stay at the peak of youth
with the kindness of the heavens.
The breeze of this country
is a companion of your breath
as long as you breathe.
Although times are difficult,
the sweetness of your memory
lessens the bitterness of days.

The poet writes his salutation
in the name of your beauty!

'Tumhaare Husn Ke Naam'

salaam likhta hai shaa'yir tumhaare husn ke naam

bikhar gaya jo kabhi rang-e pairahan sar-e baam
nikhar gaaii hai kabhi sub-h daupahar kabhi shaam
kahien jo qaamat-e zeba pe saj gaaii hai qaba
chaman mein sarv o sanobar sanvar gaye hain tamaam
bani bisaat-e ghazal jab dabo li ye dil ne
tumhaar-e saaya-e rukhsaar o lab mein saaghar o jam

salaam likhta hai shaa'yir tumhaare husn ke naam

tumhaare haath pe hai taabish-e henna jab tak
jahaan mein baaqi hai dildaari-e u'rus-e sukhan
tumhaara husn javaan hai to meharbaan hai falak
tumhaara dam hai to damsaaz hai havaa-e vatan
agarche tang hain auqaat sakhat hain aalaam
tumhaari yaad se shiiriin hai talkhi-e ayyaam

salaam likhta hai shaa'yir tumhaare husn ke naam

'तुम्हारे हुस्न के नाम'

सलाम लिखता है शायर तुम्हारे हुस्न के नाम

बिखर गया जो कभी रंग-ए पैरहन सर-ए बाम
निखर गई है कभी सुब्ह दोपहर कभी शाम
कहीं जो क़ामत-ए ज़ेबा पे सज गई है क़बा
चमन में सर्व ओ सनोबर सँवर गए हैं तमाम
बनी बिसात-ए ग़ज़ल जब डुबो लिए दिल ने
तुम्हारे साया-ए रुख़सार ओ लब में साग़र ओ जाम

सलाम लिखता है शायर तुम्हारे हुस्न के नाम

तुम्हारे हाथ पे है ताबिश-ए हिना जब तक
जहाँ में बाक़ी है दिलदारी-ए उरूस-ए सुख़न
तुम्हारा हुस्न जवाँ है तो मेहरबाँ है फ़लक
तुम्हारा दम है तो दम-साज़ है हवा-ए वतन
अगरचे तंग हैं औक़ात सख़्त हैं आलाम
तुम्हारी याद से शीरीं है तल्ख़ी-ए अय्याम

सलाम लिखता है शायर तुम्हारे हुस्न के नाम

◆

'TWO LOVES'

This poem is not very different from 'Mauzo-e-Sukhan' that we read in the first chapter, but it is much more open and clear. There are two objects, the poet says, that are at the centre of his passionate love and ardent adoration: the beloved and the land and its people. Both 'passions' are equal in intensity, and they touch the poet's heart in the same manner. There is a mix of love and reality, the latter born from the social and political situation of the land: '*is i'shq n us i'shq pe naadam hai magar dil*' (The heart has no excuses for this love or the other love). We are going to revisit this issue later in the book to highlight the fact that, with time, the poet's love became more revolutionary and all embracing.

1

It is fresh in my memory, O rose-like Saqi,
days that had the shine of my beloved's face.
We met face to face like flowers opening
when hope palpitated like a heart.

I hope that poor heart's luck had taken a turn for good.
The night of love's longing was over at last.
The dreamless stars of grief finally found a resting place—
I hope that the luck of impatient eyes will brighten now.

The sun of your beauty will emerge from this roof.
Henna-coloured rays will break out from a tiny nook.
From this door will flow the quicksilver of your brisk walk.
This pathway will blossom the twilight of your apparel.

I have once again seen the burning days of separation;
worries about my heart and soul made me forget my wailing.
Every night was filled with the cargo of heart-killing load.
The morning's flame would hit my chest like an arrow.

In my solitude, I remembered you in different ways.

My heart searched for other ways to gain some
comfort.
I put the hand of morning breeze next to my eyes.
Sometimes, I even put my arms around the moon.

2

With the same zeal, I have loved my beloved country.
My heart has pulsated with the same devotion to her.
My passion has looked for resting places at the
journey's end.
In the curves of her cheeks, in the curls of her tresses.

I looked at her with the same heart and eyes.
I called her in joy, and I have shouted her name
while I was crying.
All longings I have tried to fulfill.
I tried to make her painless of pain and her
griefless of grief.

No demand to show madness and passion was
overlooked.
No sound of bell reverberated without
accompanying music.
Safety of life, the well-being of the body, healthy
demeanour—
all was forgotten, even the advice for prudence
meant for lusty folks.

Over this path, we suffered like everyone else.
Sometimes in prison, sometimes dishonoured in
public.
The preachers sounded alarms from their pulpits.
Threats came from the guardians of law, close to
authorities.

Strangers did not spare any darts of infamy.
Even the folks who were our own acted quite
disgracefully.
The heart has no excuses for this love or the
other love.
My heart carries all kinds of scars, except scars of
regrets.

'Do I'shq'

1

taaza hain abhi yaad mein ae saaqi-e gulfaam
voh a'ks-e rukh-e yaar se lahke hue ayyaam
voh phuul si khilti hui diidaar ki saa'at
voh dil sa dharakata hua ummid ka hangaam

ummid k lo jaaga gham-e dil ka nasiiba
lo shauq ki tarsi hui shab ho gaaii aakhir
lo duub gaaye dard k bekhwaab sitaarey
ab chamkega besabr nigaahoon ka muqqaddar

is baam se niklega tere husn ka khurshiid
us kunj se phuutegi kiran rang-e hina ki
is dar se bahega teri raftaar ka simaab
is rah pe phailegi shafaq teri qaba ki

phir dekhe hain voh hijr ke tapte hue din bhi
jab fikr-e dil o jaan mein fughaan bhuul gaaii hai
har shab vo siyaah bojh k dil baith gaya hai
har sub-h ki lau tiir si siine mein lagi hai

tanhaaii mein kya kya n tujhe yaad kia hai
kya kya dil-zaar ne dhuundhi hain panahein
aankhon se lagaaya hai kabhi dast-e saba ko
daali hain kabhi gardan-e mahtaab mein baahein

2

chaaha hai isi rang mein laila-e vatan ko
tarpa hai isi taur se dil us ki lagan mein
dhuundhi hai yuunhi shauq ne aasaaish-e manzil
rukhsaar ke kham mein kabhi kaakul ki shikan mein

is jaan-e jahaan ko bhi yuun hi qalb o nazar ne
hans hans ke sada di kabhi ro ro ke pukaara
puure kiye sab harf-e tamanna ke taqaaze
har dard ko ujiyaala har ik gham ko sanvaara

vaapis nahien phera koi farmaan junuun ka
tanha nahien lauti kabhi aavaaz jaras ki
khairiyat-e jaan raahat-e tan sehat-e daamaan
sab bhuul gaaiin maslahatein ahl-e havas ki

is raah mein jo sab pe guzarti hai voh guzri
tanha pas-e zindaan kabhi rusva sar-e bazaar
garje hain bahut sheikh sar-e gosha-e mimbar
karke hain bahut ahl-e hakam bar sar-e darbaar

chhora nahien ghairon ne koi naavak-e dushnaam
chhuuti nahien apnon se koi tarz-e mulaamat
is i'shq n us i'shq pe naadam hai magar dil
har daagh hai is dil pe b-juz daagh-e nadamat

'दो इश्क़'

1

ताज़ा हैं अभी याद में ऐ साक़ी-ए गुलफ़ाम
वो अक्स-ए रुख़-ए यार से लहके हुए अय्याम
वो फूल सी खुलती हुई दीदार की सा'इत
वो दिल सा धड़कता हुआ उम्मीद का हंगाम

उम्मीद कि लो जागा ग़म-ए दिल का नसीबा
लो शौक़ की तरसी हुई शब हो गई आख़िर
लो डूब गए दर्द के बेख़्वाब सितारे
अब चमकेगा बेसब्र निगाहों का मुक़द्दर

इस बाम से निकलेगा तेरे हुस्न का ख़ुर्शीद
इस कुंज से फूटेगी किरन रंग-ए हिना की
इस दर से बहेगा तेरी रफ़्तार का सीमाब
उस राह पे फैलेगी शफ़क़ तेरी क़बा की

फिर देखे हैं वो हिज्र के तपते हुए दिन भी
जब फ़िक्र-ए दिल ओ जाँ में फुग़ाँ भूल गई है
हर शब वो सियह बोझ कि दिल बैठ गया है
हर सुब्ह की लौ तीर सी सीने में लगी है

तन्हाई में क्या क्या न तुझे याद किया है
क्या क्या न दिल-ए ज़ार ने ढूँडी हैं पनाहें
आँखों से लगाया है कभी दस्त-ए सबा को
डाली हैं कभी गर्दन-ए महताब में बाहें

2

चाहा है इसी रंग में लैला-ए वतन को
तड़पा है इसी तौर से दिल उस की लगन में
ढूँडी है यूँही शौक़ ने आसाइश-ए मंजिल
रुख़्सार के ख़म में कभी काकुल की शिकन में

उस जान-ए जहाँ को भी यूँही क़ल्ब ओ नज़र ने
हँस हँस के सदा दी कभी रो रो के पुकारा
पूरे किए सब हर्फ़-ए तमन्ना के तक़ाज़े
हर दर्द को उजयाला हर इक ग़म को सँवारा

वापस नहीं फेरा कोई फ़रमान जुनूँ का
तन्हा नहीं लौटी कभी आवाज़ जरस की
ख़ैरिय्यत-ए जाँ राहत-ए तन से सेहत-ए दामाँ
सब भूल गईं मस्लहतें अहल-ए हवस की

इस राह में जो सब पे गुज़रती है वो गुज़री
तन्हा पस-ए ज़िंदाँ कभी रुस्वा सर-ए बाज़ार
गरजे हैं बहुत शैख़ सर-ए गोशा-ए मिम्बर
कड़के हैं बहुत अहल-ए हकम बर-सर-ए दरबार

छोड़ा नहीं ग़ैरों ने कोई नावक-ए दुश्नाम
छूटी नहीं अपनों से कोई तर्ज-ए मलामत
उस इश्क़ न उस इश्क़ पे नादिम है मगर दिल
हर दाग़ है इस दिल में ब-जुज़ दाग़-ए नदामत

♦

GHAZAL

The colour of your alluring garment and
the fragrance of your fluttering tresses—
the spring season is nothing
but your appearance on the roof's parapet.

Friends, let us talk about her eyes and lips
without which there is no joy
in the ambiance of the garden and the tavern.

Once again, I had the vision of fragrant flowers
and candles lighted in my thoughts.
Once again, my imagination enthused over
going to that assembly.

Any talk about loveliness
invites people to talk about it.
Fairy-like beloveds do not flutter
their tresses anymore.

No Laila is ready to play
the part of a beloved now.
The name of everyone

who suffers from love's madness
is badly tarnished.

Hail the Sheikh!
Thanks to him that despite his strictures,
the libertine, Saqi, wine, wine jar and goblet—
they all enjoy high stature.

Controllers of the garden
tell the ones who are exiled:
Give a good name
to the deserted place
where you live.

Faiz, she wants a pledge of fidelity
from the likes of us
for whom the name of an unknown
is dearer than that of a friend.

'Rang Pairaahan Ka Khushbu Zulf Lehraane Ka Naam'

rang pairaahan ka khushbu zulf lehraane ka naam
mausam-e gul hai tumhaare baam par aane ka naam

dosto us chashm o lab ki kuchh kaho jis ke baghair
gulistaan ki baat rangiin hai n maikhaane ka naam

phir nazar mein phuul mehke dil mein phir sham'ein
jaliin
phir tasavvur ne liya us bazm mein jaane ka naam

dilbari thahra zabaan-e khalq khulvaane ka naam
ab nahien lete pari ru zulf bikhraane ka naam

ab kisi laila ko bhi iqraar-e mahbuubi nahien
in dinon badnaam hai har ek diivaane ka naam

mohtasib ki khair uuncha hai usi ke faiz se
rind ka saaqi ka mai ka khum ka paimaane ka naam

ham se kahte hain chaman vaale ghariibaan-e chaman
tum koi achha sa rakh lo apne viiraane ka naam

Faiz un ko hai taqaaza-e vafa ham se jinhein
aashna ke naam se pyaara hai be-gaane ka naam

'रंग पैराहन का ख़ुशबू ज़ुल्फ़ लहराने का नाम'

रंग पैराहन का ख़ुशबू ज़ुल्फ़ लहराने का नाम
मौसम-ए गुल है तुम्हारे बाम पर आने का नाम

दोस्तो उस चश्म ओ लब की कुछ कहो जिस के बग़ैर
गुलसिताँ की बात रंगीं है न मयख़ाने का नाम

फिर नज़र में फूल महके दिल में फिर शमएँ जलीं
फिर तसव्वुर ने लिया उस बज़्म में जाने का नाम

दिलबरी ठहरा ज़बान-ए ख़ल्क़ खुलवाने का नाम
अब नहीं लेते परी-रू ज़ुल्फ़ बिखराने का नाम

अब किसी लैला को भी इक़रार-ए महबूबी नहीं
इन दिनों बदनाम है हर एक दीवाने का नाम

मोहतसिब की ख़ैर ऊँचा है उसी के फ़ैज़ से
रिंद का साक़ी का मय का ख़ुम का पैमाने का नाम

हम से कहते हैं चमन वाले ग़रीबान-ए चमन
तुम कोई अच्छा सा रख लो अपने वीराने का नाम

'फ़ैज़' उन को है तक़ाजा-ए वफ़ा हम से जिन्हें
आश्ना के नाम से प्यारा है बेगाने का नाम

The couplet 'Hail the Sheikh! ... enjoy high stature' is an excellent example of how Faiz makes a bold, even a revolutionary, statement without any noise, using language that also appears to praise the adversary.

Maikhaana (tavern) where mai, sharaab (wine), is served, is a signature word in Faiz's revolutionary poetry. The elements of the underlying metaphorical triangle are saaqi (bartender), mai and mohtasib (Sheikh). The couplet opens with mohtasib, who is the symbol of oppression, as he reprimands people that drinking is taboo in Islamic society. However, drinking subtly inspires people to fall in love or show greater love for their progressive ideology. The speaking voice, the voice of the revolutionary poet, does not denounce or condemn the mohtasib; instead he obliquely welcomes him as a blessing in disguise. If there is oppression, there is bound to be dissent, and the struggle will intensify. All the five key words in the second line—rind (libertine), saaqi, mai, khum (decanter) and paimana (glass, goblet)—are associated images of maikhaana, and they signify the celebration of ideological inspiration that is required to create revolutionary fervour in a repressive atmosphere. They are welcome as they invigorate the challenge to an oppressive system. The facade of praising the Sheikh is an oriental mannerism, with a touch of irony. It, therefore, hides the disdain in which he is held and how his admonishments generate great revolutionary zeal.

◆

GHAZAL

Unremembered and left behind
griefs and frustrations of your love
enter my heart in the same way
as the expelled idols return to the Ka'ba.

One by one, stars are illuminating the sky,
just as your feet are progressing carefully
to the place, which is my final refuge.

Let the dance of wine gain traction.
Let the music become louder.
The believers are leaving
their places in the mosque
and are coming to the tavern.

Please tell the night of separation
that it should stay a little longer.
The heart's suffering is less
and her memory too
is beginning to fade at this time.

'Dil Mein Ab Yuun Tere Bhuule Hue Gham Aate Hain'

dil mein ab yuun tere bhuule hue gham aate hain
jaise bichhre hue kaa'be mein sanam aate hain

ek ik karke hue jaate hain taare raushan
meri manzil ki taraf tere qadam aate hain

raqs-e mai tez karo saaz ki lai tez karo
suu-e maikhaana safiiraan-e haram aate hain

aur kuchh der n guzre shab-e furqat se kaho
dil bhi kam dukhta hai voh yaad bhi kam aate hain

'दिल में अब यूँ तेरे भूले हुए ग़म आते हैं'

दिल में अब यूँ तेरे भूले हुए गम आते हैं
जैसे बिछड़े हुए काबे में सनम आते हैं

एक इक कर के हुए जाते हैं तारे रौशन
मेरी मंजिल की तरफ़ तेरे क़दम आते हैं

रक़्स-ए मय तेज़ करो साज़ की लय तेज़ करो
सू-ए मयख़ाना सफ़ीरान-ए हरम आते हैं

और कुछ देर न गुज़रे शब-ए फ़ुर्क़त से कहो
दिल भी कम दुखता है वो याद भी कम आते हैं

◆

'NO SAVIOUR FOR THE BROKEN GLASSES'

This poem was written a few years after Independence. Progressive poets like Faiz had invested a lot of energy in dreaming up a future—a post-Independence future—in which there was supposed to be an end to peoples' sufferings, freedom from want and access to a fair justice system. Freedom came, but nothing changed. The country moved from a situation that was bad to something much worse. Before Independence, foreign rulers were the principal exploiters. Now their place was taken over by professional politicians, capitalists and a host of other characters who were interested in serving their vested interests. In a situation like this, people wait for a saviour to appear, but the poet has to remind everyone that the one they are waiting for is not going to show up. Therefore, what should be done? 'If your hands are empty, raise them. / This battle is calling you!' People have to fight their own battles. No one else will do this work for them. Waiting for a messiah is a waste of time. Furthermore, the poem also alludes to the reality that once a glass is broken, it is a messianic job to fix it, but it might be replaced. The broken pieces of the glass are symbolic of the divide between people, mutual disputes and disunity.

In an interview with Tahir Mirza, Faiz used some lines

from this poem to explain why it was important to retain one's hope in a period of despair. He said,

> You have got to retain your hope, your belief in tomorrow. There may be periods of despair, utter, black despair. You may feel that everything is over. But these are subjective reactions to temporary situations. It would be dishonest to say that everything is all right. That there is no ugliness, injustice, oppression, exploitation. There is. But this is not the whole reality—only a first subjective impression—'*tum naa-haq tukre chun chun kar daaman mein chhuupaaye baithe ho / shiishon ka masiiha koi nahien / kya aas lagaaye baithe ho*'. But the second impression is based on the dialectical and historical perspective. You retain your hope—'*yaan parbat parbat hiire hain / yaan saagar saagar moti hain / uttho sab khaali haathon ko / is ran se bulaave aate hain*'.[38]

Whether it is a pearl, a wine glass,
or a plate,
once it is broken, it is done forever.
You can't bind it with tears.
If it is broken, it is gone for good.

Why do you needlessly pick up
bits and pieces of glass and
hide them in the folds of your apparel?
There is no saviour for slivers of glass.
You shouldn't be nursing any hopes.

Perhaps in these broken pieces
is hidden the heart of a wine glass

---

[38]Hameed, ed., *Daybreak*, p. 362.

in which the fairy representing
the beloved's eternal grief
used to descend with one hundred
flirtatious moves.

Then some crafty people of the world usurped
this glass of joy from you and
broke it into pieces.
The wine that remained in the glass
was poured on the soil
and the royal visitor was crushed.

These colourful particles are remnants
of those dazzling and precious dreams
with which you embellished the days
of your youthful solitude.

The dreams were smashed by the onslaught of
helplessness,
drudgery, hunger and grief.
Merciless was the four-faced flood of stones.
How could these glass creations survive?

Or perhaps in these slivers of glass
there was hidden the pearl of your honour
and your grace that those with incredible heights
felt envious at your modesty.

In pursuit of this precious treasure
are both genuine traders and daredevil robbers.
In this city of swindlers, the poor man is lucky
if he can save his life while sacrificing his dignity.

These precious wine glasses,
these stones, gems and pearls

carry value for their wholeness
but if they are broken into pieces,
they can stab you with their sharpness
and make you shed tears of blood.

Why do you needlessly pick up
bits and pieces of glass and then hide them
in the folds of your apparel?
There is no saviour for slivers of glass.
You shouldn't be nursing any hopes.

By repairing the collars of memories
you can't make the heart to stay healthy.
Mending one seam here and one seam there—
you can't spend your life doing that.

In this churning workshop of life
where these glass objects are shaped,
there is a substitute for everything,
and something real for wishes to come true.

The hands that stretch get rewarded,
the eye that looks straight is deemed lucky.
There is no shortage of material wealth,
but there are muggers and embezzlers
in wait, if you aren't alert.

But robbers and takers can't empty the stores.
There are mountains filled with diamonds
and oceans that hide pearls in their depths.

Some people try to hide their wealth
in the cavities behind their walls;
trying to auction mountains and oceans
they do not own.

And some people are aware
how to fight and break barriers.
They are the ones who reach those cavities.
They are the ones who understand
all the moves of lifters and freeloaders.

A fight starts between these two groups,
in each neighbourhood, in towns and cities,
it goes into the very heart of every living home
and to the forehead of every busy intersection.

One group spreads blackness and
the other lights lamps.
One group sets things on fire and
the other extinguishes those fires.

All wine glasses, precious stones and pearls are
bets in this game.
If your hands are empty, raise them.
This battle is calling you!

'Shiishon Ka Masiha Koi Nahien'

moti ho k shiisha jaam k dur
jo tuut gaya so tuut gaya
kab ashkon se jur sakta hai
jo tuut gaya so chhuut gaya

tum naa-haq tukre chun chun kar
daaman mein chhuupaaye baithe ho
shiishon ka masiiha koi nahien
kya aas lagaaye baithe ho

shaayad k inhiin tukron mein kahien
voh saaghar-e dil hai jis mein kabhi
sad naaz se utra karti thi
sahbaaye-e gham-e jaanaan ki pari

phir duniya vaalon ne tum se
ye saaghar le ke phor diya
jo mai thi baha di mitti mein
mahmaan ka shahpar tor diya

ye rangiin reze hain shaayad
in shokh billoriin sapnon ke
tum mast javaani mein jin se
khalvat ko sajaaya karte the

naadaari-e daftar bhuuk aur gham
in sapnon se takraate rahe
beraham tha chaumukh pathraao
ye kaanch ke dhaanche kya karte

yaa shaayad in zarron mein kahien
moti hai tumhaari izzat ka
voh jis se tumhaare a'jz pe bhi
shamshaad qadon ne rashk kiya

us maal ki dhun mein phirte the
taajar bhi bahut rahzan bhi kaaii
hai chor-nagar yaan muflis ki
gar jaan bachi to aan gaaii

ye saaghar shiishe l'al o gohar
saalam hon to qiimat paate hain
yuun tukre tukre hon to faqat
chubhte hain rulvaate hain

tum naa-haq shiishe chun chun kar
daaman mein chhuupaaye baithe ho
shiishon ka masiiha koi nahien
kya aas lagaaye baithe ho

yaadon ke garibaanon ke rafu

par dil ki guzar kab hoti hai
ik bakhia udhera ek siya
yuun u'mr basar kab hoti hai

is kaar-gah-e hasti mein jahaan
ye saaghar shiishe dhalte hain
har shai ka badal mil sakta hai
sab daaman pur ho sakte hain

jo haath barhe yaavar hai yahaan
jo aankh uthe voh bakhtaavar
yaan dhan daulat ka ant nahien
hon ghaat mein daaku laakh agar

kab luut jhapat se hasti ki
dukaanein khaali hoti hain
yaan parbat parbat hiire hain
yaan saagar saagar moti hain

kuchh log hain jo is daulat par
parde latkaate phirte hain
har parbat ko har saagar ko
niilaam charaahte phirte hain

kuchh voh bhi hain jo lar bhirkar
ye parde noch giraate hain
hasti ke uthaaii giiron ki
har chaal uljhaae jaate hain

in donon mein ran parta hai
nit basti basti nagar nagar
har baste gharke sine mein
har chalti raah ke maathe par

ye kaalak bharte phirte hain
voh jot jagaate rahte hain

ye aag lagaate phirte hain
voh aag bujhaate rahte hain

sab saaghar shiishe l'al o gohar
is baazi mein bad jaate hain
uttho sab khaali haathon ko
is ran se bulaave aate hain

'शीशों का मसीहा कोई नहीं'

मोती हो कि शीशा जाम कि दुर
जो टूट गया सो टूट गया
कब अश्कों से जुड़ सकता है
जो टूट गया सो छूट गया

तुम नाहक़ टुकड़े चुन चुन कर
दामन में छुपाए बैठे हो
शीशों का मसीहा कोई नहीं
क्या आस लगाए बैठे हो

शायद कि इन्हीं टुकड़ों में कहीं
वो साग़र-ए दिल है जिस में कभी
सद-नाज़ से उतरा करती थी
सहबा-ए ग़म-ए जानाँ की परी

फिर दुनिया वालों ने तुम से
ये साग़र ले कर फोड़ दिया
जो मय थी बहा दी मिट्टी में
मेहमान का शहपर तोड़ दिया

ये रंगीं रेज़े हैं शायद
उन शोख़ बिलोरीं सपनों के
तुम मस्त जवानी में जिन से
ख़ल्वत को सजाया करते थे

नादारी दफ़्तर भूक और ग़म
उन सपनों से टकराते रहे

बेरहम था चौमुख पथराओ
ये काँच के ढाँचे क्या करते

या शायद इन ज़रों में कहीं
मोती है तुम्हारी इ'ज़्ज़त का
वो जिस से तुम्हारे इ'ज़्ज़ पे भी
शमशाद-क़दों ने रश्क किया

इस माल की धुन में फिरते थे
ताजिर भी बहुत रहज़न भी कई
है चोर-नगर याँ मुफ़लिस की
गर जान बची तो आन गई

ये साग़र शीशे ला'ल ओ गुहर
सालिम हों तो क़ीमत पाते हैं
यूँ टुकड़े टुकड़े हों तो फ़क़त
चुभते हैं लहू रुलवाते हैं

तुम नाहक़ शीशे चुन चुन कर
दामन में छुपाए बैठे हो
शीशों का मसीहा कोई नहीं
क्या आस लगाए बैठे हो

यादों के गिरेबानों के रफ़ू
पर दिल की गुज़र कब होती है
इक बख़िया उधेड़ा एक सिया
यूँ उम्र बसर कब होती है

इस कार-गह-ए हस्ती में जहाँ
ये साग़र शीशे ढलते हैं
हर शय का बदल मिल सकता है
सब दामन पुर हो सकते हैं

जो हाथ बढ़े यावर है यहाँ
जो आँख उठे वो बख़्तावर
याँ धन-दौलत का अंत नहीं
हों घात में डाकू लाख मगर

कब लूट-झपट से हस्ती की
दुकानें ख़ाली होती हैं
याँ परबत परबत हीरे हैं
याँ सागर सागर मोती हैं

कुछ लोग हैं जो इस दौलत पर
पर्दे लटकाते फिरते हैं
हर पर्बत को हर सागर को
नीलाम चढ़ाते फिरते हैं

कुछ वो भी हैं जो लड़ भिड़ कर
ये पर्दे नोच गिराते हैं
हस्ती के उठाई-गीरों की
हर चाल उलझाए जाते हैं

इन दोनों में रन पड़ता है
नित बस्ती बस्ती नगर नगर
हर बस्ते घर के सीने में
हर चलती राह के माथे पर

ये कालक भरते फिरते हैं
वो जोत जगाते रहते हैं
ये आग लगाते फिरते हैं
वो आग बुझाते रहते हैं

सब सागर शीशे लाल ओ गुहर
इस बाज़ी में बद जाते हैं
उट्ठो सब ख़ाली हाथों को
इस रन से बुलावे आते हैं

♦

GHAZAL

The chances of spring's arrival
have somewhat brightened.

Flowers are tearing their cloaks
as petals are parting.

Autumn is still ruling,
but here and there in the garden
some buds can be seen opening.

The night's darkness is stuck at one place
but some colours of dawn
can be seen revealing themselves.

Whether they burnt our blood
or our soul and heart,
a few lamps have lighted the assembly.

Yes, tilt your turbans somewhat
because after losing everything,
we are now free
from the revolution of time.

Those who are in prison
will open their eyes in the garden.
There have been some vows and pledges
with the morning breeze.

Desert is still nothing more than a desert,
but with a stream of blood flowing
from my bleeding feet, Faiz,
some thorns have been nourished.

'Raushan Kahien Bahaar Ke Imkaan Hue To Hain'

raushan kahien bahaar ke imkaan hue to hain
gulshan mein chaak chand garebaan hue to hain

ab bhi khizaan ka raaj hai lekin kahien kahein
goshe rah-e chaman mein ghazal khwaan hue to hain

thahri hui hai shab ki siyaahi vahiin magar
kuchh kuchh sahar ke rang par-afshaan hue to hain

in mein lahu jala ho hamaara k dil
mahfil mein kuchh charaagh furozaan hue to hain

haan kaj karo kulaah k sab kuchh lutake ham
ab benayaaz-e gardish-e dauraan hue to hain

ahl-e qafas ki subh-e chaman mein khule gi aankh
baad-e saba se vaa'da o paimaan hue to hain

hai dasht ab bhi dasht magar khuun-e paa se Faiz
sairaab chand khaar-e mughiilaan hue to hain

'रौशन कहीं बहार के इम्काँ हुए तो हैं'

रौशन कहीं बहार के इम्काँ हुए तो हैं
गुलशन में चाक चंद गरेबाँ हुए तो हैं

अब भी ख़िज़ाँ का राज है लेकिन कहीं कहीं
गोशे रह-ए चमन में ग़ज़ल-ख़्वाँ हुए तो हैं

ठहरी हुई है शब की सियाही वहीं मगर
कुछ कुछ सहर के रंग पर-अफ़्शाँ हुए तो हैं

इन में लहू जला हो हमारा कि जान ओ दिल
महफिल में कुछ चराग़ फ़रोज़ाँ हुए तो हैं

हाँ कज करो कुलाह कि सब कुछ लुटा के हम
अब बेनियाज़-ए गर्दिश-ए दौराँ हुए तो हैं

अहल-ए कफ़स की सुब्ह-ए चमन में खुले गी आँख
बाद-ए सबा से वादा ओ पैमाँ हुए तो हैं

है दश्त अब भी दश्त मगर ख़ून-ए पा से 'फ़ैज़'
सैराब चंद ख़ार-ए मुग़ीलाँ हुए तो हैं

◆

'YOUR STREETS BE BLESSED'

This poem has the feel of a lover's yearning for his land; the beloved in this poem is the country. The poet's love for his native land is unconditional. No doubt, there is social injustice. No doubt, there is political injustice. But while locked up in prison, the poet is thinking of the streets and alleys of the land and he feels pain, having been separated from them. He is ready, however, to forgive and forget. This forced seclusion is temporary. The more important thing is that the bond of fidelity to the soil will always stay unbroken.

> May your streets be blessed,
> my country,
> where custom requires
> no one should walk
> with his head held high.
> And if a lover goes
> in search of his loved one,
> he has to hide his eyes,
> he has to keep his soul
> and heart under control.

> For those with a loving heart,
> there is a new law
> and a new order:
> stones and bricks
> are locked up,
> but dogs roam freely.

> Looking for a pretext to punish,
> there are hands of those
> who will act in your name?
> Those who seek personal gratification

have become prosecutors
as well as judges.
Who should I ask
to defend my case?
And from whom should I seek
any justice?

Time passes aimlessly.
In painful separation,
I spend my mornings and evenings
in this aimless cycle.

When the light passing through
the window of the jail cell
becomes dark,
my heart knows your hair-parting
must have been filled with the stars.
When the chains emit some shine,
I know daybreak must have spread
its light over your beautiful face.

In short, I live keeping alive
the image before my eyes
of evenings and mornings.
I live in the grip of the shadows
of walls and doors.

People have fought
against tyranny.
Neither the practice
of oppression is new,
nor the willingness of victims
to suffer.
I have made sparks
to glow in the fire.

Neither their defeat is new,
nor is my triumph fresh.

That is why
I don't blame my stars.
I don't take your separation
to my heart.
Separate today,
I might see you tomorrow.
This disconnect for a night
is not a big deal.
If the rival's star is up today,
it doesn't matter.
This brutal posture of a few days
doesn't mean anything.

Those who honour the vows
of fidelity for you,
they know, they understand
how to overcome obstacles
of days and nights.

'Nisaar Main Teri Galiyon Ke'

nisaar main teri galiyon ke ae vatan k jahaan
chali hai rasm k koi n sar utha k chale
jo koi chaahne vaala tavaaf ko nikle
nazar chura ke chale jism o jaan bacha ke chale
hai ahl-e dil ke liye ab ye nazm-e bast o kushaad
'k sang o khisht muqaiyad hain aur sag aazaad[39]

bahut hai zulm ke dast-e bahana-juu ke liye
jo chand ahl-e junuun tere naam leva hain

---

[39]A line borrowed from a Persian master poet.

bane hain ahl-e havas mudda'ii bhi munsif bhi
kise vakiil karein kis se munsifi chaahein
magar guzaarne vaalon ke din guzarte hain
tere firaaq mein yuun sub-h o shaam karte hain

bujha jo rauzan-e zindaan to dil ye samjha hai
k teri maang sitaaron se bhar gaaii ho gi
chamak uthe hain salasal to ham ne jaana hai
k ab sahar tere rukh par bikhar gaaii ho gi
gharaz tasavvur-e shaam o sahar mein jiite hain
girift-e saaya-e diivaar o dar mein jiite hain

yuunhi hamesha uljhati rahi hai zulm se khalaq
n un ki rasm naaii hai n apni riit naaii
yuunhi khilaaye hain ham ne aag mein phuul
n un ki haar naaii hai n apni jiit naaii
isi sabab se falak ka gila nahien karte
tere firaaq mein ham dil bura nahien karte

gar aaj tujh se juda hain to kal baham honge
ye raat bhar ki judaaii to koi baat nahien
gar aaj auj pe hai taal'-e raqiib to kya
ye chaar din ki khudaaii to koi baat nahien

jo tujh se a'hd-e vafa ustuvaar rakhte hain
i'laaj-e gardish-e lail o nahaar rakhte hain

'निसार मैं तेरी गलियों के'

निसार मैं तेरी गलियों के ऐ वतन कि जहाँ
चली है रस्म कि कोई न सर उठा के चले
जो कोई चाहने वाला तवाफ़ को निकले
नज़र चुरा के चले जिस्म ओ जाँ बचा के चले
है अहल-ए दिल के लिए अब ये नज़्म-ए बस्त ओ कुशाद
'कि संग ओ ख़िश्त मुक़य्यद हैं और सग आज़ाद'

बहुत है ज़ुल्म के दस्त-ए बहाना-जू के लिए
जो चंद अहल-ए जुनूँ तेरे नाम-लेवा हैं
बने हैं अहल-ए हवस मुद्दा'ई भी मुंसिफ़ भी
किसे वकील करें किस से मुंसिफ़ी चाहें
मगर गुज़ारने वालों के दिन गुज़रते हैं
तेरे फ़िराक़ में यूँ सुब्ह ओ शाम करते हैं

बुझा जो रौज़न-ए ज़िंदाँ तो दिल ये समझा है
कि तेरी माँग सितारों से भर गई होगी
चमक उठे हैं सलासिल तो हम ने जाना है
कि अब सहर तेरे रुख़ पर बिखर गई होगी
ग़रज़ तसव्वुर-ए शाम ओ सहर में जीते हैं
गिरफ़्त-ए साया-ए दीवार ओ दर में जीते हैं

यूँही हमेशा उलझती रही है ज़ुल्म से ख़ल्क़
न उन की रस्म नई है न अपनी रीत नई
यूँ ही हमेशा खिलाए हैं हम ने आग में फूल
न उन की हार नई है न अपनी जीत नई
इसी सबब से फ़लक का गिला नहीं करते
तेरे फ़िराक़ में हम दिल बुरा नहीं करते

गर आज तुझ से जुदा हैं तो कल बहम होंगे
ये रात भर की जुदाई तो कोई बात नहीं
गर आज औज पे है ता'ला-ए रक़ीब तो क्या
ये चार दिन की ख़ुदाई तो कोई बात नहीं
जो तुझ से अ'हद-ए वफा उस्तुवार रखते हैं
इ'लाज-ए गर्दिश-ए लैल ओ नहार रखते हैं

◆

GHAZAL

Two couplets of this ghazal (the first and the last) include
significant statements about what the poet feels about his
poetry. The love for freedom is expressed in a language

that may be called the style of madness or insanity, but it
has become the mode of expression that can't be stopped.
The poet takes pride in having created this metaphorical
structure of communication while he suffered the pain
of isolation in his jail cell. He is pleased that others are
impressed, and they are trying to speak in this very style.

Passion now is the medium of discourse
on everyone's lips everywhere.
What has gained momentum
can't be stopped.

Whatever was forbidden
by esteemed Sheikh as not permissible,
the same thing is comforting
everyone's soul.

People are saying
that the preacher is evasive.
Our conversation was really about the alley
of the idol.

This is Laila's beauty;
this is Shiirin's face.
The eye of desire
sees this wherever it stops.

The night of union passed in a jiffy.
The night of separation—
hard, heavy and bone-breaking.

Once we miss it
there is no way to catch
the tide of fragrance.
Once it leaves the heart,
the cry of grief

does not stay on the lips.

Hands of the hunter
and the flower-picker
have been jammed.
There is nothing now to stop
the fragrance of flowers or
the nightingale's song.

The spring must have taken a break
while it was on its way.
The autumn that was ready to depart
it has taken a moment to stop for no reason.

The style of expressing the suffering
I had invented in the prison
is now the way of divulgence
in the whole garden.

'Ab Vohi Harf-e Junuun Sab Ki Zabaan Thahri Hai'

ab vohi harf-e junuun sab ki zabaan thahri hai
jo bhi chal nikli hai voh baat kahaan thahri hai

aajtak sheikh ke ikraam mein jo shai thi haraam
ab voh hi dushman-e diin raahat-e jaan thahri hai

hai vohi aariz-e laila vohi shiiriin ka dahan
nigeh-e shauq ghari bhar ko jahaan thahri hai

hai khabar garm k phirta hai gurezaan naaseh
guftaguu aaj sar-e kuue butaan thahri hai

vasl ki shab thi to kis darja subak guzri thi
hijr ki shab hai to kya sakht garaan thahri hai

bikhri ikbaar to haath aaii hai kab mauj-e shamiim
dil se nikli hai to kab lab pe fughaan thahri hai

dast-e sayyaad bhi aa'jiz hai kaf-e gulchiin bhi
buue gul thahri n bulbul ki zabaan thahri hai

aate aate yunhi dam bhar ko ruki ho gi bahaar
jaate jaate yunhi pal bhar ko khizaan thahri hai

ham ne jo tarz-e fughaan ki hai qafas mein iijaad
Faiz gulshan mein voh i tarz-e biyaan thahri hai

'अब वही हर्फ़-ए जुनूँ सब की जबाँ ठहरी है'

अब वही हर्फ़-ए जुनूँ सब की जबाँ ठहरी है
जो भी चल निकली है वो बात कहाँ ठहरी है

आज तक शैख़ के इकराम में जो शय थी हराम
अब वही दुश्मन-ए दीं राहत-ए जाँ ठहरी है

है ख़बर गर्म कि फिरता है गुरेज़ाँ नासेह
गुफ़्तुगू आज सर-ए कू-ए बुताँ ठहरी है

है वही आरिज़-ए लैला वही शीरीं का दहन
निगह-ए शौक़ घड़ी भर को जहाँ ठहरी है

वस्ल की शब थी तो किस दर्जा सुबुक गुज़री थी
हिज्र की शब है तो क्या सख़्त गिराँ ठहरी है

बिखरी इक बार तो हाथ आई है कब मौज-ए शमीम
दिल से निकली है तो कब लब पे फ़ुग़ाँ ठहरी है

दस्त-ए सय्याद भी आ'जिज़ है कफ़-ए गुल-चीं भी
बू-ए गुल ठहरी न बुलबुल की ज़बाँ ठहरी है

आते आते यूँही दम भर को रुकी होगी बहार
जाते जाते यूँही पल भर को ख़िज़ाँ ठहरी है

हम ने जो तर्ज़-ए फ़ुग़ाँ की है क़फ़स में ईजाद
'फ़ैज़' गुलशन में वही तर्ज-ए बयाँ ठहरी है

◆

GHAZAL

Clouds come, and wine pours.
After this, torment follows,
and all are welcome.

Moon may come down
from the decanter's top.
And sun may descend into
Saqi's hands.

I wish each vein filled with blood
be illuminated once again,
so that I see her face to face,
fully unveiled.

My heart is keeping its sight
on each page of my life
while I bump into
chapters of your fidelity.

While I was counting the wounds
inflicted by the world,
I remembered you over and over.

The kingdom of your grief
never budged an inch,
though my heart moved
from one insurgence to the other.

In the assembly of the other,
doors and walls were illuminated
as soon as ruined and desolate like us
showed up.

Strange was the echo of my silence.
Reciprocations came from all sides.

Faiz, I stayed on the path
and kept going successfully,
always hitting the target.

'Aae Kuchh Abr Kuchh Sharaab Aae'

aae kuchh abr kuchh sharaab aae
is ke baa'd aae jo a'zaab aae

baam-e miina se mahtaab utre
dast-e saaqi mein aaftaab aaye

har rag-e khuun mein phir charaaghaan ho
saamne phir voh beniqaab aae

u'mr ke har varq pe dil ko nazar
teri mehr o vafa ke baab aae

kar raha tha gham-e jahaan ka hisaab
aaj tum yaad behisaab aae

na gaii tere gham ki sardaari
dil mein yuun roz inqilaab aae

jal uthe bazm-e ghair ke dar o baam
jab bhi ham khaanma-kharaab aae

is tarah apni khaamoshi guunji
goya har samt se javaab aae

Faiz thi raah sar-b-sar manzil
ham jahaan pahunche kaamyaab aae

'आए कुछ अब्र कुछ शराब आए'

आए कुछ अब्र कुछ शराब आए
इस के बा'द आए जो अज़ाब आए

बाम-ए मीना से माहताब उतरे

दस्त-ए साक़ी में आफ़्ताब आए

हर रग-ए ख़ूँ में फिर चरागाँ हो
सामने फिर वो बेनक़ाब आए

उ'मर के हर वरक़ पे दिल की नज़र
तेरी मेहर ओ वफ़ा के बाब आए

कर रहा था ग़म-ए जहाँ का हिसाब
आज तुम याद बेहिसाब आए

न गई तेरे गम की सरदारी
दिल में यूँ रोज़ इंक़लाब आए

जल उठे बज़्म-ए ग़ैर के दर ओ बाम
जब भी हम ख़ानुमाँ-ख़राब आए

इस तरह अपनी ख़ामोशी गूँजी
गोया हर सम्त से जवाब आए

'फ़ैज़' थी राह सर-ब-सर मंज़िल
हम जहाँ पहुँचे कामयाब आए

◆

'AN EVENING IN THE JAILHOUSE'

This poem 'Zindaan Ki Ek Shaam' and the next one 'Zindaan Ki Ek Sub-h' should be read together because they have a discrete link. They have the same setting: the jailhouse (which is involuntarily the poet's home). Another common feature is the intense imagery of the night, moon, stars, trees and sounds, which are detected in the stillness of the night. The first poem shows defiance towards the end and tells the oppressors: '*chaand ko gul karein to ham jaanein!* (We shall greet them if they succeed

in smothering moon's brightness!)'. The second poem
starts with the powerful imagery of the personification
of the moon but then slowly slithers away and what we
get are the sights and sounds of prison. There is some
anticipation and hope but darkness reigns. The second
poem is marked incomplete, and it gives a feeling of
having arrived at the last couple of lines.

The night is coming down the stairs,
one step at a time.
The fragrant wind crosses me like
someone is whispering a feeling of love.
In the jailhouse's backyard,
there are trees
that are missing their native lands.
Their heads are looped downward.
They are busy imprinting
on the space of the sky
images and portrayals.
On the crest of the prison's roof
there is shine and sparkle
and the beautiful hand
of the magnanimous moonlight.

The liquid core of the cosmic bodies
has been reduced to dust.
The blue sky has fully dissolved itself
into the wide-open dimness.
In some emerald corners,
there are dark grey shades.
They move back and forth
like the wave of separation from the beloved
that hits the heart.

A thought continuously rises:
life is just too sweet in this moment.
Those who mix the poison of oppression
shall neither succeed today nor tomorrow.
So what if they have doused
the lamps of the pleasure chambers of the union?
We shall greet them if they succeed
in smothering the moon's brightness!

'Zindaan Ki Ek Shaam'

shaam ke pech o kham sitaaron se
ziina ziina utar rahi hai raat
yuun saba paas se guzarti hai
jaise kah di kisi ne pyaar ki baat
sahn-e zindaan ke bevatan ashjaar
sar-niguun mahv hain banaane mein
daaman-e aasmaan pe naqsh o nigaar
shaana-e baam par damakta hai
mehrbaan chaandni ka dast-e jamiil
khaak mein ghul gaaii hai aab-e najuum
nuur mein ghul gaya hai a'rsh ka niil
sabz goshon mein niil guun saaye
lah lahaate hain jis tarah dil mein
mauj-e dard-e firaaq-e yaar aaye

dil se paiham khayaal kahta hai
itni shiiriin hai zindagi is pal
zulm ka zahr gholne vaale
kaamraan ho sakein ge aaj n kal
jalvah gaah-e visal ki sham'ayein
voh bujha bhi chuke agar to kya
chaand ko gul karein to ham jaanein

'जिन्दाँ की एक शाम'

शाम के पेच ओ ख़म सितारों से
ज़ीना ज़ीना उतर रही है रात
यूँ सबा पास से गुज़रती है
जैसे कह दी किसी ने प्यार की बात
सेहन-ए ज़िंदाँ के बेवतन अश्जार
सर-निगूँ महव हैं बनाने में
दामन-ए आसमाँ पे नक़्श। ओ निगार
शाना-ए बाम पर दमकता है
मेहरबाँ चाँदनी का दस्त-ए जमील
ख़ाक में घुल गई है आब-ए नुजूम
नूर में घुल गया है अर्श का नील
सब्ज़ गोशों में नील-गूँ साए
लहलहाते हैं जिस तरह दिल में
मौज-ए दर्द-ए फ़िराक़-ए यार आए

दिल से पैहम ख़याल कहता है
इतनी शीरीं है ज़िंदगी इस पल
ज़ुल्म का ज़हर घोलने वाले
कामराँ हो सकेंगे आज न कल
जल्वा-गाह-ए विसाल की शमा'एं
वो बुझा भी चुके अगर तो क्या
चाँद को गुल करें तो हम जानें!

◆

'A MORNING IN THE JAILHOUSE'

Faiz once told an interviewer that he wanted to make this a really long poem but he couldn't, so he left it incomplete.[40]

---

[40]Hameed, ed., *Daybreak*, p. 359.

The night was still young
when the moon reached me
while I was sleeping and said:
'Get up! The wine of dreams
that was your share
has gone down
from the top of the cup
to nearly hit the bottom.'
I said goodbye
to the image of my beloved
that I was holding and
raised my eyes.
On the black covering
of the night's settled waters
whirlpools of silver
appeared and started to dance
and slowly dwindled.
From the moon's hand
lotuses of stars fell one by one,
they sank, they swam,
they withered,
and they blossomed.
Night and day stayed
in an embrace for
a long while.

In the prison's backyard
the golden images
of friends emerged
at a leisurely pace,
spreading radiance.
The dewdrops of sleepiness
had washed from those faces

the grief of the land,
the misery of separation.

The sound of a drum
in the backdrop.
The impatient feet
started to move.
Pale-faced guards,
bitten by hunger,
the dreadful cries
of prisoners.
Everything aligned
with everything else.

The breeze drunk
with the delights of sleep
was awakened.
The prison sounds
were filled with poison and
were sadly broken.
They awakened.
Far away,
a door opened and
another one closed.
Far away,
a chain muttered and whined and
then it cried.
Far away,
someone put a dagger
into the heart of a bolt.

The window lost its cool
as if it witnessed
the rising of enemies of being,

demons shaped by stone and steel,
in whose grip
lies the lament of the night and day.
The dainty fairies
of my useless days and nights—
my co-prisoners—
are waiting for their wings
in whose quiver are hidden
flaming arrows of hope.
(Incomplete)

'Zindaan Ki Ek Sub-h'

raat baaqi thi abhi jab sar-e baalein aa kar
chaand ne mujh se kaha 'jaag! sahar aaii hai
jaag! is shab jo mai-e khwaab tera hissa thi
jaam ke lab se tah-e jaam utar aaii hai'
aks-e jaanaan ko vid'a kar ke uthi meri nazar
shab ke thahre hue paani ki siyaah chaadar par

ja-b-ja raqs mein aane lage chaandi ke bhanvar
chaand ke haath se taaron ke kanval gir gir kar
duubte tairte murjhaate rahe khilte rahe
raat aur sub-h bahut der gale milte rahe

sahn-e zindaan mein rafiiqon ke sunehare chehre
sat-ha-e zulmat se damakte hue ubhre kamkam
niind ki os ne un chehron se dho dala tha
des ka dard firaaq-e rukh-e mahbuub ka gham

duur naubat hui phirne lage bezaar qadam
zard faaqon ke sitaaye hue pehre vaale
ahle zindaan ke ghazab naak khroshaan naale
jinki baahon mein phira karte hain baahein daale

lazzat-e khwaab se makhmuur havaaein jaagiin

jail ki zahrbhari chor sadaaein jaagiin
duur darvaaza khula koi koi band hua
duur machli koi zanjiir machal ke rooii
duur utra kisi taale ke jigar mein khanjar

sar tapakne laga rah rah ke dariicha koi
goya phir khwaab se bedaar hue dushman-e jaan
sang o faulaad se dhaale hue jannaat-e giraan
jin ke chungal mein shab o roz hain faryaad kunaan
mere be-kaar shab o roz ki naazuk pariyaan
apne shahpuur ki raah dekh rahi hain ye asiir
jis ke tarkash mein hain ummiid ke jalte hue tiir

'ज़िन्दाँ की एक सुब्ह'

रात बाक़ी थी अभी जब सर-ए बालीं आ कर
चाँद ने मुझ से कहा 'जाग सहर आई है
जाग इस शब जो मय-ए ख़्वाब तेरा हिस्सा थी
जाम के लब से तह-ए जाम उतर आई है'
अक्स-ए जानाँ को विदा' कर के उठी मेरी नज़र
शब के ठहरे हुए पानी की सियह चादर पर

जा-ब-जा रक़्स में आने लगे चाँदी के भँवर
चाँद के हाथ से तारों के कँवल गिर गिर कर
डूबते तैरते मुरझाते रहे खिलते रहे
रात और सुब्ह बहुत देर गले मिलते रहे

सेहन-ए जिंदाँ में रफ़ीक़ों के सुनहरे चेहरे
सतह-ए ज़ुल्मत से दमकते हुए उभरे कम कम
नींद की ओस ने उन चेहरों से धो डाला था
देस का दर्द फ़िराक़-ए रुख़-ए महबूब का ग़म

दूर नौबत हुई फिरने लगे बेज़ार क़दम
ज़र्द फ़ाक़ों के सताए हुए पहरे वाले
अहल-ए ज़िंदाँ के ग़ज़बनाक ख़रोशाँ नाले
जिन की बाहों में फिरा करते हैं बाहें डाले

लज़्ज़त-ए ख़्वाब से मख़मूर हवाएँ जागीं
जेल की ज़हर-भरी चूर सदाएँ जागीं
दूर दरवाज़ा खुला कोई कोई बंद हुआ
दूर मचली कोई ज़ंजीर मचल के रोई
दूर उतरा किसी ताले के जिगर में ख़ंजर

सर पटकने लगा रह रह के दरीचा कोई
गोया फिर ख़्वाब से बेदार हुए दुश्मन-ए जाँ
संग ओ फ़ौलाद से ढाले हुए जन्नात-ए गिराँ
जिन के चंगुल में शब ओ रोज़ हैं फ़रियाद-कुनाँ
मेरे बेकार शब ओ रोज़ की नाज़ुक परियाँ
अपने शहपूर की रह देख रहे हैं ये असीर
जिस के तरकश में हैं उम्मीद के जलते हुए तीर

◆

'MEMORY'

'Memory' ('Yaad') is an incredibly sensuous poem, perhaps the best and profusely complimented by even brutal critics. The beloved's image no doubt stays with the lover at all times, but it does attain special significance depending on how beautifully and richly she is remembered. This poem talks about a lonely place away from home (dasht—that evokes memories associated with Majnun's wanderings), possibly as far away from human habitation as possible. Nature, of course, plays an integral part in such a setting. But the beloved's memory comes with such force that it alters the visual spectacle. Where there was just dust and barrenness, there are now are jasmines and roses, there is fragrance on her breath and there are sparkling dewdrops falling slowly from the sky. Such is the impact of memory changing the natural scenery, that the night of separation does not look like a night of separation but the night of fulfillment of hope. The poem should be read just for the beauty of its heart-touching thoughts and its extremely rich and gratifying visualization.

In the stillness of wilderness,
O my life, are quivering
echoes of your voice and
mirages of your lips.

In this lonely place in the desert,
burdened by the dust and dirt,
are blossoming jasmines and roses,
finding joy in your arms.

There is a rising, close to you,
the tenderness of your breath
glowing in its fragrance
at a slow pace.

In the distance, beyond the horizon,
there are sparkling dewdrops
of your captivating eyes
that are falling, one drop at a time.

Your memory is back, O my life,
and it has kept its hand gently
on the cheeks of my heart.

I feel that our separation is over,
and the night of union is here,
although it was just the beginning
of our ongoing detachment.

'Yaad'

dasht-e tanhaaii mein ae jaan-e jahaan larzaan hain
teri aavaaz ke saaye tere honton ke saraab

dasht-e tanhaaii mein duuri ke khas o khaak tale
khil rahe hain tere pahlu ke saman aur gulaab

uth rahi hai kahien qurbat se teri saans ki aanch
apni khushbu mein sulagati hui madham madham

duur ufq paar chamakati hui qatra qatra
gir rahi hai teri dildaar nazar ki shabnam

is qadar pyaar se ae jaan-e jahaan rakha hai
dil ke rukhsaar pe is vaqat teri yaad ne haat

yuun gumaan hota hai garche hai abhi sub-h-e firaaq
dhal gaya hijar ka din aa bhi gaii vasl ki raat

'याद'

दश्त-ए तन्हाई में ऐ जान-ए जहाँ लज़ाँ हैं
तेरी आवाज़ के साए तेरे होंटों के सराब

दश्त-ए तन्हाई में दूरी के ख़स ओ ख़ाक तले
खिल रहे हैं तेरे पहलू के समन और गुलाब

उठ रही है कहीं क़ुर्बत से तेरी साँस की आँच
अपनी ख़ुशबू में सुलगती हुई मद्धम मद्धम

दूर उफ़ुक़ पार चमकती हुई क़तरा क़तरा
गिर रही है तेरी दिलदार नज़र की शबनम

इस क़दर प्यार से ऐ जान-ए जहाँ रखा है
दिल के रुख़सार पे इस वक़्त तेरी याद ने हाथ

यूँ गुमाँ होता है गरचे है अभी सुब्ह-ए फ़िराक़
ढल गया हिज्र का दिन आ भी गई वस्ल की रात

three

DAWNS AND DUSKS OF THE JAILHOUSE

In the arrogance of my grief, I kept my head high and never lowered my gaze before anyone; how difficult this was, how agonizing, only my heart knows. But now I am alone with my grief inside my jail cell and I do not have to hold my head high any longer. There is no shame here in surrendering to the tyranny of my pain. But please do not worry. This wound is sudden and unwarranted but I am strong enough to bear it and not bow my head. I only wish I was outside and could offer the strength of my arms to those weaker than I, whose sorrow is more burdensome than my grief.

—Faiz's letter to Alys from his prison cell[41]

THE PRISON LETTERS

While Faiz was in prison, he wrote many letters to Alys. The authorities read them, but nothing much was redacted. Written in English, they number 135. Here is the breakdown: Hyderabad Prison: 92 letters from June 1951 to June 1953; Karachi Prison and Jinnah Hospital in Karachi: 8

---

[41]Hashmi, *Love and Revolution,* p. 170.

letters from June 1953 to August 1954; Montgomery Prison: 35 letters from October 1954 to April 1955. In all, the letters covered a period of three years and 11 months.

The publication of these letters in their Urdu translation is itself an interesting story. As Faiz celebrated his sixtieth birthday in February 1971, he was pressured by his friends to write an autobiography, but by temperament, he was reticent about sharing details of his personal life. He also felt that it would not be a good use of his time. As a compromise, Alys offered to share for publication the letters she had received from Faiz while he had been in prison. This was a good solution, but the language in which the letters were written (English) was a problem. It was felt that if the letters were published in the form they had been written, they would have limited appeal. At the request of Mirza Zafarul Hasan, Faiz agreed to dictate the translation of the letters in conversational Urdu. This work took several weeks because Faiz often travelled from Karachi to Lahore for various activities. It was thanks to the total devotion of Mirza Zafarul Hasan that the work on the Urdu publication was completed in June 1971, which incidentally marked the twentieth anniversary of the first letter that Faiz wrote from prison. The book, titled *Salibein Mere Dariche Mein,* was later published both in Pakistan and India. Faiz made it clear in his introductory note that the letters were not literary creations. These were personal communications, written under tremendous pressure. The primary objective was to tell the family how he was coping with the stresses of jail life and, therefore, any philosophical reflections or ruminations were purely incidental.

Not everything written in the letters will be of interest to today's readers, but here are some excerpts (in my translation from the Urdu text) that contain some observations of lasting value:[42]

> The three or four days that I spent in Lahore were certainly the most painful of my stay in prison so far. I realized for the first time that to harm others for their benefit, some people will be ready to do something that is wrong. One can try to justify it as idealism or something which is based on principles, but in reality, it is selfishness. While strictly following their own principles, people can forget what the victims value. This way you hurt others only to promote your interests.

◆

> If in your heart you have guilt, you can bear all kinds of difficulties. But when something is imposed on you from the outside, it would always remain external to your being. You will have that feeling for life.

◆

> I wish you were here. But it is good that you are not here. The outcome of such meetings is always more pain and more yearning.

◆

> The philosophy of pleasure does not answer a simple question: if temporary pleasure is followed by pain, how should we avoid such transient pleasure? This question is difficult to answer because the proportionality of pleasure and pain can't be determined in advance.

◆

---

[42]Urdu text drawn from Abdul Qayyuum, 'Faiz Ke Khatuut', in *Shabistan* Faiz Number, pp. 179–83. Translation mine.

After a certain age, it is difficult for a man to change himself fundamentally. All this excitement about personal change is a wasteful self-deception. It is also true that unless we are forced to go through difficult challenges, we neither get to know the truth or falsehood of our identity nor do we know how to distinguish our true self (which is real) from the self that we present to others as an act of showmanship.

◆

The legal system that British left behind has many good aspects. But the endless routines and formalities (the purpose of which was to safeguard the interests of the innocent) are a big drain on one's time and financial resources. The common man has no money and no patience. Therefore, the system is a burden on him.

◆

I have concluded that selfishness is the source of man's anger and unhappiness. People attach too much importance to themselves. Beneath the layers of anxiety, lack of effort, self-flagellation lies the complaint that the creator didn't design the universe to take care of our aspirations.

◆

In life, struggle is not enough. It is also necessary that the human being should fight the battle with optimism and good temper and should not allow oneself to become a victim of thoughts of grievance and self-victimization. This would make the challenges even more severe. To some extent, this depends on one's temperament. We can't always do what we want to do.

However, there is no alternative to what is a right and proper effort.

◆

I know your opinion and I don't disagree with you. These small things have many dimensions that should be kept in view. To always see the choice as black or white is not right ... I know in your 'downright' philosophy these things have no place. But think of the more fragile multitudes who can't always follow one and the only one true path.

◆

My talent is limited. There are many more people who are much more talented than I am. But hard work counts, and it makes a difference.

◆

All literature—whether its objective is to promote a political viewpoint or a personal philosophy or it is an expression of national heritage, whatever be the circumstances—is a service to one's nation. It deserves recognition. The writer should, therefore, have enough freedom so that he may fully express himself.

Faiz's third poetry collection *Zindaan Nama* was published in 1956 after his release from prison. The book had no dedication and no celebratory book launch, as Faiz saw this work as a continuation of his second poetry book, *Dast-e Saba*. There was a preface by Sajjad Zaheer and a long essay by one of the co-conspirators and Faiz's prisonmates, Maj. Mohammad Ishaaq. This chapter contains a selection of some of the best ghazals and poems from *Zindaan Nama*.

GHAZAL

I kept a good social distance
from the honourable Sheikh.
Thank goodness, I didn't ruin my life.

When I saw you
it was a gift for my sight.
When I fell in love with you,
I reached the love's end.

Your oppressive hand
knows no modesty.
Non-believer that my heart is,
it didn't show its agony.

On the night of separation
there were many other concerns.
I didn't care much about
my withered heart.

Faiz, name a killer in town
with whom my friends didn't have
some kind of a conventional relationship.

'Sheikh Sahib Se Rasm o Raah N Ki'

sheikh sahib se rasm o raah n ki
shukr hai zindagi tabaah n ki

tujh ko dekha to ser-chashm hue
tujh ko chaaha to aur chaah n ki

tere dast-e sitam ka i'jaz nahien
dil hi kaafir tha jis ne aah n ki

the shab-e hijr kaam aur bahut
ham ne fikr-e dil-e tabaah n ki

kaun qaatil bacha hai shahar mein Faiz
jis se yaaron ne rasm o raah n ki

'शैख़ साहिब से रस्म ओ राह न की'

शैख़ साहिब से रस्म ओ राह न की
शुक्र है ज़िंदगी तबाह न की

तुझ को देखा तो सेर-चश्म हुए
तुझ को चाहा तो और चाह न की

तेरे दस्त-ए सितम का इ'ज़्ज़ नहीं
दिल ही काफ़िर था जिस ने आह न की

थे शब-ए हिज्र काम और बहुत
हम ने फ़िक्र-ए दिल-ए तबाह न की

कौन क़ातिल बचा है शहर में 'फ़ैज़'
जिस से यारों ने रस्म ओ राह न की

♦

GHAZAL

After being killed in your presence,
we feel free and relieved.
We have returned from our journey's end.

The candle of sight,
stars of imagination,
wounds of the heart.
All the luminosity has radiated
from your meeting place.

I got up and left your niche
and it seemed like a simple act.
But my heart knows
how much pain I had to go through

to do that.

Each step was like the call of death.
Each point in time was life.
We loitered and returned from
the alley of the assassins.

Say thanks, Faiz, to the autumn's breeze;
its hands have brought messages
sent by a springtime beauty.

'Sab Qatl Ho Ke Tere Muqaabil Se Aaye Hain'

sab qatl ho ke tere muqaabil se aaye hain
ham log surkhuru hain k manzil se aaye hain

sham'a-e nazar khayal ke anjum jigar ke daagh
jitney charaagh hain teri mahfil se aaye hain

uth kar to aa gaye hain teri bazm se magar
kuchh dil hi jaanta hai k kis dil se aaye hain

har ik qadam ajal tha har ik gaam zindagi
ham ghuum phir ke kuucha-e qaatil se aaye hain

baad-e khizaan ka shukr karo Faiz jis ke haath
naame kisi bahaar shimaa'il se aaye hain

'सब क़त्ल हो के तेरे मुक़ाबिल से आए हैं'

सब क़त्ल हो के तेरे मुक़ाबिल से आए हैं
हम लोग सुर्ख़-रू हैं कि मंज़िल से आए हैं

शम-ए नज़र ख़याल के अंजुम जिगर के दाग़
जितने चराग़ हैं तेरी महफ़िल से आए हैं

उठ कर तो आ गए हैं तेरी बज़्म से मगर
कुछ दिल ही जानता है कि किस दिल से आए हैं

हर इक क़दम अजल था हर इक गाम जिंदगी
हम घूम फिर के कूचा-ए क़ातिल से आए हैं

बाद-ए ख़िज़ाँ का शुक्र करो 'फ़ैज़' जिस के हाथ
नामे किसी बहार शिमा'ईल से आए हैं

◆

GHAZAL

Don't ask about the evening of separation.
It came and went by.
It was my heart that soothed
and it was my life that regained its balance.

In the assemblage of my imagination,
the candle of your beauty was lit up.
The moon of suffering was doused;
the night of separation dwindled.

Your memory made the morning fragrant
and even more aromatic.
When I awakened the pain of our separation,
night sulked and fidgeted away.

Before I came, I had sorted out
all my issues with my heart.
But when I faced her,
I couldn't keep my talk straight.

The fellow travellers
of the latter part of the evening—
Faiz, where did they go?
Where did we leave the gentle breeze?
Where did the morning go?

(Jinnah Hospital, Karachi, July 1953)

'Shaam-e Firaaq Ab N Puuchh Aaii Aur Aa Ke Tal Gaaii'

shaam-e firaaq ab n puuchh aaii aur aa ke tal gaii
dil tha k phir behal gaya jaan thi k phir sambhal gaii

bazm-e khayal mein tere husn ki sham'a jal gaii
dard ka chaand bujh gaya hijr ki raat dhal gaii

jab tujhe yaad kar liya sub-h mehak mehak uthi
jab tera gham jaga liya raat machal machal gaii

dil se to har m'uaamla kar ke chale the saaf ham
kahne mein un ke saamne baat badal badal gaii

aakhr-e shab ke ham-safar Faiz na-jaane kya hue
rah gaii kis jagaah saba sub-h kidhar nikal gaii

'शाम-ए फ़िराक़ अब न पूछ आई और आ के टल गई'

शाम-ए फ़िराक़ अब न पूछ आई और आ के टल गई
दिल था कि फिर बहल गया जाँ थी कि फिर सँभल गई

बज़्म-ए ख़याल में तेरे हुस्न की शमा जल गई
दर्द का चाँद बुझ गया हिज्र की रात ढल गई

जब तुझे याद कर लिया सुब्ह महक महक उठी
जब तेरा ग़म जगा लिया रात मचल मचल गई

दिल से तो हर मोआमला कर के चले थे साफ हम
कहने में उन के सामने बात बदल बदल गई

आख़िर-ए शब के हम-सफ़र 'फ़ैज़' न जाने क्या हुए
रह गई किस जगह सबा सुब्ह किधर निकल गई

◆

'COMING TOGETHER'

This poem, written in October 1953 in Montgomery Jail, is one of Faiz's masterful creations. It has the same sensual feel as the two prison poems that we read in the last chapter. But in many ways, this poem is so unique that it can stand on its own merits. The setting is the poet's favourite—the night in its pristine darkness, but there are some new symbols. A tree, which is generally viewed as a symbol of knowledge, is presented here as a tree of suffering; it is so powerful that it has transformed the night into its persona. And this tree is more significant than everything else: even the caravans of stars have lost their paths under its branches. But there is something bigger than this tree, and that is the memory of the beloved. The fallen leaves of this tree, when they become entangled with the curls of the beloved, transform into pomegranate flowers.

As we come to the second part of the poem, the tone changes. A river of blood emerges from the darkness of the night: this refers to the revolutionary struggle and the way oppressors cause misery and inflict pain on those who are protesting. The imagery of the beloved provides some relief, but it has receded into the background.

The third part of the poem presents the meeting point. There is the beloved and there is the pain of suffering, as well as the struggle to attain freedom: but these things are not separate. They meet here and become one: '*jahaan par ham tum khare hain dono / sahar ka raushan ufq yahien hai* (The place where both of us are standing / is dawn's bright horizon)'. This is the gift of the night that should be cherished.

1

This night is a tree of suffering
which is higher than you and me.
Higher because in its branches
caravans of millions of torch-carrying stars
have lost their paths.
Hundreds of moons under its shadow
have lost their splendour.
This night is a tree of suffering
which is higher than you and me.
But from this night's tree
few yellow leaves have fallen
and once they got entangled in your curls
they have become pomegranate flowers.
As its dewdrops of tranquility rained on your
forehead,
they became threaded diamonds and jewels.

2

This is a night
but from this darkness emerges
the river of blood
which is my clarion call.
In its shadow, there is a light,
which is a wave of substance,
resembling your alluring eyes.
The pain that is burning at this time
in the rose-garden of your arms.
(That pain is the fruit of this night.)
If the flames of sighs heat it,
it could become a spark.
From each arch of the dark branch

the arrows that have hit my heart
and have broken into pieces,
I have pulled them out
and I have used them
to forge hatchets of my own.

3

The morning of unfortunate ones
and those with broken hearts
is not visible in the skies.
The place where both of us are standing
is dawn's bright horizon.
Here the sparks of sorrow
when they blossom
become pomegranate flowers
of morning's twilight.
Here the axes of murderous sorrows,
line after line,
become flaming garlands of rays.
This sadness,
which is a gift of this night,
is a belief about the certainty of the coming
dawn—
a belief which is more forgiving
than the sorrow itself,
about the morning that is greater than the night.

'Mulaaqaat'

1

ye raat jo is dard ka shajar hai
jo mujh se tujh se a'ziim-tar hai

a'ziim-tar hai k is ki shaakhon
mein laakh mish'al-b-kaf sitaaron
ke kaarvaan ghir ke kho gaye hain
hazaar mahtaab is ke saaye
mein apna sab nuur ro gaye hain
ye raat is dard ka shajar hai
jo mujh se tujh se aziim-tar hai
magar isi raat ke shajar se
ye chand lamhon ke zard patte
gire hain aur tere gesuon mein
ulajh ke gulnaar ho gaye hain
isi ki shabnam se khaamshi ke
ye chand qatre teri jabiin par
baras ke hiire piro gaye hain

2

bahut siyaah hai ye raat lekin
isi siyaahi mein ruunuma hai
voh nehre-khuun jo meri sada hai
isi ke saaye mein nuurgar hai
voh mauj-e zar jo teri nazar hai
voh gham jo is vaqt teri baahon
ke gulsitaan mein sulag raha hai
(voh gham jo is raat ka samar hai)
kuchh aur tap jaaye apni aahon
ki aanch mein to yahi sharar hai
har ik siyaah shaakh ki kamaan se
jigar mein tuute hain tiir jitney
jigar se noche hain aur har ik
ka ham ne tesha bana liya hai

3

alam nasiibon jigar figaaron
ki sub-h aflaak par nahien hai
jahaan par ham tum khare hain dono
sahar ka raushan ufq yahien hai
yahien pe gham ke sharaar khilkar
shafaq ka gulzaar ban gaye hain
yahien pe qaatil dukhon ke teshe
qataar andar qataar kirnon
ke aatshiin haar ban gaye hain
ye gham jo is raat ne diya hai
ye gham sahar ka yaqiin bana hai
yaqiin jo gham se kariim-tar hai
sahar jo shab se a'ziim-tar hai

'मुलाक़ात'

1

ये रात उस दर्द का शजर है
जो मुझ से तुझ से अज़ीम-तर है
अ'ज़ीम-तर है कि इस की शाख़ों
में लाख मिशअल-ब-कफ़ सितारों
के कारवाँ घिर के खो गए हैं
हज़ार महताब इस के साए
में अपना सब नूर रो गए हैं
ये रात उस दर्द का शजर है
जो मुझ से तुझ से अज़ीम-तर है
मगर इसी रात के शजर से
ये चंद लम्हों के ज़र्द पत्ते
गिरे हैं और तेरे गेसुओं में
उलझ के गुलनार हो गए हैं
इसी की शबनम से ख़ामुशी के

ये चंद क़तरे तेरी जबीं पर
बरस के हीरे पिरो गए हैं

2

बहुत सियाह है ये रात लेकिन
इसी सियाही में रूनुमा है
वो नहर-ए ख़ूँ जो मेरी सदा है
इसी के साए में नूरगर है
वो मौज-ए ज़र जो तेरी नज़र है
वो ग़म जो इस वक़्त तेरी बाँहों
के गुलसिताँ में सुलग रहा है
(वो ग़म जो इस रात का समर है)
कुछ और तप जाए अपनी आहों
की आँच में तो यही शरर है
हर इक सियह शाख़ की कमाँ से
जिगर में टूटे हैं तीर जितने
जिगर से नोचे हैं और हर इक
का हम ने तेशा बना लिया है

3

अलम-नसीबों जिगर-फ़िगारों
की सुब्ह अफ़्लाक पर नहीं है
जहाँ पे हम तुम खड़े हैं दोनों
सहर का रौशन उफ़ुक़ यहीं है
यहीं पे ग़म के शरार खिल कर
शफ़क़ का गुलज़ार बन गए हैं
यहीं पे क़ातिल दुखों के तेशे
क़तार अंदर क़तार किरनों
के आतिशीं हार बन गए हैं
ये ग़म जो इस रात ने दिया है
ये ग़म सहर का यक़ीं बना है

यक़ीं जो ग़म से करीम-तर है
सहर जो शब से अ'ज़ीम-तर है

◆

QAT'A

Don't take too much pleasure so that tomorrow
becomes awful.
It is not a night that is not spent wrapped in
beloved's curls.
This longing is something quite significant, my
friend.
Union with the beloved, however, is something
beyond longing.

n aaj lutf kar itna k kal guzar n sake
voh raat jo k tere gesuon ki raat nahien
ye aarzu bhi bari chiiz hai magar hamdam
visaal-e yaar faqat aarzu ki baat nahien

न आज लुत्फ़ कर इतना कि कल गुज़र न सके
वो रात जो कि तेरे गेसुओं की रात नहीं
ये आरज़ू भी बड़ी चीज़ है मगर हमदम
विसाल-ए यार फ़क़त आरज़ू की बात नहीं

◆

GHAZAL

This matter is already in the zone
where nothing is under my control.
My heart is feeling better.

Frenzy is crossing its limits.
My disposition seems
somewhat relaxed.

My tears are nothing
but water and blood.
The colour of my grief
is changing.

Either the candles are dousing
for no particular reason,
or the night of separation
is getting close to its end.

Millions of messages—
when the gentle breeze
runs for a moment.

Stars, please go away
and have some rest.
The night of suffering
is near its demise.

(Montgomery Jail, November 1953)

'Baat Bas Se Nikal Chali Hai'

baat bas se nikal chali hai
dil ki haalat sambhal chali hai

ab junuun had se barh chala hai
ab tab'iiyat behal chali hai

ashk khuun-aab ho chale hain
gham ki rangat badal chali hai

ya yuun hi bujh rahi hain sham'a-ein
ya shab-e hijr tal chali hai

laakh paighaam ho gaye hain
jab saba ek pal chali hai

jaao ab so raho sitaaro
dard ki raat dhal chali hai

'बात बस से निकल चली है'

बात बस से निकल चली है
दिल की हालत सँभल चली है

अब जुनूँ हद से बढ़ चला है
अब तबी'अत बहल चली है

अश्क ख़ूनाब हो चले हैं
ग़म की रंगत बदल चली है

या यूँही बुझ रही हैं शमा'एं
या शब-ए हिज्र टल चली है

लाख पैग़ाम हो गए हैं
जब सबा एक पल चली है

जाओ अब सो रहो सितारो
दर्द की रात ढल चली है

◆

GHAZAL

There is no time
when you are not in my thoughts.
There is no time
when my hand is not in your hand.
It is a blessing that there is no night
that is a night of separation!

If conditions are difficult
in the alley of the beloveds,
what should we do?
Should we sell our hearts,

or give away our souls?
Are the conditions so bad?

The way someone enters the
place of execution,
the style, and the honour,
it stays in people's memory.
Life and death are routine matters.
Life, as such, has little meaning.

The field of love
is not like the royal court.
Your name or lineage
has little recognition.
The passion of love
is not anyone's monopoly
and love itself is not
someone's caste.

If this is a gamble of love,
play the game without fear.
If you win, it is a celebration.
If you lose, it is not a loss.

*'Kab Yaad Mein Tera Saath Nahien Kab Haath Mein
Tera Haath Nahien'*

*kab yaad mein tera saath nahien kab haath mein tera
haath nahien*
sad-shukr k apni raaton mein ab hijr ki koi raat nahien

*mushkil hain agar haalaat vahaan dil bech aayein
jaan de aayein*
*dil vaalo kuucha-e jaanaan mein aise bhi haalaat
nahien*

*jis dhaj se koi maqtal mein gaya voh shaan salaamat
rehti hai
ye jaan to aani jaani hai is jaan ki to koi baat nahien*

*maidaan-e vafa dar baar nahien yaan naam o nasab
ki puuchh kahaan
aa'shiq to kisi ka naam nahien kuchh i'shq kisi ki zaat
nahien*

*gar baazi i'shq ki baazi hai jo chaaho laga do dar kaisa
gar jiit gaye to kya kehna haare bhi to baazi maat nahien*

'कब याद में तेरा साथ नहीं कब हाथ में तेरा हाथ नहीं'

कब याद में तेरा साथ नहीं कब हाथ में तेरा हाथ नहीं
सद-शुक्र कि अपनी रातों में अब हिज्र की कोई रात नहीं

मुश्किल हैं अगर हालात वहाँ दिल बेच आएँ जाँ दे आएँ
दिल वालो कूचा-ए जानाँ में क्या ऐसे भी हालात नहीं

जिस धज से कोई मक़तल में गया वो शान सलामत रहती है
ये जान तो आनी जानी है इस जाँ की तो कोई बात नहीं

मैदान-ए वफ़ा दरबार नहीं याँ नाम ओ नसब की पूछ कहाँ
आशिक़ तो किसी का नाम नहीं कुछ इ'श्क़ किसी की ज़ात नहीं

गर बाज़ी इ'श्क़ की बाज़ी है जो चाहो लगा दो डर कैसा
गर जीत गए तो क्या कहना हारे भी तो बाज़ी मात नहीं

◆

GHAZAL

Others are spreading the word
that I'm in love with you.
It is not something bad.
It is not a blame. It's an honour.

What I am blamed for
is not a crime.
My passion is a waste
and my love is a failure.

My heart is happy
with the humiliating words
of the plaintiff, but, my beloved,
your blame is nothing
more than a name.

My heart has not lost hope,
though it has already failed me.
The evening of despair is long,
but it is just an evening.

The hidden hand of the sky
is not an indicator
of how the cycle of our fate moves;
it is nothing but a circle
of the passage of time.

One day my eyes will undoubtedly see
my charming and virtuous friend,
standing on her balcony.

It's a damp evening, Faiz,
start reciting a ghazal.
The time for music
is the time for talking
about agony.

(Montgomery Jail, March 1954)

'Ham Pe Tumhaari Chaah Ka Ilzaam Hi To Hai'

ham pe tumhaari chaah ka ilzaam hi to hai

dushnaam to nahien hai ye ikraam hi to hai

karte hain jis pe taa'n koi jurm to nahien
shauq-e fuzuul o ulfat-e nakaam hi to hai

dil muddaa'ii ke harf-e malamat se shaad hai
ai jaan-e jaan ye harf tera naam hi to hai

dil naummid to nahien na-kaam hi to hai
lambi hai gham ki shaam mugar shaam hi to hai

dast-e falak mein gardish-e taqdiir to nahien
dast-e falak mein gardish-e ayyaam hi to hai

aakhir to ek roz karegi nazar vafa
voh yaar-e khush-khisaaal sar-e baam hi to hai

bhiigi hai raat Faiz ghazal ibtada karo
vaqt-e suruud dard ka hangaam hi to hai

'हम पर तुम्हारी चाह का इल्ज़ाम ही तो है'

हम पर तुम्हारी चाह का इल्ज़ाम ही तो है
दुश्नाम तो नहीं है ये इकराम ही तो है

करते हैं जिस पे ता'न कोई जुर्म तो नहीं
शौक़-ए फ़ुज़ूल ओ उल्फ़त-ए नाकाम ही तो है

दिल मुद्दाई के हर्फ़-ए मलामत से शाद है
ऐ जान-ए जाँ ये हर्फ़ तेरा नाम तो नहीं

दिल नाउमीद तो नहीं नाकाम ही तो है
लम्बी है ग़म की शाम मगर शाम ही तो है

दस्त-ए फ़लक में गर्दिश-ए तक़दीर तो नहीं
दस्त-ए फ़लक में गर्दिश-ए अय्याम ही तो है

आख़िर तो एक रोज़ करेगी नज़र वफ़ा
वो यार-ए खुश-ख़िसाल सर-ए बाम ही तो है

भीगी है रात 'फ़ैज़' ग़ज़ल इब्तिदा करो
वक़्त-ए सरोद दर्द का हंगाम ही तो है

◆

'O THE CITY OF LIGHTS'

There is a stamp of Faiz's aesthetic sensibility in every word
and every line of this poem. It was written in Montgomery
Jail in March–April 1954. Sitting amidst the loneliness of a
prison cell, the poet was missing Lahore, his favourite city.
The subject matter of the poem is simple: a city is divided
along the lines of residents' living conditions and income
levels. These differentiations are visible in all big cities,
be it Lahore or Delhi, Karachi or Mumbai, New York or
Washington, D.C. The geography and architecture of the two
sides in each case speaks for itself. But this obvious truth is
not what makes this poem enjoyable. The soul of the city
hides behind its appearance. Bright lights make everything
beautiful, but there is a layer that we don't see. It is 'poison of
loneliness drubbing the walls', 'murky tide giving a misty look
of sparsely populated sorrows and griefs' and behind 'this
hazy and smoggy layer lives a city of lights'. This city of lights
is, in reality, a city of pain. Wherever you look there is another
city: you don't have to be fooled by the luminosity. Those who
live in the city of exclusion also need lamps: '*thak kar har suu
baith rahi hai shauq ki maand sipaah / aaj mera dil fikr mein hai /
ae raushaniyon ke shahar*' (Tired and worn out, / an indistinct
army of muffled desires / is sitting everywhere. / My heart is
showing its concern. / O the city of lights). The poem ends
with a prayer for the beautiful fairies of the city and a request:
'*aaj ki shab jab diye jalaayein uunchi rakhein lau*' (Tonight when
you light the lamps, / just keep the beam high).

It is noontime and
the anemic yellow sunlight is shriveling up.
The poison of loneliness
is beating the walls.
Far away, touching the ends of the sky
it is diminishing, bulging, soaring, descending—
a murky tide that is giving a misty look
of sparsely populated sorrows and griefs.
Behind this hazy and smoggy layer,
lives a city of lights.
O the city of lights!

Who could find the
source of your luminosity?
In each direction, there is another city,
glow-less, the town of exclusion,
of dispossession.
Tired and worn out,
an indistinct army of muffled desires
is sitting everywhere.
My heart is showing its concern.
O the city of lights!

This deluge of desires should not
turn its face from
the bloodied night.
May your beautiful fairies live happily!
Please tell all of them:
tonight when you light the lamps,
just keep the beam high.

'Ae Raushaniyon Ke Shahar'

sabza sabza suukh rahi hai phiiki zard daupahr
diivaaron ko chaat raha hai tanhaaii ka zahr

duur ufq tak ghat-ti barhti utthti girti rahti hai
kohr ki suurat beraunaq dardon ki gadli lahr
basta hai is kohr ke piichhe raushaniyon ka shahar
ae raushniyon ke shahar

kaun kahe kis simt hai teri raushaniyon ki raah
har jaanib benuur khari hai hijr ki shahar-panaah
thak kar har suu baith rahi hai shauq ki maand
sipaah
aaj mera dil fikr mein hai
ae raushaniyon ke shahar

shab-khuun se munh pher n jaaye armaanon ki rau
khair ho teri laila-on ki in sab se kah do
aaj ki shab jab diye jalaayein uunchi rakhein lau

'ऐ रौशनियों के शहर'

सब्ज़ा सब्ज़ा सूख रही है फीकी जर्द दोपहर
दीवारों को चाट रहा है तन्हाई का ज़हर
दूर उफ़ुक़ तक घटती बढ़ती उठती रहती है
कोहर की सूरत बेरौनक़ दर्दों की गदली लहर
बस्ता है इस कोहर के पीछे रौशनियों का शहर
ऐ रौशनियों के शहर

कौन कहे किस सम्त है तेरी रौशनियों की राह
हर जानिब बेनूर खड़ी है हिज़्र की शहर-पनाह
थक कर हर सू बैठ रही है शौक़ की मांद सिपाह
आज मिरा दिल फ़िक्र में है
ऐ रौशनियों के शहर

शब-खूँ से मुँह फेर न जाए अरमानों की रौ
ख़ैर हो तेरी लैलाओं की उन सब से कह दो
आज की शब जब दिए जलाएँ ऊँची रखें लौ

◆

GHAZAL

Let the breeze of the new spring
pour more colour into flowers.
I want you to come back
for the garden to grow more.

The jailhouse is sorrowful.
Friends, say something to the breeze.
With the grace of God,
please do talk about love.

Let the dawn sometimes start its trip
touching the corner of your lips.
Let the night spread its wings
while carrying the fragrance
of your curls.

The wealth of pain is immense
but my heart is lacking.
When your name is divulged,
grief-stricken will get together.

Whatever happened to me,
O night of separation,
my tears groomed your persona
for this life and the next.

Faiz, you have touched each spot
on this pathway of desire.
Coming from the alley of love,
you went straight to the hanging post.

(Montgomery Jail, January 1954)

'Gulon Mein Rang Bhare Baad-e Nau-Bahaar Chale'

gulon mein rang bhare baad-e nau-bahaar chale
chale bhi aao k gulshan ka kaaro-baar chale

qafas udaas hai yaaro saba se kuchh to kaho
kahien to bahr-e khuda aaj zikr-e yaar chale

kabhi to sub-h tere kunj-e lab se ho aaghaaz
kabhi to shab sar-e kaakul se mushk baar chale

bara hai dard ka rishta ye dil ghariib sahi
tumhaare naam pe aayein ge gham gusaar chale

jo ham pe guzri so guzri magar shab-e hijraan
hamaare ashk teri a'qbat sanvaar chale

maqaam Faiz koi raah mein jacha hi nahien
jo kuue yaar se nikle to suue daar chale

'गुलों में रंग भरे बाद-ए नौ-बहार चले'

गुलों में रंग भरे बाद-ए नौ-बहार चले
चले भी आओ कि गुलशन का कारोबार चले

क़फ़स उदास है यारो सबा से कुछ तो कहो
कहीं तो बहर-ए ख़ुदा आज ज़िक्र-ए यार चले

कभी तो सुब्ह तेरे कुंज-ए लब से हो आग़ाज़
कभी तो शब सर-ए काकुल से मुश्क-बार चले

बड़ा है दर्द का रिश्ता ये दिल ग़रीब सही
तुम्हारे नाम पे आएँगे ग़म-गुसार चले

जो हम पे गुज़री सो गुज़री मगर शब-ए हिज्राँ
हमारे अश्क तेरी आ'क़बत सँवार चले

मक़ाम 'फ़ैज़' कोई राह में जचा ही नहीं
जो कू-ए यार से निकले तो सू-ए दार चले

◆

'WE WERE KILLED IN THE DARK ALLEYS'

The poem, written in Montgomery Jail in May 1954, was inspired by the letters of Julius and Ethel Rosenberg, two American citizens who were arrested, tried and executed in 1953 for providing secrets relating to atomic weapons to the Soviet Union. The letters were published both in the United States and in England.[43] It is not clear how Faiz gained access to these letters. Coppola writes:[44]

> An important point to remember while reading this poem is the fact that the narrator's mention of the Rosenbergs in the parenthetical remark is incidental to the spirit of the poem; the poem could maintain itself as a viable work of art without this specific reference.

From the opening line until the end, the poem reads like an exceptional love poem, capturing the thoughts and feelings of a lover in a metaphorical language: a the lover who is facing execution for the crime of love.

> For the love and craving
> of the blossoms of your lips
> I was hanged
> from the scaffold of the dry branch of a tree.
> I yearned to touch
> the luminescence of your hands,
> but I was killed
> in the dim light of the dark alleys.

---

[43] *Death House Letters of Ethel and Julius Rosenberg*, New York: Jero Pub. Co., 1953 and Michael Meeropol, ed., *The Rosenberg Letters*, London: D. Dobson, 1953.

[44] Coppola, *Urdu Poetry*, p. 382.

I didn't witness your death
and your crucifixion
that happened away from me
and from my lips,
but the redness of your lips
caught my attention,
the intemperance of your tresses
continued to rain,
the silver of your hands
continued to shine.

When the night of oppression
joined with your pathway,
I moved toward you
as far as my feet could take me,
with verses of an ode on my lips
and shining a paper lantern
of grief in my heart.
My sorrow was a testament to your beauty,
and both of us were bound by
that testament.
We were killed in the dark alleys.

If our helplessness was
part of our fate,
my love for you was
my commitment.
Who can complain
that fragments of our desire
went straight to the slaughterhouses
of separation.

Lovers who will follow us
will pick up the banner

from the slaughterhouses
and places of execution
and new caravans of desire
will start their journeys.
Their aspirations will follow
in our footsteps and
would reduce the distance
of pain that separated us.
It is for them
we have made a new world.
By giving up my life
I have saved the secret
of your beauty and your loveliness.
We were killed in the dark alleys.

'Ham Jo Taariik Raahon Mein Maare Gaye'

tere honton ke phuulon ki chaahat mein ham
daar ki khushk tahni pe vaarey gaye
tere haaton ki sham'aon ki hasrat mein ham
niim taariik raahon mein maarey gaye

suulion par hamaare labon se pare
tere honton ki laali lapakti rahi
teri zulfon ki masti barasti rahi
tere haathon ki chaandi damakti rahi

jab ghuli teri raahon mein shaam-e sitam
ham chale aaye laaye jahaan tak qadam
lab pe harf-e ghazal dil mein qandiil-e gham
apna gham tha guvaahi tere husn ki
dekh qaayam rahe us guvaahi p ham
ham jo taariik raahon mein maarey gaye

na-rasaaii agar apni taqdiir thi
teri ulfat to apni hi tadbiir thi
kis ko shikvah hai gar shauq ke silsile
hijar ki qatl-gaahon se sab ja mile

qatl-gaahon se chunkar hamaare i'lm
aur nikleinge u'shaaq ke qaafle
jinki raah-e talab se hamaare qadam
mukhtsar ho chale dard ke faasle
kar chale jinki khaatir jahaangiir ham
jaan gunvaan kar teri dilbari ka bharam
ham jo taariik raahon mein maarey gaye

'हम जो तारीक राहों में मारे गए'

तेरे होंटों के फूलों की चाहत में हम
दार की खुश्क टहनी पे वारे गए
तेरे हातों की शमा'आं की हसरत में हम
नीम-तारीक राहों में मारे गए

सूलियों पर हमारे लबों से परे
तेरे होंटों की लाली लपकती रही
तेरी जुल्फों की मस्ती बरसती रही
तेरे हाथों की चाँदी दमकती रही

जब घुली तेरी राहों में शाम-ए सितम
हम चले आए लाए जहाँ तक कदम
लब पे हर्फ-ए ग़ज़ल दिल में किंदील-ए ग़म
अपना ग़म था गवाही तेरे हुस्न की
देख कायम रहे इस गवाही पे हम
हम जो तारीक राहों पे मारे गए

ना-रसाई अगर अपनी तक़दीर थी
तेरी उल्फ़त तो अपनी ही तदबीर थी
किस को शिकवा है गर शौक़ के सिलसिले
हिज्र की क़त्ल-गाहों से सब जा मिले

क़त्ल-गाहों से चुन कर हमारे अलम
और निकलें गे उ'श्शाक के क़ाफिले
जिन की राह-ए तलब से हमारे क़दम
मुख़्तसर कर चले दर्द के फ़ासले
कर चले जिन की ख़ातिर जहाँगीर हम
जाँ गँवा कर तेरी दिलबरी का भरम
हम जो तारीक राहों में मारे गए

◆

'THE WINDOW'

This poem, written in Montgomery Jail, is a comment on
different faiths and their gods. The main image is drawn
from the cross, a reference to the crucifixion of Jesus Christ,
for which the poet finds a parallel in the crosses of the
window of his jail cell. The second stanza is a somewhat
satirical description of how these gods, messiahs and
prophets play an essential role in people's lives. The poet
separates himself from these people because he is a non-
believer, but wonders to what length people go to please
these deities. Of course, the language which he uses is
highly poetic, but words like 'sacrifice' and 'martyrdom'
tell the story of what happens in real life. For a person
in prison, who is denied his fundamental human rights,
this does not mean much. He can look at these 'deities
of compassion and heavenliness' the same way he looks
at other beings. The images of martyred bodies arise in
his mind. He observes what ordinary people do in this
situation: ceremonially wash the dead and bury them.
The poet's window is a symbol of his imprisonment, but
in a broader context, it is a window to the religious lives
of people that the poet can watch from some distance.

He does not, however, see himself as a partner in these ritualistic practices.

Fastened on my window
are several crosses,
each one carrying
the colour of the blood of its messiah.
Each one stretching out
aspiration for a divine unification.

For some
we sacrifice the cloud of spring.
For another
the bright moon is martyred.
For yet another one
the garden of mystification is cut into half.
For one more
the morning breeze is taken
to the chopping block.

Not a day passes
without these deities of compassion
and heavenliness
coming into my hearth of lament,
dripping blood.
And every day in front of my eyes
their martyred bodies are washed,
groomed and embellished.

(Montgomery Jail, December 1954)

'Dariicha'

gari hain kitni saliibein mere dariiche mein
har ek apne masiiha ke khuun ka rang liye
har ek vasl-e khudaavand ki umang liye

kisi pe karte hain abr-e bahaar ko qurbaan
kisi pe qatl maah-e taabnaak karte hain
kisi pe hoti hai sarmast shaakhsaar-e do niim
kisi pe baad-e saba ko halaaq karte hain

har aaye din ye khuda vandgaan-e mehr o jamaal
lahu mein gharq mere gham kade mein aate hain
aur aaye din meri nazron ke saamne un ke
shahiid jism salaamat uthaaye jaate hain

'दरीचा'

गड़ी हैं कितनी सलीबें मिरे दरीचे में
हर एक अपने मसीहा के ख़ूँ का रंग लिए
हर एक वस्ल-ए ख़ुदा-वंद की उमंग लिए

किसी पे करते हैं अब्र-ए बहार को क़ुर्बाँ
किसी पे क़त्ल मह-ए ताबनाक करते हैं
किसी पे होती है सरमस्त शाख़-सार-ए दो-नीम
किसी पे बाद-ए सबा को हलाक करते हैं

हर आए दिन ये ख़ुदा वंदगान-ए मेहर ओ जमाल
लहू में ग़र्क़ मिरे ग़म-कदे में आते हैं
और आए दिन मेरी नज़रों के सामने उन के
शहीद जिस्म सलामत उठाए जाते हैं

◆

'PAIN WILL WALK IN SOFTLY'

This is another poem written in jail which focuses on loneliness and the cause of a lot of pain in that environment: involuntary isolation. The thoughts expressed by the poet are not very different from some of the other 'jail poems', but the combination of words used and their lyrical flair are unique. There is an interesting reference to a brigade on the other side of the 'dark' boundaries. These are forces comprising sacrifices of other friends, that are bringing the dawn a little closer. Dawn ends the suffering of loneliness and opens prison doors.

> After some time,
> my heart will once again
> be captured by worries
> about finding a remedy
> for loneliness.
> The pain will come softly,
> carrying a red lantern.
> About the grief that is palpitating
> close to my heart.

> The spark of agony will grab me
> by my side.
> On the wall of my heart
> each wound will glitter.
> The circle of tresses here
> and the refuge of cheeks there,
> the desert of separation here
> and the garden of discernment there,
> the tale of pleasure here
> and the promise of love there.

> I will have a talk with
> my heart calling it, O my heart.
> The one who is the beloved of your lonely hours,
> she is a guest of a few hours,
> and she will leave soon.
> She will not treat the malady you have.

> These blazing wild shadows will arise.
> They will move away and some remnants

will be left behind.
The whole night you will have a
bloody struggle with them.
This is war, not a game, my dear heart.
These are enemies of your well-being
and they are all murderers.
This difficult night, these shadows
and this loneliness.
There is no meeting point between
the grief and the war.
Let us start a fire with the full force
of our resentments.
Where is the fire of our rage?
Bring it here.
Where is the smouldering bed of roses?
Bring it here.
I'm talking about the one
that has warmth, motion and strength.

It could be a brigade that belongs
to our tribe,
waiting on the other side
of the dark boundaries.
We shall sing a flaming song of victory
that tells them who we are.
Even if they don't reach the spot where we are,
they will give us a shout.
How long do we have to wait for the dawn?
They will let us know.

(Montgomery Jail, December 1954)

'Dard Aayega Dabe Paaon'

aur kuchh der mein jab phir mere tanha dil ko
fikar aa le gi k tanhaaii ka kya chaara kare
dard aayega dabe paaon liye surkh charaagh
voh jo ik dard dharakta hai kahiin dil se pare

sho'la-e dard jo pahlu mein lapak uthe ga
dil ki diivaar pe har naqsh damak uthe ga
halka-e zulf kahien gosha-e rukhsaar kahien
hijr ka dasht kahien gulshan-e diidaar kahien
lutf ki baat kahien pyaar ka iqraar kahien

dil se phir ho gi meri baat k ae dil ae dil
ye jo mahbuub bana hai teri tanhaaii ka
ye to mahmaan hai ghari bhar ka chala jaaye ga
us se kab teri musiibat ka madaava ho ga

mushtaa'il ho ke abhi uthein ge vahshi saaye
ye chala jaayega rah jaayein ge baaqi saaye
raat bhar jin se tera khuun kharaaba ho ga
jang thahri hai koi khel nahien hai ae dil
dushman-e jaan hain sabhi saare ke saare qaatil
ye kari raat bhi ye saaye bhi tanhaaii bhi
dard aur jang mein kuchh mel nahien hai ae dil
laao sulgaao koi josh-e ghazab ka angaar
taish ki aatish-e jarraar kahaan hai laao
voh dahakta hua gulzaar kahaan hai laao
jis mein garmi bhi hai harkat bhi tavaanaaii bhi

ho n ho apne qabiile ka bhi koi lashkar
muntazir ho ga andhere ki fasiilon ke udhar
un ko sho'lon ke rajaz apna pata to dein ge
khair ham tak voh n pahunchein bhi sada to dein ge
duur kitni hai abhi sub-h bata to deinge

'दर्द आएगा दबे पाँव'

और कुछ देर में जब फिर मेरे तन्हा दिल को
फ़िक्र आ लेगी कि तन्हाई का क्या चारा करे
दर्द आएगा दबे पाँव लिए सुर्ख़ चराग़
वो जो इक दर्द धड़कता है कहीं दिल से परे

शो'ला-ए दर्द जो पहलू में लपक उट्ठेगा
दिल की दीवार पे हर नक़्श दमक उट्ठेगा
हल्क़ा-ए ज़ुल्फ़ कहीं गोशा-ए रुख़्सार कहीं
हिज्र का दश्त कहीं गुलशन-ए दीदार कहीं
लुत्फ़ की बात कहीं प्यार का इक़रार कहीं

दिल से फिर होगी मेरी बात कि ऐ दिल ऐ दिल
ये जो महबूब बना है तेरी तन्हाई का
ये तो मेहमाँ है घड़ी-भर का चला जाएगा
उस से कब तेरी मुसीबत का मुदावा होगा

मुश्ता'ईल हो के अभी उट्ठेंगे वहशी साए
ये चला जाएगा रह जाएँगे बाक़ी साए
रात-भर जिन से तेरा ख़ून-ख़राबा होगा
जंग ठहरी है कोई खेल नहीं है ऐ दिल
दुश्मन-ए जाँ हैं सभी सारे के सारे क़ातिल
ये कड़ी रात भी ये साए भी तन्हाई भी
दर्द और जंग में कुछ मेल नहीं है ऐ दिल
लाओ सुल्गाओ कोई जोश-ए ग़ज़ब का अँगार
तैश की आतिश-ए जर्रार कहाँ है लाओ
वो दहकता हुआ गुलज़ार कहाँ है लाओ
जिस में गर्मी भी है हरकत भी तवानाई भी

हो न हो अपने क़बीले का भी कोई लश्कर
मुंतज़िर होगा अंधेरे की फ़सीलों के उधर
उन को शो'लों के रजज़ अपना पता तो देंगे
ख़ैर हम तक वो न पहुँचें भी सदा तो देंगे
दूर कितनी है अभी सुब्ह बता तो देंगे

◆

QAT'A

With the explosive rise of dawn, I found on your sky
the sprinkling of the colour of your cheeks.
When the night covered the face of the earth,
a waterfall of your tresses hit everywhere.

sub-h phuuti to aasmaan pe tere
rang-e rukhsaar ki phuhaar giri
raat chhaaii to ruue a'alam par
teri zulfon ki aabshaar giri

सुब्ह फूटी तो आसमाँ पे तेरे
रंग-ए रुख़्सार की फुहार गिरी
रात छाई तो रूए आ'लम पर
तेरी ज़ुल्फ़ों की आबशार गिरी

◆

'A LOVER TO A BELOVED'

Faiz wrote two poems using the same title with a gap of nearly 25 years. The first poem, published in 1956, departs from classical Urdu poetry, where it is customary for a lover to seek the love and affection of his beloved until his last breath. At no time would he say, 'If you don't love me, that is okay too.' In this modern version of the classical relationship between lover and beloved, Faiz brings the idea of an affection that is based entirely on the free will of the involved parties. Two individuals have the same rights. Both of them can reach 'a bend in the road' at any time, and the parting of ways can occur as a matter of routine. Faiz, as a progressive poet, could not have visualized a man-woman love in any other way.[45]

> On the path of memories,
> maintaining the same old visage,
> you have been walking for a long time.
> If this passage ends, walk a few steps more,
> up to the point where there is a bend in the road
> for those going to forgetfulness.
> Beyond that point, there is neither *you* nor *me*.
> My eyes are alert because I'm not sure
> when you might return or look back at me.
> My eyes know that it is a deception.
> If they visually embraced you at any point,
> a new path will emerge.
> That will be the start of a new journey—
> of the shadow of tresses
> and the movement of the arms.
>
> This is an illusion, of course.
> My heart knows that there is no bend in the road,
> no desert, no bank of a river,
> where my current obsession can find
> a place to submerge myself.
> When you walk on this path, it will go on moving.
> If you didn't look back, that is okay too.

'Koi Aashiq Kisi Mahbuuba Se (1)'

yaad ki raahguzar jis p isi suurat se
muddatein biit gayi hain tumhein chalte chalte
khatam ho jaye jo do chaar qadam aur chalo
mor parta hai jahaan dasht-e faraamoshi ka
jis se aage n koi main huun n koi tum ho

---

[45]From *Zindaan Nama* (1956).

saans thaame hain nigaahein k n jaane kis dam
tum palat aao guzar jaao ya mur kar dekho

garche vaaqif hain nigahein k ye sab dhoka hai
gar kahien tum se ham-aaghoosh hui phir se nazar
phuut niklegi vahaan aur koi raah guzar
phir isi tarah jahaan hoga muqaabil paiham
saaya-e zulf ka aur jumnbish-e baazu ka safar

duusri baat bhi jhuuti hai k dil jaanta hai
yaan koi mor koi dasht koi ghaat nahien
jiske parde mein mera maah-e ravaan duub sake
tum se chalti rahe ye raah yuun hi achha hai
tum ne mur kar bhi n dekha to koi baat nahien

'कोई आशिक़ किसी महबूबा से (1)'

याद की राहगुज़र जिस पे इसी सूरत से
मुद्दतें बीत गई हैं तुम्हें चलते चलते
ख़त्म हो जाए जो दो चार क़दम और चलो
मोड़ पड़ता है जहाँ दश्त-ए फ़रामोशी का
जिस से आगे न कोई मैं हूँ न कोई तुम हो
साँस थामे हैं निगाहें कि न जाने किस दम
तुम पलट आओ गुज़र जाओ या मुड़ कर देखो

गरचे वाक़िफ़ हैं निगाहें कि ये सब धोका है
गर कहीं तुम से हम-आग़ोश हुई फिर से नज़र
फूट निकलेगी वहाँ और कोई राहगुज़र
फिर इसी तरह जहाँ होगा मुक़ाबिल पैहम
साया-ए ज़ुल्फ़ का और जुम्बिश-ए बाज़ू का सफ़र

दूसरी बात भी झूटी है कि दिल जानता है
याँ कोई मोड़ कोई दश्त कोई घात नहीं
जिस के पर्दे में मेरा माह-ए रवाँ डूब सके
तुम से चलती रहे ये राह यूँही अच्छा है
तुम ने मुड़ कर भी न देखा तो कोई बात नहीं

'A LOVER TO A BELOVED'

This second version of the poem, published in 1981, is consistent with the spirit of the '80s. There was a renewed emphasis on the importance of dialogue. Meeting someone and having a conversation that was free of any demands or blame was considered key to sustaining romance. This was a new belief. Love can bring two people together, but the continuation of a healthy partnership, based on free will and free choice, depends on how the dialogue (sitting together, speaking freely, listening and listening to unspoken words) bolsters the connection over time.[46]

If in the garden of memory,
after the morning breeze starts,
someone wants to scatter fresh flowers,
let that happen.
If there is a grief that is alive
in the crevice of a past moment
and it wants to come back shining,
let it happen.
You can go on meeting me like a stranger,
as you do now.
Come and sit in front of me
for a moment or two.
If we meet, we shall feel our loss
much more acutely.
If we continue to speak
the same language,
then in between us, we shall find
a veil of unspoken words.
I shall not remind you

[46]From *Mere Dil Mere Musafir* (1981).

of any broken promises.
We shall not talk about
staying loyal or not.
If you want to wash the dust off
the face of memory of the days past,
our eyes might meet.
You can hear what you want;
and do not listen to what you don't want.
If my runaway eyes try to blame,
you can say what you like;
and do not say what you
don't want to say.

'Koi Aashiq Kisi Mahbuuba Se (2)'

gulshan-e yaad mein gar aaj dam-e baad-e saba
phir se chaahe k gul afshaan ho to ho jaane do
u'mr-e rafta ke kisi taaq pe bisra hua dard
phir se chaahe k frozaan ho to ho jaane do
jaise begaane se ab milte ho vaise hi sahi
aao do chaar ghari mere muqaabil baitho
garche mil baitheinge ham tum to mulaqaat ke baa'd
apna ehsaas-e ziaan aur zyaada hoga
ham-sukhan honge jo ham donon to har baat ke biich
an-kahi baat ka mauhuum sa parda hoga
koi iqraar n main yaad dilaaun ga tumhein
koi mazmuun vafa ka n jafa ka hoga
gard-e ayyaam ki tahriir ko dhone ke liye
tum se goya hon dam-e diid jo meri palkein
tum jo chaaho to suno aur jo n chaho n suno
aur jo harf karein mujh se gurezaan ankhein
tum jo chaaho to kaho aur jo n chaho n kaho

'कोई आशिक़ किसी महबूबा से (2)'

गुलशन-ए याद में गर आज दम-ए बाद-ए सबा
फिर से चाहे कि गुल-अफ़शाँ हो तो हो जाने दो
उ'मर-ए रफ़्ता के किसी ताक़ पे बिसरा हुआ दर्द
फिर से चाहे कि फ़रोज़ाँ हो तो हो जाने दो
जैसे बेगाने से अब मिलते हो वैसे ही सही
आओ दो चार घड़ी मेरे मुक़ाबिल बैठो
गरचे मिल-बैठेंगे हम तुम तो मुलाक़ात के बा'द
अपना एहसास-ए ज़ियाँ और ज़्यादा होगा
हम-सुख़न होंगे जो हम दोनों तो हर बात के बीच
अन-कही बात का मौहूम सा पर्दा होगा
कोई इक़रार न मैं याद दिलाऊँगा तुम्हें
कोई मज़मून वफ़ा का न जफ़ा का होगा
गर्द-ए अय्याम की तहरीर को धोने के लिए
तुम से गोया हों दम-ए दीद जो मेरी पलकें
तुम जो चाहो तो सुनो और जो न चाहो न सुनो
और जो हर्फ़ करें मुझ से गुरेज़ाँ आँखें
तुम जो चाहो तो कहो और जो न चाहो न कहो

◆

QAT'A

When the flowers of beauty blossomed in a window,
dawn swayed and suddenly turned itself into a bed
of roses.
Wherever the rays of illumination of your eyes fell,
everything at once became graceful and elegant.

(Jinnah Hospital, Karachi)

khile jo ek dariiche mein aaj husn ke phuul
to sub-h jhuum ke gulzaar ho gaaii yaksar
jahaan kahien bhi gira nuur un nigaahon se
har ek chiiz tarahdaar ho gaaii yaksar

खिले जो एक दरीचे में आज हुस्न के फूल
तो सुब्ह झूम के गुलज़ार हो गई यक-सर
जहाँ कहीं भी गिरा नूर उन निगाहों से
हर एक चीज़ तरह-दार हो गई यक-सर

◆

GHAZAL

Since the day I pinned my hope on you
and started to wait for your arrival,
my night has no quibble with the day
and my day is happy with the night.

I attribute anyone's suffering
to your name.
Whatever gripe I have with anyone,
it is because of you.

Since the day my impatient heart
has gone out of control,
my conversation with you
and the way I see you
has reached a new level of respect.

If it is a spark, it should flare up.
If it is a flower, it should blossom.
I have different kinds of demands
from your colourful lips.

Where are those folks who were awake
during the night of separation?
The morning star has been engaged
in a conversation for quite some time.

'Teri Ummiid Tera Intizaar Jab Se Hai'

teri ummiid tera intizaar jab se hai
n shab ko din se shikayaat n din ko shab se hai

kisi ka dard ho karte hain tere naam raqm
gila hai jo bhi kisi se tere sabab se hai

hua hai jab se dil-e na-subuur beqaabu
kalaam tujh se nuzar ko bare adab se hai

agar sharar hai to bharke jo phuul hai to khile
tarah tarah ki talab tere lab-e rang se hai

kahaan gaye shab-e furqat ke jaagne vaale
sitaara-e sahri ham-kalaam kab se hai

'तेरी उम्मीद तेरा इंतिज़ार जब से है'

तेरी उम्मीद तेरा इंतिज़ार जब से है
न शब को दिन से शिकायत न दिन को शब से है

किसी का दर्द हो करते हैं तेरे नाम रक़म
गिला है जो भी किसी से तेरे सबब से है

हुआ है जब से दिल-ए ना-सुबूर बेक़ाबू
कलाम तुझ से नज़र को बड़े अदब से है

अगर शरर है तो भड़के जो फूल है तो खिले
तरह तरह की तलब तेरे रंग-ए लब से है

कहाँ गए शब-ए फ़ुर्क़त के जागने वाले
सितारा-ए सहरी हम-कलाम कब से है

◆

QAT'A

The night is softening into our hearts.
Let the fire find its flare in the goblets.
Get some news about lovers' hearts.
Flowers bloom in these months.

raat dhalne lagi hai siinon mein
aag sulgaao aab giino mein
dil-e u'shhaaq ki khabar lena
phuul khilte hain in mahinoon mein

रात ढलने लगी है सीनों में
आग सुल्गाओ आबगीनों में
दिल-ए उ'श्शाक की ख़बर लेना
फूल खिलते हैं इन महीनों में

four

LOOKING DOWN FROM THE STARS: TOWARDS A COSMIC VISION

Today, when we can look down upon our world from the stars, these irrational selfish attempts to grasp a few bits of Earth, to establish our dominion over a few people seem beyond reason ... Are there not enough people among us who can convince the others to sink these guns, bombs, rockets and cannons into the sea and instead of trying to subjugate one another, set out together to conquer the heavens, where there is no shortage of space and no one need fight another, where there are countless skies and uncounted worlds?

—From the Lenin Peace Prize acceptance speech[47]

A NEW REALITY

When Faiz returned from prison, he made an effort to take control of his life, but the country had changed in fundamental ways. People, especially writers, were afraid of expressing their opinions. Faiz joined *Pakistan Times* and its associated publications, but the work climate had changed

---

[47]Hashmi, *Love and Revolution*, pp. 202–3.

radically. Progressive ideas were getting a pushback. The government was not tolerating any criticism. There were people within the news organization who were undercutting his contribution as a thinker and an opinion writer. *Zindaan Nama* had been published, but the public response had been subdued, compared to *Dast-e Saba*.

Some good news came in 1956 when Faiz got an invitation to attend the first Afro-Asian Writers' Conference in Delhi. He was not sure whether the government would allow him to travel to Delhi. But with help from Raja Ghazanfar Ali Khan, who was Pakistan's top diplomat in New Delhi, Faiz was allowed to travel. In India, Faiz was received like royalty. He met with Sarvepalli Radhakrishnan, leading philosopher and India's president, Prime Minister Nehru and other high-level officials, thinkers, poets and writers. This trip was useful in lifting the poet's spirits. He had seen much in Pakistan since his release from prison to dampen his optimism about the country's future.

Another important trip happened soon after his return from Delhi. Faiz had always wanted to visit China to see what difference the Revolution had made in improving the lives of ordinary citizens. He was chosen to accompany Prime Minister Suhrawardy, who was leading an official delegation. But somehow that trip was cancelled; Faiz went to China as part of a journalists' delegation. Two poems that he wrote on this trip captured Faiz's impressions of post-Revolution China.

In 1958, the government allowed Faiz and Hafiz Jalandhari to attend the second Afro-Asian Writers' Conference in Tashkent, Uzbekistan (which was part of the Soviet Union at that time). While Faiz was in Tashkent, a major political development happened back home: Gen. Ayub Khan staged a coup and took control of the government. After Tashkent, Faiz visited Moscow and London. He was concerned that he might be arrested on arrival in Karachi, but nothing unusual happened and Faiz reached Lahore safely. That satisfaction was however short-lived, as police showed up a few days later and Faiz was back in jail, this time on the suspicion of being a Soviet agent. He got another shock when he heard the news that Mian Iftikharuddin had died. Mian was the person who had introduced Faiz to the world of journalism by appointing him as the chief editor of *Pakistan Times*. He was also the one who had lent Faiz rupees 300 to buy a wedding ring for Alys.

Faiz was freed in April 1959, but the world around him had changed once again. His link with the *Pakistan Times* and thereby the world of journalism was finally broken, as he refused to honour the government's wish to be an editor because that job required him to be a spokesperson for the military regime.

LAHORE ARTS COUNCIL, HEART ATTACK AND THE PRIZE

At the request of some of his artist friends, in 1959, Faiz accepted the responsibility of becoming the director of the Lahore Arts Council, which was located in a rundown abandoned property that resembled an animal shelter. With his personal efforts, this organization gained popular recognition and its activities attracted the notice of critics both inside and outside the government. It was quite obvious that artistic activities that were the products of free minds would be seen as a threat by the dictatorial regime and religious conservatives.

In February 1962, Faiz suffered a heart attack and

fortunately survived, but this was a stark reminder that years of stress and chainsmoking were catching up to him. He stayed in the hospital for days and returned home with instructions from doctors for a special diet and exercise. Five years later, he captured his feelings about this episode in a poem titled 'Heart Attack'. Here is the first part of the poem:

> That night, the pain was so intense
> and my wild heart
> was ready to pick a fight with every vein,
> with the root of every hair,
> and at some distance in your home garden
> every leaf after being washed in the blood
> of my wretched heart
> was wearily looking at the moon's beauty.

Faiz eventually decided to give up his position at the arts council to spend more time with his family. It was on one of those days when his entire attention was focused on recuperation and spending time with his daughters that he received a phone call informing him that he had been awarded the Lenin Peace Prize, the Soviet equivalent of the Nobel Prize. He took this as a prank, but soon thereafter the news was confirmed by press reports. It was also worth noting that Faiz shared the prize with the great painter Pablo Picasso. Previous recipients of this honour included people like Chilean poet Pablo Neruda and German playwright Bertolt Brecht. Not knowing how the Ayub administration would react to this news, Faiz reluctantly sent a message of thanks to the Soviets, accepting the honour. To his surprise, Faiz was told by the government that he was free to go to Moscow to accept the prize. Because of his health, he chose to travel by ship and train along with his eldest daughter, Salima. He travelled from Karachi to Naples, Italy, and then took the train from Rome to Moscow, crossing countries such as Hungary, Czechoslovakia and Poland to reach his destination. Considering his fragile health, officials in Moscow sent Faiz to a sanatorium in Sochi, where he had a remarkable first meeting with the poet Pablo Neruda, who was already under treatment there.

The prize ceremony itself was held in the Grand Kremlin Palace in front of a global audience of artists and writers. The speech that Faiz delivered that day is one of the best speeches he gave anywhere. Here are some excerpts:

> Everyone can imagine that peace is amber waves of grain and eucalyptus trees, it is the veil of a newly-wed bride and the gleeful hands of children, the pen of the poet and the brush of the painter and that freedom is the guarantor of tyranny, the murderer of all these things that differentiate humans from animals: intelligence and awareness, justice and truth, bravery and chivalry, goodness and compassion ... the two forces that have been locked in the struggle since the dawn of humankind: creation and destruction, progress and decline, light and darkness, love of freedom and hatred for it ... before today humans had so little control over the bounties of nature that every group could not hope to satisfy their basic needs and so there was at least some justification for snatching and looting, but not any more. Human ingenuity, science and industry have progressed to the point where today, everyone can be fed, clothed and satisfied, provided these boundless treasures of nature and production are not used just to satisfy the lusts of a

few people but for all of humankind.[48]

Dast-e-Tah-e-Sang, the fourth collection of Faiz's poems, named after an expression used by Ghalib, was published in July 1965 and it contained the full text of the above address in Urdu as the preface. This chapter contains several compositions (qat'as, ghazals and poems) from this work.

QAT'A

Is this the smell of blood or the fragrance of my beloved's lips?
Which direction is the gentle breeze coming from? Look.
Has the spring arrived in the garden, or the jailhouse got filled?
Which direction is the sound of melodies coming from? Look.

ye khuun ki mehak hai k lab-e yaar ki khushbu
kis raah ki jaanib se saba aati hai dekho
gulshan mein bahaar aaii k zindaan hua aabaad
kis samt se naghmon ki sada aati hai dekho

ये खूँ की महक है कि लब-ए यार की खुशबू
किस राह की जानिब से सबा आती है देखो
गुलशन में बहार आई कि ज़िंदाँ हुआ आबाद
किस सम्त से नग़मों की सदा आती है देखो

◆

'HAND TRAPPED UNDER A STONE'

---

[48]Hashmi, *Love and Revolution*, pp. 202–3.

Most of us will read this poem, inspired by an enigmatic expression by Ghalib, as yet another passionate love-centric work by Faiz. That would be a mistake. In a scholarly treatise titled 'How Not To Read Faiz' Professor Gopi Chand Narang unravels the secret.

> The poem, which revolves around the helplessness of love, is not a love poem, nor it is an overly political poem … The central portion of the poem begins with 'let us raise our glasses and remember those lips'. Glasses of what? Here, the reference is not to the glass of wine. It can be said that the meaning of wine has been repressed. Similarly, 'lips' should invoke the lips of the beloved; the human beloved is not being referred to here. The image of the form and beauty of the beloved, which sneaked in through the doorway of lyrical aesthetics, wants to take over the poem, but the ideological project represses it. The repressed meaning wants to come to the surface; but when it cannot, its form changes. Repressed by ideology, it turns into absence or silence. For example, consider: 'A gift of the aching heart.' Whose heart? Or: 'When the morning comes, the rose garden shows her spring-like face.' Whose face? Consider further: 'Every night that is moist is filled with dewdrops of her tresses.' One can say that Faiz permits repression in his poetic expression because the rhetorical conventions of the oriental lyrical taghazzul aesthetics are an integral part of his consciousness. It is known that Faiz as a poet had made his mark with the publication of his first collection *Naqsh-e-Faryadi*. The later collections *Dast-e Saba* and *Zindaan Nama* completed the poetic identity of Faiz. There was all along an inner contradiction within Faiz

himself, even if he wanted to close the hidden door of subconscious creativity or the innate pull of the Indo-Persian taghazzul aesthetics of ruby lips and rose garden, he could not do so. As a result, those portions are most compelling where the repression runs wild, or where absences and silences speak in their repressed language, or where the text between-the-lines glows with pleasure. The effect in such cases is fascinating. This is the real Faiz, what Faiz is, the tension or pulls between the overt and covert that makes his poetry enjoyable and his words brilliant.[49]

Ailing domain and the breeze that is distressing.
It seems that all my old friends had had enough
of me.
My friends, you had enough to drink,
and elements are showing their colours.
The climate is just right for a stroll in the garden.
But there is a rainstorm of indictments from all
sides.
The dark clouds of reprimand follow me
everywhere.
The wine container is boiling gently, and
every cup of wine brims with deadly poison.
Never mind, let us raise our glasses, and
remember those lips filled with a taste of honey.
Haven't we drunk this poison before?
This, heartfelt emotion has no penalty or reward.
The place where this desire takes us
knows neither constancy nor faithlessness.
The awareness of the heart's pain is a gift of the

---

[49]Narang, Gopi Chand, trans. Baidar Bakht. 'How Not To Read Faiz Ahmed Faiz', *Indian Literature I*, vol. 53 no. 1 (249) (2009): 44–56.

aching heart.
It is a gift that her beauty has left behind.
When morning comes,
the rose garden shows me her spring-like face.
Each flower is nothing but a footprint of her
memory.
Every moist night is filled with dewdrops of her
tresses.
The setting sun is reminiscent of the closing of
her lips.
Every pathway leads me to the door of her love.
Every desire that shows up is the sound of her
footsteps.
I don't blame the politics or the oppressive moves
of my enemies.
This is something that I have inflicted on my wild
and unbroken heart.
I have trapped myself in the love of my friend.
There are neither handcuffs nor shackles.
'Our powerlessness when we are taken prisoner by
love
is nothing but a hand trapped under a stone.'
(Ghalib)[50]

'Dast-e Tah-e Sang Aamdah'

bezaar faza darpai-e aazaar saba hai
yuun hai k har ik hamdam-e deriina khafa hai
haan baada-kasho aaya hai ab rang pe mausam

---

[50]'When you have made a pledge / to stay in the prison of love, / your claim of fidelity / is like your hand / placed under a heavy stone.' Surinder Deol, *The Treasure: A Modern Rendition of Ghalib's Lyrical Love Poetry*, 2nd ed., New Delhi: Partridge Publishing, 2018, p. 432.

ab sair ke qaabil ravish-e aab o hava hai
umdi hai har ik samt se ilzaam ki barsaat
chhaaii hui har daang malaamat ki ghata hai
voh cheez bhari hai k sulagati hai suraahi
har kaasa-e mai zehr-e halaa-hal se siva hai
haan jaam uthaao k bayaad-e lab-e shiirin
ye zahr to yaaron ne kaaii baar piya hai
is jazba-e dil ki n saza hai n jaza hai
maqsuud rah-e shauq vafa hai n jafa hai
ehsaas-e gham-e dil jo gham-e dil ka sila hai
us husn ka ehsaas hai jo teri a'ta hai
har sub-h-e gulistaan hai tera ruu-e bahaariin
har phuul teri yaad ka naqsh-e kaf-e paa hai
har bhiigi hui raat teri zulf ki shabnam
dhalta hua suraj tere honton ki faza hai
har raah pahunchti hai teri chaah ke dar tak
har harf-e tamanna tere qadmon ki sada hai
taa'ziir-e siyaasat hai n ghairon ki khata hai
voh zulm jo ham ne dil-e vahshi pe kya hai
zindaan-e rah-e yaar mein paaband hue ham
zanjiir bakaf hai n koi band bapa hai
'majbuuri o daa'va-e giraftaarii-e u'lfat
dast-e tah-e sang aamdah paimaan-e vafa hai' [Ghalib]

'दस्त-ए तह-ए संग'

बेज़ार फ़ज़ा दरपा-ए आज़ार सबा है
यूँ है कि हर इक हमदम-ए देरीना ख़फ़ा है
हाँ बादा-कशो आया है अब रंग पे मौसम
अब सैर के क़ाबिल रविश-ए आब ओ हवा है
उमड़ी है हर इक सम्त से इल्ज़ाम की बरसात
छाई हुई हर दाँग मलामत की घटा है
वो चीज़ भरी है कि सुलगती है सुराही
हर कासा-ए मय ज़हर-ए हलाहल से सिवा है

हाँ जाम उठाओ कि ब-याद-ए लब-ए शीरीं
ये ज़हर तो यारों ने कई बार पिया है
इस जज़्बा-ए दिल की न सज़ा है न जज़ा है
मक़्सूद-ए रह-ए शौक़ वफ़ा है न जफ़ा है
एहसास-ए ग़म-ए दिल जो ग़म-ए दिल का सिला है
उस हुस्न का एहसास है जो तेरी अता है
हर सुब्ह-ए गुलिस्ताँ है तेरा रू-ए बहारीं
हर फूल तेरी याद का नक़्श-ए कफ़-ए पा है
हर भीगी हुई रात तेरी ज़ुल्फ़ की शबनम
ढलता हुआ सूरज तेरे होंटों की फ़ज़ा है
हर राह पहुँचती है तेरी चाह के दर तक
हर हर्फ़-ए तमन्ना तेरे क़दमों की सदा है
ता'ज़ीर-ए सियासत है न ग़ैरों की ख़ता है
वो ज़ुल्म जो हम ने दिल-ए वहशी पे किया है
ज़िंदान-ए रह-ए यार में पाबंद हुए हम
ज़ंजीर-ब-कफ़ है न कोई बंद बपा है
'मजबूरी ओ दा'वा-ए गिरफ़्तारी-ए उ'ल्फ़त
दस्त-ए तह-ए संग-आमदा पैमान-ए वफ़ा है' [ग़ालिब]

◆

QAT'A

Loneliness came walking like an old companion
to do the job of a Saqi as the evening shadows
lengthened.
Both of us wait, sitting idly, for the moon to rise,
and your image appears in each silhouette.

aaj tanhaaii kisi hamdam-e diiriin ki tarah
karne aaii hai meri saaqi-gari shaam dhale
muntazir baithe hain donon k mahtaab ubhre
aur tera aks jhalakne lage har saaye tale

आज तन्हाई किसी हमदम-ए देरीं की तरह
करने आई है मेरी साक़ी-गरी शाम ढले

मुंतज़िर बैठे हैं हम दोनों कि महताब उभरे
और तेरा अक्स झलकने लगे हर साए-तले

◆

'EVENING'

Evening or night at the jailhouse is something unusual. It
is the time when all the activity of the daytime slows down.
While life is hectic during the day, with people coming and
going, things settle down by evening. But this quietude,
for someone in prison, is not the same as that of a free
person. These are two very different mental states. We see
this difference in Faiz's prison poems. This poem is unique
because of its imagery. Every tree looks like a Hindu temple
('which is seeking ways to self-destruct') and the sky has
turned itself into a priest ('his body covered with ash, a
vermillion mark on his forehead'). The sound of a conch
shell, used in Hindu temples, the poet hopes, will break the
spell of silence.

> Every tree
> gives the appearance of a temple—
> some worn, dark, and an old temple.
> The one who is seeking ways
> to self-destruct.
> The roof has holes
> and each door is crying for attention.
> The sky is like a priest,
> sitting under the roof,
> his body covered with ash,
> a vermillion mark on his forehead—
> he is silently sitting in a corner,
> with his head hanging down.
> It seems

there is a magician behind the curtain,
who has spread his magic
into the heavens.
The apparels of time and the evening
have meshed with the other.
Neither the evening will be doused,
nor will there be darkness.
Neither the night will show its descent,
nor the daybreak will shine.
Skies are looking forward to
the end of this spell.
The chain of silence should break;
time's garb should be freed so that it moves.
Let some conch shell bleat and roar,
let some anklet vocalize its jingle,
let an idol wake up from its sleep,
and make some rustic beauty
unravel her veil.

'*Shaam*'

is tarah hai k har ik per koi mandir hai
koi ujra hua be-nuur purana mandir
dhuundhta hai jo kharaabi ke bahaane kab tak
chaak har baam har ik dar ka dam-e aakhir hai
aasmaan koi purohit hai jo har baam tale
jism par raakh male maathe pe sindhuur male
sar-niguun baitha hai chupchaap n jaane kab se
is tarah hai k pas-e pardah koi saahir hai

jis ne aafaaq pe phailaaya hai yuun sahar ka daam
daaman-e vaqt se paivast hai yuun daaman-e shaam
ab kabhi shaam bujhe gi n andhera ho ga
ab kabhi raat dhale gi n savera ho ga

aasmaan aas liye hai k ye jaadu tuute
chup ki zanjiir kate vaqt ka daaman chhute
de koi sankh dohaaii koi paail bole
koi but jaage koi saanvli ghuunghat khole

'शाम'

इस तरह है कि हर इक पेड़ कोई मंदिर है
कोई उजड़ा हुआ बे-नूर पुराना मंदिर
ढूँढता है जो ख़राबी के बहाने कब से
चाक-ए हर-बाम हर इक दर का दम-ए आख़िर है
आसमाँ कोई पुरोहित है जो हर बाम तले
जिस्म पर राख मले माथे पे सिन्दूर मले
सर-निगूँ बैठा है चुप-चाप न जाने कब से
इस तरह है कि पस-ए पर्दा कोई साहिर है
जिस ने आफ़ाक़ पे फैलाया है यूँ सहर का दाम
दामन-ए वक़्त से पैवस्त है यूँ दामन-ए शाम
अब कभी शाम बुझेगी न अँधेरा हो गा
अब कभी रात ढले गी न सवेरा हो गा

आसमाँ आस लिए है कि ये जादू टूटे
चुप की ज़ंजीर कटे वक़्त का दामन छूटे
दे कोई संख दुहाई कोई पायल बोले
कोई बुत जागे कोई साँवली घूँघट खोले

◆

GHAZAL

The sick are losing their breath.
Why don't you heal them?
Your credentials as a saviour
are dubious for now.
Why don't you heal?

Why don't you provide relief
for the pain of the night of separation?
The blood of my wild heart has been drawn.
Where is the compensation for that?

Will your justice come
when ordinary people
have been decimated?
If you're the judge,
why don't you bring this doomsday
to an end?

I'm calling upon discerning minds.
O instrument players, ask your devices
why don't they make any sound?

How long this oath of frenzy
will put my hands to shame?
People with a heart, please let me know
how should I show my inner commotion?

Faiz, the ruination of your heart
is not someone's oppressive act.
If she is the enemy of your well-being,
why don't you forget her?

(Lahore Prison, December 1958)

'Bedam Hue Biimaar Dava Kyon Nahien Dete'

bedam hue biimaar dava kyon nahien dete
tum achhe masiha ho shifa kyon nahien dete

dard-e shab-e hijraan ki jaza kyon nahien dete
khuun-e dil-e vahshi ka sila kyon nahien dete

mit jaayegi makhluuq to insaaf karo ge
munsif ho to ab hashar utha kyon nahien dete

haan nuktavaro laao lab o dil ki gavaahi
haan naghma garo saaz sada kyon nahien dete

paimaan-e junuun haathon ko sharmaaye ga kab tak
dilvalo gariibaan ka pata kyon nahien dete

barbaadi-e dil jabar nahien Faiz kisi ka
voh dushman-e jaan hai to bhula kyon nahien dete

'बेदम हुए बीमार दवा क्यों नहीं देते'

बेदम हुए बीमार दवा क्यों नहीं देते
तुम अच्छे मसीहा हो शिफ़ा क्यों नहीं देते

दर्द-ए शब-ए हिज्राँ की जज़ा क्यों नहीं देते
ख़ून-ए दिल-ए वहशी का सिला क्यों नहीं देते

मिट जाएगी मख़लूक़ तो इंसाफ करो गे
मुनसिफ़ हो तो अब हशर उठा क्यों नहीं देते

हाँ नुक्तावरो लाओ लबो ओ दिल की गवाही
हाँ नग़मा गरो साज़ सदा क्यों नहीं देते

पैमान-ए जनूँ हाथों को शर्माए गा कब तक
दिल वालो गरेबाँ का पता क्यों नहीं देते

बर्बादी-ए दिल जबर नहीं 'फ़ैज़' किसी का
वो दुश्मन-ए जां है तो भुला क्यों नहीं देते

◆

'LET US GO TODAY TO THE MARKETPLACE SHACKLED'

This poem, written in Lahore Jail after a few months of the
military rule imposed by Gen. Ayub Khan, is an open call

for action. The marketplace is the field of political action where the voices of people are heard. Everyone should go to the marketplace, even those who are shackled and manacled. They should go 'swaying and tripping' with 'stains of blood' on their garments. Since the ruler and his minions have all the power and there is no moral sensibility, it is a call for martyrdom. The poet knows it. That is why he has no hesitation in saying '*phir hamiin qatl ho aayein yaaro chalo*' (Let us go and get killed. / Friends, let us go).

> Moist eyes and the blustery spirit
> is not enough.
> The whispers about covert affairs
> are not enough.
> Today, let us go to the marketplace
> shackled and manacled.
>
> Waving hands, thrilled and pleased,
> swaying and tripping.
> With dust-covered hands
> and with stains of blood on our garments.
> All the city's beauties are waiting and watching.
> Let us go.
>
> The city's ruler, throngs of people,
> arrows of defamation, stones of disgrace,
> unhappy mornings, days that come to naught.
>
> Who is the champion of all this?
> Who can claim sanctity
> in this city of sweet darlings?
> Who can match the hand of the executioner?

Strengthen your heart,
victims of the afflicted heart.
Let us go and get martyred.
Friends, move.

'Aaj Bazaar Mein Paa-b-Jaulaan Chalo'

chashm-e nam jaan-e shoriidah kaafi nahien
tuhmat-e i'shq-e poshiidah kaafi nahien
aaj bazaar mein paa-b-jaulaan chalo

dast afshaan chalo mast o raqsaan chalo
khaak barsar chalo khuun b daamaan chalo
raah takta hai sab shahr-e jaanaan chalo

haakim-e shahar bhi majm'a-e aa'm bhi
tiir-e ilzaam bhi sang-e dushnaam bhi
sub-h-e naashaad bhi roz-e naakaam bhi

in ka damsaaz apne siva kaun hai
shahr-e jaanaan mein ab baa-safa kaun hai
daste qaatil ke shaayaan raha kaun hai

rakhte dil baandh lo dil fagaaro chalo
phir hamiin qatl ho aayein yaaro chalo

'आज बाज़ार में पा-ब-जौलाँ चलो'

चश्म-ए नम जान-ए शोरीदा काफ़ी नहीं
तोहमत-ए इश्क़-ए पोशीदा काफ़ी नहीं

आज बाज़ार में पा-ब-जौलाँ चलो

दस्त-अफ़शाँ चलो मस्त ओ रक़साँ चलो
ख़ाक-बर-सर चलो ख़ूँ-ब-दामाँ चलो
राह तकता है सब शहर-ए जानाँ चलो

हाकिम-ए शहर भी मजमा-ए आम भी

तीर-ए इल्ज़ाम भी संग-ए दुश्नाम भी
सुब्ह-ए नाशाद भी रोज़-ए नाकाम भी

उन का दम-साज़ अपने सिवा कौन है
शहर-ए जानाँ में अब बा-सफ़ा कौन है
दस्त-ए क़ातिल के शायाँ रहा कौन है

रख़्त-ए दिल बाँध लो दिल-फ़िगारो चलो
फिर हमीं क़त्ल हो आएँ यारो चलो

◆

'THE LONELY JAIL CELL'

This poem, although written in prison, is very personal.
There is no trace here of the political logjam in which the
country was trapped. From his jail cell, the poet is looking
outside at the daybreak, which is a 'wave of luminescence'
that 'moved to and fro' and as 'the time passed with caution
carrying the anguish of hope'. In the end, everything
('the bitterness of the past and the poison of today')
melds together, and in this mesh of memories of drinking
buddies and the splendour of the beloved, the struggle and
celebration go on.

Far away on the horizon
a wave of luminescence
moved to and fro.
The city of grief awakened
during a dream.
Again in the middle of a dream,
eyes became restive.
Day broke into the abode of existence.
In the cup of my heart
I poured the blueprint

that the morning gave
and made a concoction
of bitterness that yesterday brought
and poison that was the gift of today.

Far away on the horizon
a wave of luminescence moved to and fro
signalling the arrival of a dawn
that my eyes couldn't fathom.
No melody, no fragrance,
no wickedly charming face.
Time passed with caution,
carrying the anguish of hope.
Making a concoction
of the bitterness of yesterday
and the poison of today
I put together my yearning
for the union and addressed it
to my drinking buddies
at home and abroad,
to the beauty of the world
around us,
and to the splendour of her lips
and cheeks.

(Lahore Jail, March 1959)

'Qaid-e Tanhaaii'

duur aafaaq pe lahraaii koi nuur ki lahar
khwaab hi khwaab mein bedaar hua dard ka shahar
khwaab hi khwaab mein be-taab nazar hone lagi
a'dam aabaad judaaii mein sahar hone lagi
kaasa-e dil mein bhari apni subuuhi main ne
ghol kar talkhi-e diiroz mein imroze ka zahar

duur aafaaq pe lahraaii koi nuur ki lahar
aankh se duur kisi sub-h ki tamhiid liye
koi naghma koi khushbu koi kaafir suurat
bekhabar guzri pareshaani-e ummid liye
ghol kar talkhi-e diiroz mein imroze ka zahr
hasrat-e roz-e mulaaqaat raqam ki main ne
des pardes ke yaaraan-e qadah khwaar ke naam
husn-e aafaaq jamaal-e lab o rukh saar ke naam

'कैद-ए तन्हाई'

दूर आफ़ाक़ पे लहराई कोई नूर की लहर
ख़्वाब ही ख़्वाब में बेदार हुआ दर्द का शहर
ख़्वाब ही ख़्वाब में बेताब नज़र होने लगी
अदम-आबाद-ए जुदाई में सहर होने लगी
कासा-ए दिल में भरी अपनी सुबूही मैंने
घोल कर तलख़ी-ए दीरोज़ में इमरोज़ का ज़हर
दूर आफ़ाक़ पे लहराई कोई नूर की लहर
आँख से दूर किसी सुब्ह की तम्हीद लिए
कोई नग़्मा कोई ख़ुशबू कोई काफ़िर सूरत
बेख़बर गुज़री परेशानी-ए उम्मीद लिए
घोल कर तलख़ी-ए दीरोज़ में इमरोज़ का ज़हर
हसरत-ए रोज़-ए मुलाक़ात रक़म की मैंने
देस परदेस के यारान-ए क़दह-ख़्वार के नाम
हुस्न-ए-आफ़ाक़ जमाल-ए लब ओ रुख़्सार के नाम

◆

'LIFE'

Life, with its varied renderings of happiness and grief, is at the very centre of every poet's fascination. Faiz is no exception. Everything he wrote was some form of commentary on a facet of life. The tone of this poem is satirical, mockingly irreverent. Each stanza presents two faces of life, but the dark side fails to push the poet over the cliff. Nothing will stop him if he decides to bet on the treasures of the sun and the moon!

> Her royal eminence of cities and towns,
> how can I express my gratitude?
> The wealth of the heart is boundless.
> I can whine a bit about what's not there.
> But let us leave it there.
>
> Those who are seduced by your charms,
> they don't have to worry about making a living.
> They sell their grief and sing melodies.
> There is no more charming business than this
> one.
>
> When the decanters of wine overflow,
> the gathering will be set for great amusement.
> Some are absent today.
> We can't share our pain with them.
> Only one teardrop makes a garden to show its
> bloom.
> Who feels terrible about spring holding something
> back?
>
> There is happiness in not seeking
> what the eyes and heart crave in temples or
> mosques.
> 'Where can we go to test our good fortune?'[51]
> Every idol is already in its right place.
>
> Is there anyone rich enough
> with whom we can have a bargaining session

---

[51]This line is borrowed from Mirza Ghalib for a somewhat satirical use.

about the treasures of the sun and moon?
Let the one who is ready to engage in a contest
first go and conquer the universe.

'Zindagi'

malikaa-e shahar zindagi tera
shukar kis taur se ada kiije
daulat-e dil ka kuchh shumaar nahien
tang dasti ka kya gila kiije

jo tere husn ke faqiir hue
un ko tashviish-e rozgaar kahaan
dard becheinge giit gaaeinge
is se khush-bakht kaarobaar kahaan

jaam chhalka to jam gaaii mahfil
minnat-e lutf-e gham gusaar kise
ashk tapka to khil gaya gulshan
ranj-e kamzarfi-e bahaar kise

khush nishiin hain k chashm o dil ki muraad
dair mein hai n khaan kaah mein hai
'ham kahaan qismat aazmaane jaaein' [Ghalib]
har sanam apni baar gaah mein hai

kaun aisa ghani hai jis se koi
naqd-e shams o qamar ki baat kare
jis ko shauq-e nabard ho ham se
jaaye taskhiir-e kaaenaat kare

' ज़िंदगी '

मलका-ए शहर-ए ज़िंदगी तेरा
शुक्र किस तौर से अदा कीजे
दौलत-ए दिल का कुछ शुमार नहीं
तंग-दस्ती का क्या गिला कीजे

जो तेरे हुस्न के फ़क़ीर हुए
उन को तशवीश-ए रोज़गार कहाँ
दर्द बेचेंगे गीत गाएँगे
इस से ख़ुश-बख़्त कारोबार कहाँ

जाम छलका तो जम गई महफ़िल
मिन्नत-ए लुत्फ़-ए ग़म-गुसार किसे
अश्क टपका तो खिल गया गुलशन
रंज-ए कम-ज़र्फ़ी-ए बहार किसे

ख़ुश-नशीं हैं कि चशम ओ दिल की मुराद
दैर में है न ख़ानक़ाह में है
'हम कहाँ क़िस्मत आज़माने जाएँ' (ग़ालिब)
हर सनम अपनी बारगाह में है

कौन ऐसा घनी है जिस से कोई
नक़्द-ए शम्स ओ क़मर की बात करे
जिस को शौक़-ए नबर्द हो हम से
जाए तसख़ीर-ए कायनात करे

◆

GHAZAL

You were searching as part of your soul's quest
those who would sacrifice their lives for you—
but those who were asking
for the sacrifice of one's head have gone away.

After surrendering to your tortuous ways,
the night of waiting slipped away.
Annoyed by my control over my despairing state,
my fellow sufferers left me too.

No questions about the union,
no expression of sorrow, no suggestions,

no complaints, and in your reign
my distressed heart lost all its privileges.

Blood was spilled on my dress
while I was walking in the street.
This was the blemish that I embellished
and then I headed straight
to the beloved's assembly.

When the frenzy of fidelity has no place left,
what are you going to do with the rope?
And the gallows?
Those who were proud of their love's madness,
those sinners have vanished too.

(July 1959)

*'Tere Gham Ko Jaan Ki Talaash Thi Tere Jaan Nisaar
Chale Gaae'*

tere gham ko jaan ki talaash thi tere jaan nisaar chale gaae
teri raah mein karte the sar talab sar-e rahguzaar chale
gaae

teri kaj-adaaii se haar ke shab-e intizaar chali gaii
mere zabt-e haal se ruuth kar mere gham-gusaar chale
gaae

n savaal-e vasl n arz-e gham n hikaayetein n
shikaaetein
tere a'hd mein dil-e zaar ke sabhi ikhtiaar chale gaae

ye hamien the jin ke libaas par sar-e rah siyaahi likhi gaii
yahi daagh the jo sajake ham sar-e bazm-e yaar chale gaae

n raha junuun-e rukh-e vafa ye rasan ye daar karoge kya
jinhein jurm-e i'shq p naaz tha voh gunahgaar chale gaae

'तेरे ग़म को जाँ की तलाश थी तेरे जाँ निसार चले गए'

तेरे ग़म को जाँ की तलाश थी तेरे जाँ निसार चले गए
तेरी राह मैं करते थे सर तलब सर-ए राहगुज़ार चले गए

तेरी कज-अदाई से हार के शब-ए इन्तिज़ार चली गई
मेरे ज़ब्त-ए हाल से रूठ कर मेरे ग़म-गुसार चले गए

न सवाल-ए वस्ल ना अर्ज़-ए ग़म न हिकायतें न शिकायतें
तेरे अहद में दिल-ए ज़ार के सभी इख़्तियार चले गए

ये हमीं थे जिन के लिबास पर सर-ए रह सियाही लिखी गई
यही दाग़ थे जो सजा के हम सर-ए बज़्म-ए यार चले गए

न रहा जनून-ए रुख़-ए वफ़ा ये रसन ये दार करोगे क्या
जिन्हें जुर्म-ए इश्क़ पे नाज़ था वो गुनाहगार चले गए

◆

QAT'A

Listen, O ripped collars, the harvest of calmness
has arrived.
Lips are sealed, though wounds might not be healed.
Friends, arrange the celebration as the spring has
arrived.
Wounds have opened, whether or not any buds
will blossom.

(April 1962)

aa gaaii fasl-e sakuun chaak-garebaan vaalo
sil gaye hont koi zakhm sile ya n sile
dosto bazm sajaao k bahaar aaii hai
khil gaye zakhm koi phuul khile n khile

आ गई फस्ल-ए सुकूँ चाक-गरेबाँ वालो
सिल गए होंट कोई ज़ख़्म सिले या न सिले

दोस्तो बज़्म सजाओ कि बहार आई है
खिल गए ज़ख़्म कोई फूल खिले या न खिले

◆

GHAZAL

When will the pain stop, O heart,
How will I spend the night of suffering?
I hear she will come in her glory.
I hear that dawn's twilight will break.

When will my breath transform itself into blood?
When will my tear become a pearl?
When are you going to have a hearing,
O my tearful eyes?

When will fragrance take over,
and when will the tavern get drunk?
When will the morning of verse arrive?
And when will I see her?

Neither preacher nor hermit,
neither counsellor nor murderer.
How will my friends and buddies
celebrate their time in the city?

How long do we have to wait for your arrival,
my towering beloved?
What is the scheduled date for the doomsday?
At least you will know this.

'Kab Thahrega Dard-e Dil Kab Raat Basar Hogi'

kab thahrega dard-e dil kab raat basar hogi
sunte the voh aaeinge sunte the sahar hogi

kab jaan lahu hogi kab ashk gohar hoga
kis din teri shunvaii ae diida-e tar hogi

kab mehkegi fasl-e gul kab mehkega maikhaana
kab sub-h-e sukhan hogi kab shaam-e nazar hogi

vaa'iz hai n zaahid hai naaseh hai n qaatil hai
ab shahar mein yaaron ki kis tarah basar hogi

kab tak abhi rah dekhein ae qaamat-e jaanaana
kab hashr mu'eiin hai tujh ko to khabar hogi

'कब ठहरेगा दर्द ऐ दिल कब रात बसर होगी'

कब ठहरेगा दर्द ऐ दिल कब रात बसर होगी
सुनते थे वो आएँगे सुनते थे सहर होगी

कब जान लहू होगी कब अश्क गुहर होगा
किस दिन तेरी शुनवाई ऐ दीदा-ए तर होगी

कब महकेगी फ़स्ल-ए गुल कब बहकेगा मयख़ाना
कब सुब्ह-ए सुख़न होगी कब शाम-ए नज़र होगी

वाइज़ है न ज़ाहिद है नासेह है न क़ातिल है
अब शहर में यारों की किस तरह बसर होगी

कब तक अभी राह देखें ऐ क़ामत-ए जानाना
कब हश्र मुअय्यन है तुझ को तो ख़बर होगी

◆

GHAZAL

There was wave after wave of grief
but it stabilized, and sufferers felt relieved.
Like the fragrance of the tresses of spring
which arrived just in time.

Like a message that promised
the sight of the beloved was received.

The one whom I desired to see,
the work of my imagination,
once again met me face to face on the pathway.
My heart started to thirst for tomorrow's dawn,
while the days went by, gained my trust.

When the season changes
you should look at the colour of my heart.
Simply looking at the colour of the garden
doesn't solve the mystery.
Was there a wound that shook up,
or a flower that blossomed?
Tears fell, or the cloud of spring arrived?

Decanters started to fill up with the blood of
lovers.
Hearts began to burn. The scars were ignited.
The assembly of pain reached its climax.
The night of desire appeared clear and
unblemished.

The rules for rebellion were changed.
Receiving an invitation for self-killing from the
city's slaughterhouse,
someone came forward with a yoke around his
neck,
someone came carrying gallows on his shoulders.

Faiz, I don't know what makes my friends
keep their hopes high and wait for the good news.
They say the morality chief shows kindness to the
drunks,

and the broken hearts have received a reprieve
from the killer.

'Aaj Yuun Mauj Dar Mauj Gham Tham Gaya'

*aaj yuun mauj dar mauj gham tham gaya is tarah
gham-zadon ko qaraar aa gaya
jaise khushbu-e zulf-e bahaar aa gaii jaise paighaam-e
diidar-e yaar aa gaya*

*jis ki diid o talab vahm samjhe the ham ru-b-ru phir
sar-e rahguzaar aa gaya
sub-h-e farda ko phir dil tarasne laga u'mr-e rafta tera
e'tibaar aa gaya*

*rut badalne lagi rang-e dil dekhna rang-e gulshan se ab
haal khulta nahien
zakhm chhalka koi ya koi gul khila ashk umde k abr-e
bahaar aa gaya*

*khuun-e u'shshaaq se jaam bharne lage dil sulagne lage
daagh jalne lage
mahfil-e dard phir rang par aa gaii phir shab-e aarzu
par nikhaar aa gaya*

*sarfroshi ke andaaz badle gaye da'avat-e qatl par
maqtal-e shahar mein
daal kar koi gardan mein toq aa gaya laad kar koi
kandhe pe daar aa gaya*

*'Faiz' kya jaaniye yaar kis aas par muntazir hain k
laaye ga koi khabar
maikashon par hua mohtisib meharbaan dil figaaron pe
qaatil ko pyaar aa gaya*

'आज यूँ मौज दर मौज ग़म थम गया'

आज यूँ मौज दर मौज ग़म थम गया इस तरह गम-ज़दों को क़रार आ गया
जैसे खुशबू-ए ज़ुल्फ़-ए बहार आ गई जैसे पैग़ाम-ए दीदार-ए यार आ
गया

जिस की दीद ओ तलब वहम समझे थे हम रू-ब-रू फिर सर-ए
रहगुज़ार आ गया
सुब्ह-ए फ़र्दा को फिर दिल तरसने लगा उम्र-ए रफ़्ता तेरा ऐतबार आ गया

रुत बदलने लगी रंग-ए दिल देखना रंग-ए गुलशन से अब हाल खुलता
नहीं
ज़ख़्म छलका कोई या कोई गुल खिला अश्क उमड़े कि अब्र-ए बहार
आ गया

खून-ए उ'श्शाक़ से जाम भरने लगे दिल सुलगने लगे दाग़ जलने लगे
महफ़िल-ए दर्द फिर रंग पर आ गई फिर शब-ए आरज़ू पर निखार आ
गया

सरफ़रोशी के अंदाज़ बदले गए दावत-ए क़त्ल पर मक़्तल-ए शहर में
डाल कर कोई गर्दन में तौक़ आ गया लाद कर कोई काँधे पे दार आ गया

'फ़ैज़' क्या जानिए यार किस आस पर मुंतज़िर हैं कि लाएगा कोई ख़बर
मयकशों पर हुआ मोहतसिब मेहरबाँ दिल-फ़िगारों पे क़ातिल को प्यार
आ गया

◆

GHAZAL

Faiz dedicated this ghazal to the memory of his friend,
Mian Iftikharuddin, who passed away while he was in
prison. 'Faiz had borrowed rupees 300 from him to buy
Alys a wedding ring.'[52]

---

[52]Hashmi, *Love and Revolution*, pp. 193–4.

Don't waste your half-drawn arrows.
My heart is already shattered.
Please save your unused stones.
Wound after wound, my body was robbed
of its wholeness.

Please share the news
with my care provider.
The whole line of my enemies
should be informed.
Whatever my body owed
to its creditors
has been paid off.

Cover up my dead body
up to my forehead
so that my killers
have no suspicion.
After my death,
I carried no memory
of the innocence
of my love's pride.

On that side,
one word could get you killed,
but here there are numerous excuses
worth mentioning.
Whatever was said,
it was listened to,
and then it was thrown to the winds.
Whatever was written,
it was read and then erased.

As long as I stayed,
it was like a mountain.

When I moved,
I passed through life.
O my love's pathway—
step by step,
I made you into a monument.

*'N Ganvaao Naavak-e Niimkash Dil-e Reza Reza Gunva
Diya'*

n ganvaao naavak-e niimkash dil-e reza reza gunva diya
*jo bache hain sang samet lo tan-e daagh daagh luta
diya*

*mere chaara-gar ko naved ho saf-e dushmanaan ko
khabar karo*
*jo voh qarz rakhte the jaan par voh hisaab aaj chuka
diya*

*karo kaj jabiin pe sar-e kafan mere qaatalon ko gumaan
n ho*
*k gharuur-e i'shq ka baankpan pas-e marg ham ne
bhula diya*

udhar ek harf k kushtani yahaan laakh uzr tha guftani
jo kaha to sun ke ura diya jo likha to parh ke mita diya

*jo ruke to koh-e giraan the ham jo chale to jaan se
guzar gaye*
*rah-e yaar ham ne qadam qadam tujhe yaadgaar bana
diya*

'न गँवाओ नावक-ए नीम-कश'

न गँवाओ नावक-ए नीम-कश दिल-ए रेज़ा-रेज़ा गँवा दिया
जो बचे हैं संग समेट लो तन-ए दाग़-दाग़ लुटा दिया

मेरे चारा-गर को नवेद हो सफ़-ए दुश्मनाँ को ख़बर करो

जो वो क़र्ज़ रखते थे जान पर वो हिसाब आज चुका दिया

करो कज जबीं पे सर-ए कफ़न मेरे क़ातिलों को गुमाँ न हो
कि गुरूर-ए इ'श्क़ का बाँकपन पस-ए मर्ग हम ने भुला दिया

उधर एक हर्फ़ कि कुश्तनी यहाँ लाख उज़्र था गुफ़्तनी
जो कहा तो सुन के उड़ा दिया जो लिखा तो पढ़ के मिटा दिया

जो रुके तो कोह-ए गिराँ थे हम जो चले तो जाँ से गुज़र गए
रह-ए यार हम ने क़दम क़दम तुझे यादगार बना दिया

◆

'WHEN IN YOUR OCEANIC EYES'

In this poem, written in London in 1963, the poet leaves
aside his usual Urdu diction with a creative mix of Persian
and adopts the language of Hindi speakers to express his
thoughts, perhaps watching a sunset away from home. This
nazm with a feel of a 'giit' is absolutely heart touching: the
simplicity of expressed feelings traps the reader in its magic.
The beloved is remembered but there is no judgement here
whether their union is true or false. But one thing is right:
the sun will set in her oceanic eyes. And what happens when
night comes? Those who have homes will have a relaxed
sleep, and those who are on a journey will move on to find
some kind of night's dwelling elsewhere. Owning a home,
in this case, is a symbolic hint, pointing to those who enjoy a
union with their beloved.

> This sunny coast and dwindling evening.
> Two time zones are meeting here.
> Neither night nor day, neither today nor
> tomorrow.
> Eternity in a moment. Smoke in a moment.

Around this sunny coast for a moment or two.
Lips are reaching out. Sound of arms moving.
This union of ours is neither false nor true.
Why object, why blame? No reason to lie.
When in your oceanic eyes
this evening's sun will set
people who own homes will have a relaxed night.
And the traveller will find his way.

'Jab Teri Samundar Aakhon Mein'

ye dhuup kinaara shaam dhale
milte hain donon vaqt jahaan
jo raat n din jo aaj n kal
pal bhar ko amar pal bhar mein dhuaan
is dhuup kinaare pal do pal
honton ki lapak banhon ki chhanak
ye mel hamaara jhuut n sach
kyon raar karo kyon dosh dharo
kis kaaran jhuuti baat karo
jab teri samundar aankhon mein
is shaam ka suuraj duubega
sukh soeinge ghar dar vaale
aur raahi apni rah lega

'जब तेरी समुंदर आँखों में'

ये धूप किनारा शाम ढले
मिलते हैं दोनों वक़्त जहाँ
जो रात न दिन जो आज न कल
पल भर को अमर पल भर में धुआँ
इस धूप किनारे पल-दो-पल
होंटों की लपक बाँहों की छनक
ये मेल हमारा झूट न सच
क्यूँ रार करो क्यूँ दोश धरो

किस कारण झूटी बात करो
जब तेरी समुंदर आँखों में
इस शाम का सूरज डूबेगा
सुख सोएँगे घर दर वाले
और राही अपनी राह लेगा

◆

'THE COLOUR OF MY HEART'

This poem, written while Faiz was in Moscow, is a creative exercise in playing with the emotions of separation and union. There is an emotion that is dominant during the union, and there is a colour of the heart that goes with it. But the poet is focused here on his emotional state and the colours of his heart in the time of separation. When the heart is reduced to blood due to the agony of separation, then the red blood colour changes its hues. Sometimes it appears golden, another time it is grey, it is red of the flaming garden, it is yellow like the autumn leaves, it is the colour of poison and it is the colour of a black night. It is like an ever-changing mirror. But when the time of union comes, everything returns to normal.

When you had not come
everything was the same, the way it is:
the sky as far away as one could see,
a pathway here and a path there,
a glass of wine here and a glass of wine there.
And now the wine glass,
the pathway, the colour of the sky,
everything is the colour of my heart
with my heart reduced to blood.
Sometimes golden.

The colour of satisfaction from meeting with you.
There is grey colour, a colour of the moment in
time.
Of yellow leaves, the colour of nature's leftovers.
Of red flowers. Of a flaming garden.
The colour of poison. The colour of blood.
The colour of a black night.
Sky, pathway, and the wine glass.
Like a wet garb. Like an aching vein.
Like an ever-changing mirror.
Since you have come,
please stay so that some colour, some season,
some objects should settle in one place.
Once again,
we should have everything the way it used to be:
the sky as far away as one could see,
a pathway here and a path there,
a glass of wine here and a glass of wine there.

'Rang Hai Dil Ka Mere'

tum n aaye the to har cheez vohi thi k jo hai
aasmaan hadd-e nazar raahguzar raahguzar shiisha-e
mai shiisha-e mai
aur ab shiisha-e mai raahguzar rang-e falak
rang hai dil ka mere 'khuun-e jigar hone tak' (Ghalib)
champaaii rang kabhi raahat-e diidaar ka rang
surmaaii rang k hai saa'at-e bezaar ka rang
zard patton ka khas o khaar ka rang
surkh phuulon ka dahakte hue gulzaar ka rang
zahr ka rang lahu rang shab-e taar ka rang
aasmaan raahguzar shiisha-e mai
koi bhiiga hua daaman koi dukhti hui rag
koi har lahza badalta hua aaiina hai

ab jo aaye ho to thahro k koi rang koi rut koi shai
ik jagaah par thahre
phir se ik baar har ik cheez vohi ho k jo hai
aasmaan hadd-e nazar raahguzar raahguzar shiisha-e
mai shiisha-e mai

'रंग है दिल का मेरे'

तुम न आए थे तो हर इक चीज़ वही थी कि जो है
आसमाँ हद्द-ए नज़र राहगुज़र राहगुज़र शीशा-ए मय शीशा-ए मय
और अब शीशा-ए मय राहगुज़र रंग-ए फ़लक
रंग है दिल का मेरे 'ख़ून-ए जिगर होने तक' (ग़ालिब)
चम्पई रंग कभी राहत-ए दीदार का रंग
सुरमई रंग कि है सा'इत-ए बेज़ार का रंग
ज़र्द पत्तों का ख़स ओ ख़ार का रंग
सुर्ख़ फूलों का दहकते हुए गुलज़ार का रंग
ज़हर का रंग लहू रंग शब-ए तार का रंग
आसमाँ राहगुज़र शीशा-ए मय
कोई भीगा हुआ दामन कोई दुखती हुई रग
कोई हर लहज़ा बदलता हुआ आईना है
अब जो आए हो तो ठहरो कि कोई रंग कोई रुत कोई शय
एक जगह पर ठहरे
फिर से इक बार हर इक चीज वही हो कि जो है
आसमाँ हद्द-ए-नज़र राहगुज़र राहगुज़र शीशा-ए मय शीशा-ए मय

◆

'STAY CLOSE TO ME'

This poem is a heartfelt request, even a prayer, for the beloved to stay close. There is a fear of being alone in the dark of the night. Why night? It is the time when most dreadful things happen. The night of course is a metaphor. If you are a fighter, your daily struggle against oppression brings up horrors that we associate with darkness. Long after we have stopped reading this poem, the last line will linger in our unconscious: '*mere qaatil mere dildaar mere paas raho* (My killer, my beloved, stay close to me)'.

Stay close to me.
My killer, my beloved, stay close to me,
as the night comes.
When the night
after having drunk the blood of the skies,
wearing the scent of musk, carrying the golden spear,
lamenting, laughing, singing,
arrives dangling the blue anklets of pain.
When the heart happens to drown
and starts watching hidden hands in the sleeves.
Hoping.
And gurgling of wine starts just like the children whimpering.
Exasperation surfaces, but nothing happens.
Nothing materializes as planned.
When the conversation comes to a standstill.
When the night falls.
When the mournful, ruined night arrives.
Stay close.
My killer, my beloved, stay close to me.

'Paas Raho'

tum mere paas raho
mere qaatil mere dildaar mere paas raho
jis ghari raat chale
aasmaanon ka lahu pii ke siyaah raat raat chale
marhame mushk liye nishtar-e almaas liye
bain karti hui hansti hui gaati nikle

dard ki kaasni paazeb bajaati nikle
jis ghari siinon mein duube hue dil
aastiinon mein nihaan haathon ki rah takne lagein
aas liye
aur bachhon ke bilakne ki tarah qulqul-e mai
bahr-e naa-suudgi machle to manaaye n mane
'jab koi baat banaye na bane'
jab n koi baat chale
jis ghari raat chale
jis ghari maatmi sunsaan si yaah raat chale
paas raho
mere qaatil mere dildaar mere paas raho

'पास रहो'

तुम मेरे पास रहो
मेरे क़ातिल मेरे दिलदार मेरे पास रहो
जिस घड़ी रात चले
आसमानों का लहू पी के सियह रात चले
मरहम-ए मुश्क लिए नश्तर-ए अल्मास लिए
बैन करती हुई हँसती हुई गाती निकले
दर्द के कासनी पाज़ेब बजाती निकले
जिस घड़ी सीनों में डूबे हुए दिल
आस्तीनों में निहाँ हाथों की राह तकने लगे
आस लिए
और बच्चों के बिलकने की तरह क़ुलक़ुल-ए मय
बहर-ए ना-सूदगी मचले तो मनाए न मने
जब कोई बात बनाए न बने
जब न कोई बात चले
जिस घड़ी रात चले
जिस घड़ी मातमी सुनसान सियह रात चले
पास रहो
मेरे क़ातिल मेरे दिलदार मेरे पास रहो

◆

'VISTA'

Faiz is very effective in portraying a natural scene. He does it with the flair of a landscape painter. But it is not just nature alone: there is always an image of the beloved lurking nearby, and then it intuitively becomes a part of the poem. The dialogic end of this poem, where the lover, the beloved and the moon utter the same word, is the climax. The poem has an undertone of sensuousness in love, when one is fully absorbed and feels everything to be silent and still.

> Pathway, shadows, trees,
> dwellings and doors, roof's end.
> The bosom of the moon
> opened over the roof, slowly.
> Like someone unfastens
> the hooks, slowly.
> Towards the edge of the roof
> blue shadows, stagnant.
> A still blue lake.
> On the lake floats a bubbled leaf.
> One moment it flows.
> It moves.
> And then the bubble bursts.
> Very slowly, very light, refreshing wine.
> Poured into the glass, slowly.
> Wine glass and a big wine container,
> your rose-like hands.
> The image of a dream
> at some distance.
> It has come into being
> on its own, and then it disappears.

My heart repeats a word slowly.
You said, 'Slowly!'
The moon bent a little and said:
'And a little more slowly!'

(Moscow, 1963)

'Manzar'

rah guzar saaye shajar manzil o dar halqa-e baam
baam par siina-e mahtaab khula aahista
jis tarah khole koi band-e qaba aahista
halqa-e baam tale saayion ka thahra hua niil
niil ki jhiil
jhiil mein chupke se taira kisi patte ka habaab
ek pal taira chala phuut gaya aahista
bahut aahista bahut halka khunak rang-e sharaab
mere shiishe mein dhala aahista
shisha o jaam suraahi tere haathon ke gulaab
jis tarah duur kisi khwaab ka naqsh
aap hi aap bana aur mita aahista.

dil ne dohraaya koi harf-e vafa aahista
tum ne kaha, 'aahista!'
chaand ne jhuk ke kaha:
'aur zara aahista!'

'मंज़र'

रह-गुज़र साए शजर मंज़िल ओ दर हल्का-ए बाम
बाम पर सीना-ए महताब खुला आहिस्ता
जिस तरह खोले कोई बंद-ए क़बा आहिस्ता
हल्का-ए बाम तले सायों का ठहरा हुआ नील
नील की झील
झील में चुपके से तैरा किसी पत्ते का हबाब
एक पल तैरा चला फूट गया आहिस्ता

बहुत आहिस्ता बहुत हल्का खुनुक-रंग शराब
मेरे शीशे में ढला आहिस्ता
शीशा ओ जाम सुराही तेरे हाथों के गुलाब
जिस तरह दूर किसी ख़्वाब का नक़्श
आप ही आप बना और मिटा आहिस्ता

दिल ने दोहराया कोई हर्फ़-ए वफ़ा आहिस्ता
तुम ने कहा 'आहिस्ता'
चाँद ने झुक के कहा
'और ज़रा आहिस्ता'

five

DEATH WILL WALK IN... QUIETLY

While one should not deny the presence of pain and despair when it is present, but at the same time, one should not lose one's faith and hope, for without faith and hope, one cannot survive and life cannot continue. In a recent ghazal, I have said: 'the heavens are in motion / you say all has already happened; it is not so.' Ghalib said it a long time ago: 'the seven heavens are in motion day and night / why should I worry, something would happen' ... so I feel the same.

—Faiz on not losing faith and hope in the face of adversity[53]

KARACHI

After receiving the Lenin Peace Prize in Moscow, Faiz went to London, where Alys was waiting for him along with their younger daughter Moneeza. He was hesitant to return to Pakistan because the military dictatorship was still going strong and freedom of expression for writers and journalists had been severely constrained. Faiz used this time to visit many countries in Western and Eastern Europe, including a trip, at the invitation of Fidel Castro, to Cuba. Eventually, feeling restless about the London weather and suffering

---

[53]Hameed, ed., *Daybreak*, p. 354.

the boredom of loneliness (Alys had taken up a teaching position, and the girls went to the school), Faiz decided to return to Pakistan, and this time he chose Karachi as his new home instead of Lahore. He also agreed to a request from an old friend, Dr Shaukat Haroon, daughter of Sir Abdullah Haroon, a leading figure in the Muslim League and an associate of Jinnah, to take care of the Abdullah Haroon School. On his advice, the family trust agreed to upgrade the school to a two-year college and finally to a degree college. While in Karachi, he also became involved in several other initiatives: rehabilitation of the Karachi Arts Council and the establishment of the Institute of Ghalib Studies (Idara-e Yaadgar-e Ghalib) that coincided with the Ghalib centenary celebration of 1969. Faiz lived in Karachi for eight years until 1972, and this period proved to be very important for the family as his daughters Salima and Moneeza got married and their eldest children were born in the city.

A number of developments that took place towards the end of his stay in Karachi and the next few years caused a lot of grief to Faiz. These included the sudden death of Dr Shaukat Haroon, a dear family friend and associate; the genocide in East Pakistan; war and loss of half of the country in 1971 and the death of a long-time friend and a comrade in arms, Sajjad Zaheer, in December 1973 at the fifth Afro-Asian Writers' Conference in Kazakhstan. Faiz travelled in the plane which carried the body for burial to New Delhi.

At the request of Prime Minister Bhutto, Faiz agreed to be a cultural advisor to the government, a position that paved the way for the establishment of the Pakistan National Council of the Arts (PNCA), with him as its chairperson. As a result, Faiz stayed in Islamabad for four years, from

1972 to 1976, and it was in his capacity as chairperson of the PNCA that he visited Bangladesh in 1974 and wrote his famous ghazal-poem 'Ham Ke Thahre Ajnabi' while returning on the plane.

BEIRUT

The idea that there ought to be a journal for African and Asian writers for the free expression of their views about the exploitation of previously colonized countries by western imperialist nations, had its roots in the 1962 conference of Afro-Asian Writers' Association (AAWA). Faiz had strongly supported the idea. A journal named *Lotus* was started in 1969 with its headquarters in Cairo, and the Egyptian writer and journalist Yusuf al-Sibai as its editor. Al-Sibai later became Egypt's minister of culture and was assassinated for his advocacy for making peace with Israel. Therefore, at the AAWA meeting in Angola in 1979, Faiz was appointed editor-in-chief of *Lotus*, and it was also decided that the headquarters of the magazine will be set up in Beirut. The considerations that weighed with the association in making this decision included Faiz's global reputation as a distinguished poet and his ability to express himself in several languages—Arabic, Persian, English and French.

Faiz had known Beirut earlier, in peacetime, when the city had been flourishing and attracting tourists from all over the world. When Faiz arrived in the city along with Alys, it was more like a war zone, and the movement of residents was severely restricted for safety reasons. Gunfire could be heard day and night. Living in a small sixth-floor apartment with a frequently non-functional elevator and blackouts was challenging. Things became really intolerable when Israel invaded Southern Lebanon in June 1982. With the airport under Israeli control, Alys was able to fly out of Beirut because of her British passport, but for Faiz, it was a different situation. He had been told that his name was on the Israeli wanted list. Finally, Faiz got out of Beirut with the help of a friend who worked for the UN, and he joined Alys in London. Going back to Pakistan was not a feasible option since the country was under the brutal military dictatorship of Zia-ul-Haq, who had already executed the former prime minister Bhutto in a trial which was nothing more than a farce. Faiz continued to play out his role as editor of *Lotus* from whichever place he called his temporary home— London, Moscow or any other city.

It should be mentioned that early in 1982, Faiz had visited Pakistan and had even met Gen. Zia-ul-Haq, who had assured him of no harm if Faiz decided to live in Pakistan. But Faiz was concerned that many people in the military regime saw him as a friend of Bhutto, and these people could cause trouble at any time. As he was planning to leave Lahore for Beirut, his breathing problems returned and, as a result, he ended up spending 10 days in the intensive care unit in the hospital. He was back in Beirut, but it was not a place where anybody could live with any peace of mind. After some more travel and time in Moscow, where he received proper medical treatment, Faiz finally decided to return to Lahore in 1983. Earlier in the year Faiz had attended a University of London seminar in his honour and he had also participated in the BBC mushaira, presided over by Professor Gopi Chand Narang, which proved to be his last mushaira and his last visit to London.

This chapter contains selections from four poetry collections, published during the period of 1971 to 1980, and one volume which was published posthumously in the mid-1980s. These works are *Sar-e Vaadiye Saina* (1970),

Shaam-e Shahr-e Yaaran (1978), *Mere Dil Mere Musafir* (1980) and *Ghubaar-e Ayyaam*, published posthumously.

'A DEDICATION'

Stylistically, this poem is somewhat different from other Faiz poems, but ideologically, it represents his core belief that a poet must speak for the hardships and tribulations of ordinary people, who continuously struggle in their lives without a spokesperson to give voice to their sufferings. The poem is marked 'incomplete' because Faiz had something in his mind about how he wanted to end it, but he either lost interest or became busy with other things. The poem reflects Faiz's personal experience of working with the federation of workers and having a deep understanding of their work-life issues. He also had deep feelings about the centuries-old oppressive system under which the farmers and the workers were being crushed.

> For today
> and
> for today's grief—
> because today's pain is not in sync with life's fully
> grown garden.
> For the withered autumn leaves—
> which is the symbol of my country,
> a congregation of agonizers that is my country.
> For the sad and pitiful lives of clerks.
> For the moth-eaten hearts and voices.
> For the postmen.
> For the horse cart drivers.
> For the rail workers.
> For the brave and hungry souls of the factories.

For the majesties, royals and god-men.
For the farmer—
whose cattle were driven away by the mighty and
cruel,
whose daughter was kidnapped by the dacoits.
His crop was partially grabbed by the petty
revenue collector,
while the government confiscated the other part.
His turban lies under the feet of the mighty,
reduced to tatters and strips.
For those grief-stricken mothers
whose children cry during the night
and they can't handle them with their
sleep-deprived arms.
They neither say what is hurting them,
nor are they pacified by entreaties and
lamentations.

For those young beauties—
the roses of whose eyes
after blossoming on the vines of bamboo screens
and windows
have wilted.
For the brides—
whose bodies,
dressed and decorated,
are tired after waiting for love-less wedding beds.
For the widows.
For filthy localities, alleys and neighborhoods
where the moon comes nightly
for its ablution.
And in whose shadows there are lamentation and
grieving.

Henna on the scarf ends.
Tinkling of bangles.
The fragrance of tresses.
The sweat of bodies of those who are desirous of
doing something.

For those who read and learn,
who learn music and acquire knowledge.
They reach the doors with their book and pen.
Pleading with open hands.
Those innocents with their chasteness and purity.
For the love of the light of their small lamps.
They finally arrive
where they are distributing shadows of endless
cloudy nights.

For those prisoners—
in whose hearts were carved tomorrow's pearls by
fireflies;
they were burnt slowly, and they became star-like
in the wild nights of the jail cell's boisterous
winds.
For the ambassadors of the coming days—
those who like the fragrance of a rose
and have fallen in love with their message.

(Incomplete)

'Intisaab'

aaj ke naam
aur
aaj ke gham ke naam
aaj ka gham k hai zindagi ke bhare gulistaan se khafa
zard patton ka ban

zard patton ka ban jo mera des hai
dard ki anjuman jo mera des hai
clerkon ki afsurdah jaanon ke naam
kiram-khuradah dilon aur zabanon ke naam
post-mainon ke naam
taange vaalon ke naam
rel-baanon ke naam
kaarkhaanon ke bhuuke jiiyaalon ke naam
baadshaah-e jahaan vaali-e maa-siva naaib ul-allah
fil-arz
dehqaan ke naam
jiske dhoron ko zaalim hanka le gaye
jiski beti ko daaku utha le gaye
haath bhar khet se ek angusht patvaar ne kaat li
duusri maaliye ke bahaane se sarkaar ne kaat li
jiski pag zor vaalon ke paaon tale
dhajjiaan ho gayi hai
un dukhi maaon ke naam
raat mein jinke bachche bilakte hain aur
niind ki maar khaaye hue baazuon mein sambhalte
nahien
dukh bataate nahien
minnaton zaariiyon se bahalte nahien

un hasinaaon ke naam
jinki aankhon ke gul
chilmano aur darichon ki belon pe bekaar khil khil ke
murjha gaye hain
un biaahtaaon ke naam
jinke badan
bemohabbat riyakaar sejon pe saj saj ke ukta gaye hain
bevaaon ke naam
katarion aur galiyon mohallon ke naam

jinki naapaak khaashaak se chaand raaton
ko aa aa ke karta hai aksar vazu
jinke saayon mein karti hai aah o buka
aanchlon ki hina
chuurion ki khanak
kaakulon ki mahak
aarzu-mand siinon ki apne pasiine mein julne ki buu

parhne vaalon ke naam
vo jo as-haab-e tabal o alam
ke daron par kitaab aur qalam
ka taqaaza liye haath phailaaye
pahunche magar laut aaye
voh maa'suum jo bholepan mein
vahaan apne nanhe charaaghon mein lau ki lagan
le ke pahunche jahaan
bat rahe the ghatatop beant raaton ke saaye

un asiiron ke naam
jinke siinon mein farda ke shabtaab gohar
jail khaanon ki shoriidah raaton ki sarsar mein
jal jal ke anjumnuma ho gaye hain
aane vaale dinon ke safiiron ke naam
voh jo khushbu-e gul ki tarah
apne paighaam par khud fida ho gaye

'इंतिसाब'

आज के नाम
और
आज के ग़म के नाम
आज का ग़म कि है ज़िंदगी के भरे गुलसिताँ से ख़फ़ा
ज़र्द पत्तों का बन
ज़र्द पत्तों का बन जो मेरा देस है
दर्द की अंजुमन जो मेरा देस है

क्लरकों की अफ़्सुर्दा जानों के नाम
किर्म-खुर्दा दिलों और ज़बानों के नाम
पोस्ट-मैनों के नाम
ताँगे वालों के नाम
रेल-बानों के नाम
कारख़ानों के भूके जियालों के नाम
बादशाह-ए जहाँ वाली-ए मा-सिवा नाएब-उल-अल्लाह फ़िल-अर्ज
दहक़ाँ के नाम
जिस के ढोरों को ज़ालिम हँका ले गए
जिस की बेटी को डाकू उठा ले गए
हाथ भर खेत से एक अंगुश्त पटवार ने काट ली है
दूसरी मालिये के बहाने से सरकार ने काट ली है
जिस की पग ज़ोर वालों के पाँव-तले
धज्जियाँ हो गई है
उन दुखी माओं के नाम
रात में जिन के बच्चे बिलकते हैं और
नींद की मार खाए हुए बाज़ुओं में सँभलते नहीं
दुख बताते नहीं
मिन्नतों ज़ारियों से बहलते नहीं

उन हसीनाओं के नाम
जिन की आँखों के गुल
चिलमनों और दरीचों की बेलों पे बेकार खिल खिल के
मुरझा गए हैं
उन बियाहताओं के नाम
जिन के बदन
बेमोहब्बत रिया-कार से जों पे सज सज के उक्ता गए हैं
बेवाओं के नाम
कटड़ियों और गलियों मोहल्लों के नाम
जिन की नापाक ख़ाशाक से चाँद रातों
को आ आ के करता है अक्सर वज़ू
जिन के सायों में करती है आह ओ बुका
आँचलों की हिना

चूड़ियों की खनक
काकुलों की महक
आरज़ू-मंद सीनों की अपने पसीने में जुल्ने की बू

पढ़ने वालों के नाम
वो जो असहाब-ए तब्ल ओ अलम
के दरों पर किताब और क़लम
का तक़ाज़ा लिए हाथ फैलाए
वो मा'सूम जो भोलेपन में
वहाँ अपने नन्हे चराग़ों में लौ की लगन
ले के पहुँचे जहाँ
बट रहे थे घटा-टोप बेअंत रातों के साए

उन असीरों के नाम
जिन के सीनों में फ़र्दा के शब-ताब गौहर
जेल-ख़ानों की शोरीदा रातों की सरसर में
जल जल के अंजुम-नुमा हो गए हैं
आने वाले दिनों के सफ़ीरों के नाम
वो जो ख़ुश्बू-ए गुल की तरह
अपने पैग़ाम पर ख़ुद फ़िदा हो गए हैं

◆

'A SEARCH FOR BLOOD'

If you see the blood, you can probably see the victim and make guesses about the motive of the murderer. But when a regime is based on oppression so that some people can enjoy unlimited power, while a lot of people have to die for want of basic necessities of life, the murder machine works silently, and it works with absolute efficiency. People go missing. People are murdered, but no trace of dead bodies is found. It is not only murder, but it is also systematic extermination, deportation, torture, rape, political persecution and other

inhumane acts. The poem speaks to all kinds of oppressive
actions which go unseen and unreported.

Not anywhere.
Nowhere is there any sign of blood.
Searched everywhere.
It is not on the hands, nails or sleeves of the
murderer.
Not on the redness of the knife, or any point of
the sword.
There is no mark on the ground, no spot on the
roof.
Searched everywhere. Blood can't be found.
It was not spilled in the service of a royal.
It was not used in a religious ritual.
It was not used on a battlefield.
It was not inscribed on a banner of victory.
It kept calling, poor orphaned blood.
No one had any desire or inclination to hear.
No witness. No sacrifice. The case was closed.
The dust nourished the blood.
And eventually, it became food for the dust.

(Karachi, January 1965)

'Lahu Ka Suraagh'

kahien nahien hai kahien bhi nahien lahu ka suraagh
n dast o naakhun-e qaatil n aastiin pe nishaan
n surkhi-e lab-e khanjar n rang-e nok-e sinaan
n khaak par koi dhahbba n baam par koi daagh
kahien nahien hai kahien bhi nahien lahu ka suraagh
n sarf-e khidmat-e shaahaan k khuun baha dete
n diin ki nazr k bai'aana-e jaza dete
n razam gaah mein barsa k mo'tabar hota

kisi a'lam pe raqam ho k mushtahar hota
pukaarta raha beaasra yatiim lahu
kisi ko bahr-e sama'at n vaqt tha n dimaagh
n mudda'ii n shahadat hisaab paak hua
ye khuun-e khaak-nishinaan tha rizq-e khaak hua

'लहू का सुराग़'

कहीं नहीं है कहीं भी नहीं लहू का सुराग़
न दस्त ओ नाख़ुन-ए क़ातिल न आस्तीं पे निशाँ
न सुख़ीं-ए लब-ए ख़ंजर न रंग-ए नोक-ए सिनाँ
न ख़ाक पर कोई धब्बा न बाम पर कोई दाग़
कहीं नहीं है कहीं भी नहीं लहू का सुराग़
न सर्फ़-ए ख़िदमत-ए शाहाँ कि ख़ूँ-बहा देते
न दीं की नज़र कि बै'आना-ए जज़ा देते
न रज़्म-गाह में बरसा कि मो'तबर होता
किसी अ'लम पे रक़म हो के मुश्तहर होता
पुकारता रहा बेआसरा यतीम लहू
किसी को बहर-ए समा'इत न वक़्त था न दिमाग़
न मुद्दा'ई न शहादत हिसाब पाक हुआ
ये ख़ून-ए ख़ाक-नशीनाँ था रिज़्क़-ए ख़ाक हुआ

◆

'LOOK AT THE CITY FROM HERE'

Although the subject of this poem is similar, it is different
from 'O the City of Lights' ('Ae Raushaniyon Ke Shahar')
that we have read before. The city should be a fun place
because there are multitudes of people who live there.
There is life bubbling at each street corner, but when an
oppressive regime controls the levers of power (think
martial law!) a city can be easily transformed into a prison.
Known distinctions disappear. Life changes its course. Fear

prevails. No voices are heard. Notice the last stanza that says it all: '*jo saaye duur chaaraaghon ke gird larzaan hain / n jaane mahfil-e gham hai k bazm-e jaam o sabu / jo rang har dar o diivaar par pareshaan hain / yahaan se kuchh nahien khulta ye phuul hain k lahu* (There are shadows in the distance, / lurking around the dim lamps. / Not clear whether this is a gathering for grievers, / or a party for drunkards. / The colours which are dispersed around doors and walls / one can't find out from here / whether these are flowers or stains of blood)'.

Looking at the city from here—
it is nothing but one circle after another.
All around, there is a wall as if it were circling a prison.
Every road, every street looks like a dungeon
with no milestone, nowhere to go,
and nothing to show for any fidelity.

If someone walks fast-paced then there is a question:
Why was there no loud shout to halt?
If someone raises his hand, then there is a doubt:
Why was there no sound of a chain or shackles?

When you look at the city from here—
the whole population appears to be devoid
of people with strong character and mature awareness.
Every grown man looks like a criminal
with a scaffold around his neck.
Every beautiful idol has a bracelet,
a symbol that marks them as slaves.

There are shadows in the distance,

lurking around the dim lamps.
Not clear whether this is a gathering for grievers,
or a party for drunkards.
The colours which are dispersed around doors
and walls
one can't find out from here
whether these are flowers or stains of blood.

(Karachi, March 1965)

'Yahaan Se Shahar Ko Dekho'

yahaan se shahar ko dekho to halqa dar halqa
khinchi hai jail ki suurat har ek samt fasiil
har ek raahguzar gardash-e asiiraan hai
n sang-e miil n manzil n mukhlasi ki sabiil

jo koi tez chale rah to puuchhta hai khayaal
k tokne koi lalkaar kyon nahien aaii
jo koi haath hilaaye to vahm ko hai savaal
koi chhanak koi jhankaar kyon nahien aaii

yahaan se shahar ko dekho to saari khalqat mein
n koi saahib-e tamkiin n koi vaali-e hosh
har ek mard-e javaan mujrim rasan-b-gulu
har ik hasiina-e ra'ina kaniiz-e halqa bagosh

jo saaye duur chaaraghon ke gird larzaan hain
n jaane mahfil-e gham hai k bazm-e jaam o sabu
jo rang har dar o diivaar par pareshaan hain
yahaan se kuchh nahien khulta ye phuul hain k lahu

'यहाँ से शहर को देखो'

यहाँ से शहर को देखो तो हल्क़ा-दर-हल्क़ा
खिंची है जेल की सूरत हर एक सम्त फ़सील
हर एक राहगुज़र गर्दिश-ए असीराँ है
न संग-ए मील न मंज़िल न मुख़्लिसी की सबील

जो कोई तेज़ चले रह तो पूछता है ख़याल
कि टोकने कोई ललकार क्यूँ नहीं आई
जो कोई हाथ हिलाए तो वहम को है सवाल
कोई छनक कोई झंकार क्यूँ नहीं आई

यहाँ से शहर को देखो तो सारी ख़िल्क़त में
न कोई साहब-ए तमकीं न कोई वाली-ए होश
हर एक मर्द-ए जवाँ मुजरिम रसन-ब-गुलू
हर इक हसीन-ए रा'ना कनीज़-ए हल्क़ा-बगोश

जो साए दूर चराग़ों के गिर्द लज़ां हैं
न जाने महफ़िल-ए ग़म है कि बज़्म-ए जाम ओ सुबू
जो रंग हर दर ओ दीवार पर परेशाँ हैं
यहाँ से कुछ नहीं खुलता ये फूल हैं कि लहू

GHAZAL

The moon appeared fully beautified,
reflecting the colour of your elegance.
The ambiance was filled with fragrance;
my confidante showed a new colour.

Veiled in the shadow of the eye,
the beauty of your illumined face.
Concealed in the redness of your lips
the colours of your voice.

I'm without a drink,
but if I can seek your indulgence
towards the end of the night
the wine glass might reveal
the colour of the daybreak!

The music was at its peak with its force.
When my heart changed its stance,

then the music made by every instrument
was toned down.

A little more mellow speech
and maybe your soft whispering
will turn the mystery of the ordinary words
into something mysteriously miraculous!

(Karachi, 1965)

'Yuun Saja Chaand K Jhalka Tere Andaaz Ka Rang'

yuun saja chaand k jhalka tere andaaz ka rang
yuun faza mehki k badla mere hamraaz ka rang

saaya-e chashm mein hairaan rukh-e raushan ka jamaal
surkhi-e lab mein parishaan teri aavaaz ka rang

be-piie huun k agar lutf karo aakhir-e shab
shiisha-e mai mein dhale sub-h ke aaghaaz ka rang

chang o nai rang pe the apne lahu ke dam se
dil ne lai badli to madham hua har saaz ka rang

ik sukhan aur k phir rang-e takkalum tera
harf-e saada ko i'nayaat kare e'jaaz ka rang

'यूँ सजा चाँद कि झलका तेरे अंदाज़ का रंग'

यूँ सजा चाँद कि झलका तेरे अंदाज़ का रंग
यूँ फ़ज़ा महकी कि बदला मेरे हमराज़ का रंग

साया-ए चशम में हैराँ रुख़-ए रौशन का जमाल
सुर्ख़ी-ए लब में परेशाँ तेरी आवाज़ का रंग

बे-पिए हूँ कि अगर लुत्फ़ करो आख़िर-ए शब
शीशा-ए मय में ढले सुब्ह के आग़ाज़ का रंग

चंग ओ नय रंग पे थे अपने लहू के दम से
दिल ने लय बदली तो मद्धम हुआ हर साज़ का रंग

इक सुख़न और कि फिर रंग-ए तकल्लुम तेरा
हर्फ़-ए सादा को इ'नायत करे इ'जाज़ का रंग

◆

'BLACKOUT'

This poem was written in September 1965, the month
and year of the first land and air war between India and
Pakistan. Until that time, there had been a free flow of
books, literary journals and films between the two countries.
It had not been difficult for writers from one country to visit
the other. These cultural exchanges mitigated the effects
of Partition because it still felt like one place. This short
but intense war changed all this. It was tough for poets
like Faiz who had dozens of dear friends across the border
and who enjoyed their visits to India more than anything
else. Therefore, the dislocation in mutual relations was
like 'losing both eyes'. The poet struggles with the tides
of poison which he hopes will dissipate. Faiz is purposely
ambiguous. There is no mention of war, India or Pakistan.
But there was no better way to express his disgust and
frustration than the manner he chose.

> Since the glittering lights
> lost their illumination
> I am trying to find in the dust,
> and not even know the place.
> I have lost both my eyes.
> If you know me, please tell me who I am.
> I feel it has descended into every vein
> a murderous river filled with poison,
> tide after tide,
> yearning for you, my love.

I do not know
which tide has swallowed my heart.
Just wait a while
something might come from the world beyond.
A flash of lightening might come
in my direction
bringing with it luminous hands
and the lost glow of my eyes,
the light of black new shiny eyes—
given back to me.
Wait and let us find
the river's depth and breadth
and a new heart of mine
washed with poison, decimated,
let it find a bank of its own.
Then I will make new offerings,
fresh eyes and a new heart
in praise of beauty,
an unending essay
on love's intoxicating passion.

'Blackout'

jab se benuur hui hain sham'ein
khaak mein dhuundhta phirta huun n jaane kis jaa
kho gaii hain meri dono aankhein
tum jo vaaqif ho bataao koi pahchaan meri
is tarah hai k har ik rag mein utar aaya hai
mauj dar mauj kisi zahr ka qaatil darya
tera armaan teri yaad liye jaan meri
jaane kis mauj mein ghaltaan hai kahaan dil mera
ek pal thahro k us paar kisi duniya se
barq aaye meri jaanib yad-e baiza le kar
aur meri aankhon ke gum gashta guhar

jaam-e zulmat se siyaah mast
naaii aankhon ke shab-taab guhar
lauta de
ek pal thahro k dariya ka kahien paat lage
aur naya dil mera
zahr mein dhulke fana ho ke
kisi ghaat lage
phir paye nazar naye diidah o dil le ke chuluun
husn ki mad-ha karuun shauq ka mazmuun likhuun

'ब्लैकआउट'

जब से बेनूर हुई हैं शमा'एं
ख़ाक में ढूँढता फिरता हूँ न जाने किस जा
खो गई हैं मेरी दोनों आँखें
तुम जो वाक़िफ़ हो बताओ कोई पहचान मेरी
इस तरह है कि हर इक रग में उतर आया है
मौज-दर-मौज किसी ज़हर का क़ातिल दरिया
तेरा अरमान तेरी याद लिए जान मेरी
जाने किस मौज में ग़लताँ है कहाँ दिल मेरा
एक पल ठहरो कि उस पार किसी दुनिया से
बर्क़ आए मेरी जानिब यद-ए बैज़ा ले कर
और मेरी आँखों के गुम-गश्ता गुहर
जाम-ए ज़ुल्मत से सियह-मस्त
नई आँखों के शब-ताब गुहर
लौटा दे
एक पल ठहरो कि दरिया का कहीं पाट लगे
और नया दिल मेरा
ज़हर में धुल के फ़ना हो के
किसी घाट लगे
फिर पए-नज़्र नए दीदा ओ दिल ले के चलूँ
हुस्न की मदह करूँ शौक़ का मज़मून लिखूँ

◆

'A PRAYER'

This poem, which was originally written in connection to the celebration of Pakistan's twentieth Independence Day in 1967, was later read by most people as a challenge to Zia's Islamist military coup.[54]

Come, let us raise our hands in prayer.
We are the ones
who have forgotten the rules of prayer.
We are the ones
who without the burning fire of love
do not remember any idol or any god.
Let us pray that this enchanted life
should show kindness
and pour some sweetness of tomorrow
into the poison of today,
and for those who can't bear the burden of days
please lessen the weight of days
and nights on their eyelashes.
And for those who can't even enjoy daybreak,
let them have a candle to brighten their nights.
Those whose feet can't find a path to walk on
make their eyes see a shining passage before them.
And those who use their faith to lie and
can't give them the courage to know their wrongs
and
help them find the right way.
Those whose heads are awaiting the oppressor's
sword,
provide them with the courage to shake off the
murderer's attack.

---

[54]Coppola, *Urdu Poetry*, p. 336.

The secret of love is merely a soul on fire;
let us make a new compact to diminish the heat
we bear.
Truth pulsates in the depths of the heart like a
barb.
Let us come to an agreement and free ourselves
of love's agony.

'Dua'

aaiye haath uthaaein ham bhi
ham jinhein rasm-e dua yaad nahien
ham jinhein soz-e mohabbat ke siva
koi but koi khuda yaad nahien

aaiye a'rz guzaarein k nigaar-e hasti
zahr-e imroz mein shiiriini-e farda bhar de
voh jinhein taab-e giraan baari-e ayyaam nahien
unki palkon pe shab o roz ko halka kar de

jin ki aankhon ko rukh-e sub-h ka yaaraa bhi nahien
un ki raaton mein koi sham'a munavvar kar de
jin ke qadmon ko kisi rah ka sahaara bhi nahien
un ki nazron pe koi raah ujaagar kar de

jinka diin pairavi-e kizb o riya hai un ko
himmat-e kufr mile jurrat-e tahqiiq mile
jinke sar muntazir-e tegh-e jafa hain unko
dast-e qaatil ko jhatak dene ki taufiiq mile

i'shq ka sir-e nihaan jaan ta paan hai jis se
aaj iqraar karein aur tapish mit jaae
harf-e haq dil mein khatakta hai jo kaante ki tarah
aaj izhaar karein aur khalish mit jaae

'दुआ'

आइए हाथ उठाएँ हम भी
हम जिन्हें रस्म-ए दुआ याद नहीं
हम जिन्हें सोज़-ए मोहब्बत के सिवा
कोई बुत कोई ख़ुदा याद नहीं

आइए अ'र्ज़ गुज़ारें कि निगार-ए हस्ती
ज़हर-ए इमरोज़ में शीरीनी-ए फ़र्दा भर दे
वो जिन्हें ताब-ए गिराँ-बारी-ए अय्याम नहीं
उन की पलकों पे शब ओ रोज़ को हल्का कर दे

जिन की आँखों को रुख़-ए सुब्ह का यारा भी नहीं
उन की रातों में कोई शम्'अ मुनव्वर कर दे
जिन के क़दमों को किसी रह का सहारा भी नहीं
उन की नज़रों पे कोई राह उजागर कर दे

जिन का दीं पैरवी-ए किज़्ब ओ रिया है उन को
हिम्मत-ए कुफ़्र मिले जुरअत-ए तहक़ीक़ मिले
जिन के सर मुंतज़िर-ए तेग़-ए जफ़ा हैं उन को
दस्त-ए क़ातिल को झटक देने की तौफ़ीक़ मिले

इ'श्क़ का सिर्र-ए निहाँ जान-ए तपाँ है जिस से
आज इक़रार करें और तपिश मिट जाए
हर्फ़-ए हक़ दिल में खटकता है जो काँटे की तरह
आज इज़हार करें और ख़लिश मिट जाए

◆

'HEART ATTACK'

Faiz took up smoking early in his life. The love of Scotch
came later. These personal habits, coupled with a lack of
physical exercise and a stressful work environment, took a
toll on his health. In February 1962, he was taken ill with
severe breathing problems. The doctors told him that he

had had a mild heart attack. He resigned from his position in the arts council and agreed to go on a special diet and lead a less stressful life. After this close brush with death due to a heart attack, fear found a permanent place in his psyche. He had also suffered the loss of friends to heart attacks. The pain caused by this incident, which was a stark reminder of one's mortality, lingered on for a long time. It was not until 1967 that Faiz picked up his pen and wrote about it.

> That night, the pain was so intense
> and my wild heart
> was ready to pick up a fight with every vein,
> with the root of each hair,
> and at some distance in your home garden
> every leaf after being washed in the blood
> of my wretched heart
> was wearily looking at the moon's beauty.
> As if in the desolation of my body's tent
> ropes of all my troubling nerves were freed
> and began to announce ominously
> the departure of the caravan of craving,
> and in the dying candles of memory
> was found somewhere, one bit,
> one moment of your loving kindness.
> The pain was so intense that I wanted to go beyond it.
> I wished, but the heart had his way.

'Heart Attack'

dard itna tha k us raat dil-e vahshi ne
har rag-e jaan se ulajhna chaaha
har bun-e muu se tapakna chaaha
aur kahien duur tere sehn mein goya

patta patta mere afsurdah lahu mein dhul kar
husn-e mahtaab se aazurdah nazar aane laga
mere viirana-e tan mein goya
saare dukhte hue reshon ki tanaabein khulkar
silsila vaar pata dene lagiin
rukhsat-e qaafla-e shauq ki taiyaari ka
aur jab yaad ki bujhti hui sham'on mein nazar aaya
kahien
ek pal aakhri lamha teri dildaari ka
dard itna tha k us se bhi guzarna chaaha
ham ne chaaha bhi magar dil n thaharna chaaha

'हार्ट अटैक'

दर्द इतना था कि उस रात दिल-ए वहशी ने
हर रग-ए जाँ से उलझना चाहा
हर बुन-ए मू से टपकना चाहा
और कहीं दूर तेरे सहन में गोया
पत्ता पत्ता मेरे अफ़्सुर्दा लहू में धुल कर
हुस्न-ए महताब से आज़ुर्दा नज़र आने लगा
मेरे वीराना-ए तन में गोया
सारे दुखते हुए रेशों की तनाबें खुल कर
सिलसिला-वार पता देने लगीं
रुख़्सत-ए क़ाफ़िला-ए शौक़ की तय्यारी का
और जब याद की बुझती हुई शम्ओं में नज़र आया कहीं
एक पल आख़िरी लम्हा तेरी दिलदारी का
दर्द इतना था कि उस से भी गुज़रना चाहा
हम ने चाहा भी मगर दिल न ठहरना चाहा

✦

QAT'A

A determination for self-control and a promise to
curb desire—
I want to go beyond the limits of resolution and
commitment.
The pain was so intense that it felt like the day of
resurrection.
And there was tranquility and a feeling of just
embracing death.

(1968)

zabt ka a'hd bhi hai shauq ka paimaan bhi hai
a'hd o paimaan se guzar jaane ko ji chaahta hai
dard itna hai k har rag mein hai mahshar barpa
aur sakuun aisa k mar jaane ko ji chaahta hai

ज़ब्त का अ'हद भी है शौक़ का पैमाँ भी है
अहद ओ पैमाँ से गुज़र जाने को जी चाहता है
दर्द इतना है कि हर रग में है महशर बरपा
और सकूँ ऐसा कि मर जाने को जी चाहता है

◆

GHAZAL

This ghazal is one of the three ghazals that Faiz wrote
and gave them a common title 'Marsiay' (elegies). He was
deeply troubled by the sudden death of a family friend,
Dr Shaukat Haroon, and two other deaths that had
happened around that time (passing of his mother and
that of his dear friend and ideological companion, Sajjad
Zaheer).

How long should I wish my heart well?
How long will you make me wait?
How long will you allow me to stay calm?
How long will you spare me of your memory?

The season when there was hope of seeing you is
over.
Now the dust is pouring into my eyes.
When are you going to direct the cloud of suffering?
When are you going to send some rain clouds?

You make the compact of being faithful,
or you can break the bond of love.
Nothing is under my control.
What do you want me to do differently?

Who has watched the sunny day of the union?
Who has suffered the night of separation?
Who were those sweethearts with beautiful tresses?
What can you say about them?

Faiz, it is written in the fate of hearts
that they will gain possessions
and that they will get robbed.
How long do you plan to put on air?

(October 1968)

*'Kab Tak Dil Ki Khair Manaaein Kab Tak Rah
Dikhlaaoge'*

*kab tak dil ki khair manaaein kab tak rah dikhlaaoge
kab tak chain ki mohlat doge kab tak yaad n aaoge*

*biita diid ummiid ka mausam khaak urti hai aankhon
mein*

kab bhejoge dard ka badal kab barkha barsaaoge

a'hd-e vafa ya tarke mohabbat jo chaaho so aap karo
apne bas ki baat hi kya hai ham se kya munvaaoge

kis ne vasl ka suuraj dekha kis par hijr ki raat dhali
gesuon vaale kaun the kya the un ko kya jatlaaoge

Faiz dilon ke bhaag mein hai ghar bharna bhi lut jaanu bhi
tum is husn ke lutf o karam par kitne din itraaoge

'कब तक दिल की ख़ैर मनाएँ कब तक राह दिखलाओगे'

कब तक दिल की ख़ैर मनाएँ कब तक राह दिखलाओगे
कब तक चैन की मोहलत दोगे कब तक याद न आओगे

बीता दीद उम्मीद का मौसम ख़ाक उड़ती है आँखों में
कब भेजोगे दर्द का बादल कब बरखा बरसाओगे

अ'हद-ए वफ़ा या तर्क-ए मोहब्बत जो चाहो सो आप करो
अपने बस की बात ही क्या है हम से क्या मनवाओगे

किस ने वस्ल का सूरज देखा किस पर हिज्र की रात ढली
गेसुओं वाले कौन थे क्या थे उनको क्या जतलाओगे

'फ़ैज़' दिलों के भाग में है घर भरना भी लुट जाना भी
तुम इस हुस्न के लुत्फ़ ओ करम पर कितने दिन इतराओगे

◆

'KEEP YOURSELF AT SOME DISTANCE FROM ME'

While the national election at the end of 1970 was a great victory for democracy, the joy was short-lived. Pakistan's army and Bhutto's political party refused to honour the results of the election. This led to civil strife and a new war with India and eventually, the loss of East Pakistan. Faiz was deeply hurt by listening to the stories of atrocities committed by the Pakistani armed forces against Bengali civilians. He expressed his feelings of disgust in two poems, and here is the first of the two. No names are mentioned, but every line of this poem speaks of the tragedy that resulted in the dismemberment of the country and the loss of countless lives.

How can I celebrate
this festival of mass killing?
Whose attention
the blood of my wailing heart
will attract?
How much blood
do you think
my frail body already has?
You can't fill a lamp with this,
or fill a wine glass.
You can't use it as a fuel for the fire,
or quench someone's thirst.
How much blood do you think
my wounded body has?
Every vein is filled with poison—
such poison
that each drop has more venom
than a cobra's.
Each drop contains the pain
and longing of ages.
Each drop carries a seal of rage,
fury and anger.
Be careful.
My body is a flowing river
of poison.
Be cautious.

My body is a dried up piece of wood
in the desert.
If you burn it,
the garden's courtyard will see the blossoming of
my bones like acacia.
You won't find
what you usually see—cypress or jasmine.
If you spread it in a forest,
it will turn into a dust bowl of my scorched soul.
Could you leave me alone?
My heart is thirsting for blood.

(March 1971)

'Hazar Karo Mere Tan Se'

saje to kaise saje qatl-e aam ka mela
kise lubha-e ga mere lahu ka vaa vaila
mere nazaar badan mein lahu hi kitna hai
charaagh ho koi raushan n koi jaam bhare
n is se aag hi bharke n is se pyaas bujhe
mere figaar badan mein lahu hi kitna hai
magar voh zahr-e halaa-hal bhara hai nas nas mein
jise bhi chhero har ik buund qahr-e af'ii hai
har ik kashiid hai sadiyon ke dard o hasrat ki
har ik mein moh-b-lab ghaiz o gham ki garmi hai
hazar karo mere tan se ye sam ka dariya hai
hazar karo k mera tan voh chob-e sahra hai
jise jalaao to sehn-e chaman mein dahkeinge
bajaae sarv o saman meri haddion ke babuul
ise bakhera to dasht o daaman mein bikhregi
bajaae mushk-e saba meri jaan-e zaar ki dhuul
hazar karo k mera dil lahu ka pyaasa hai

'हज़र करो मेरे तन से'

सजे तो कैसे सजे क़त्ल-ए आम का मेला
किसे लुभाए गा मेरे लहू का वावैला
मेरे नज़ार बदन में लहू ही कितना है
चराग़ हो कोई रौशन न कोई जाम भरे
न इस से आग ही भड़के न उस से प्यास बुझे
मेरे फ़िगार बदन में लहू ही कितना है
मगर वो ज़हर-ए हलाहल भरा है नस नस में
जिसे भी छेड़ो हर इक बूँद क़हर-ए अफ़'ई है
हर इक कशीद है सदियों के दर्द ओ हसरत की
हर इक में मोहर-ब-लब ग़ैज़ ओ ग़म की गर्मी है
हज़र करो मेरे तन से ये सम का दरिया है
हज़र करो कि मेरा तन वो चोब-ए सहरा है
जिसे जलाओ तो सेहन-ए चमन में दहकेंगे
बजाए-सर्व ओ समन मेरी हड्डियों के बबूल
इसे बिखेरा तो दश्त ओ दमन में बिखरेगी
बजाए मुश्क-ए सबा मेरी जान-ए ज़ार की धूल
हज़र करो कि मिरा दिल लहू का प्यासा है

♦

'LAYER AFTER LAYER'

This is the second poem written by Faiz about the East
Pakistan tragedy. There is blood everywhere. There is so
much blood that people wash their faces with blood!

Layer after layer
my heart's resentment
when it reached my eyes
I needed help.
I took the healer's word of advice.
And I washed my dust-filled eyes
with blood.

Now every face and appearance,
everything in the present world,
is of the same colour as my eyes—
sun's gold-coloured blood,
moon's silver-tinged blood,
dawn's laughter is blood,
a cry at night is also blood.
Every tree a pillar of blood.
The eye of every flower is
also filled with blood.
Each eye is an arrow of blood.
Each image a mash of blood.
As long as the tide of blood is flowing
its colour is red.
The desire to be martyred.
The colour of pain and grief.
If it is dammed,
then it can shrink, and it can become
the colour of hate,
the colour of the night,
the colour of death—
a tone of every colour's mournful dirge.
Healer, please let this not happen.
Bring from somewhere
the flood of tears,
for ablution with water,
if it washes, then it might clean my eyes,
the blood of my dust-filled eyes.

(April 1971)

'Tah B Tah'

tah b tah dil ki kaduurat

meri aankhon mein umand aaii to kuchh chaarah n tha
chaarah gar ki maan li
aur main ne gard aaluuda ankhon ko lahu se dho liya
main ne gard aaluuda ankhon ko lahu se dho liya
aur ab har shakl o suurat
aa'lam-e maujuud ki har ek shai
meri aankhon ke lahu se is tarah ham rang hai
khurshiid ka kundan lahu
mahtaab ki chaandi lahu
sub-hon ka hansna bhi lahu
raaton ka rona bhi lahu
har shajar miinaar-e khuun har phuul khuunien diidah hai
har nazar ik taar-e khuun har a'ks khuun maaliida hai
mauj-e khuun jab tak ravaan rahti hai us ka surkh rang
jazba-e shauq shahadat dard ghaiz o gham ka rang
aur tham jaae to kajla kar
faqat nafrat ka shab ka maut ka
har ik rang ke maatam ka rang
chaarah gar aisa n hone de
kahien se la koi sailaab-e ashk
aab vuzu
jismein dhul jaaein to shaayad dhul sake
meri aankhon meri gard aluuda ankhon ka lahu

'तह-ब-तह'

तह-ब-तह दिल की कुदूरत
मेरी आँखों में उमँड आई तो कुछ चारा न था
चारा-गर की मान ली
और मैं ने गर्द-आलूद आँखों को लहू से धो लिया
मैं ने गर्द-आलूद आँखों को लहू से धो लिया
और अब हर शक्ल ओ सूरत

आ'लम-ए मौजूद की हर एक शय
मेरी आँखों के लहू से इस तरह हम-रंग है
ख़ुर्शीद का कुंदन लहू
महताब की चाँदी लहू
सुब्हों का हँसना भी लहू
रातों का रोना भी लहू
हर शजर मीनार-ए ख़ूँ हर फूल ख़ूनीं-दीदा है
हर नज़र इक तार-ए ख़ूँ हर अक्स ख़ूँ-गालीदह है
मौज-ए ख़ूँ जब तक रवाँ रहती है उस का सुर्ख़ रंग
जज़्बा-ए शौक़-ए शहादत दर्द ग़ैज़ ओ ग़म का रंग
और थम जाए तो कजला कर
फ़क़त नफ़रत का शब का मौत का
हर इक रंग के मातम का रंग
चारा-गर ऐसा न होने दे
कहीं से ला कोई सैलाब-ए अश्क
आब वज़ू
जिस में धुल जाएँ तो शायद धुल सके
मेरी आँखों मेरी गर्द-आलूद आँखों का लहू

◆

'THE DAY DEATH COMES'

Ghalib's ghazal poetry was a great source of inspiration for
Faiz. Mirza made several references to death and dying in
his couplets. It was, therefore, natural for Faiz to write a
meditation of his own about death. A better part of this
poem is devoted to contemplating the different ways death
might consider arriving, before she actually comes. But in
the end, it does not matter. Death brings everything to an
end. While expressing his thanks for death's arrival, the
poet says, 'God be praised,' but he does not forget to say
thanks to the one 'whose lips are filled with sweetness'.

How will it come the day death comes?
Perhaps during the early hours of the evening,
unwanted, pressing forward,
with a compassionate kiss on the lips,
magical doors start to open in all directions,
and from a faraway place
an unknown spring of roses,
without any good reason,
begins to torment the moon's heart.
Dawn rising from half-opened green buds
suddenly starts to flutter in the chamber of the
beloved.
And from the silent windows
at the time of the departure
a tinkling sound comes from the stars.

How will it come the day death comes.
Perhaps like a vein that is touched by a pointed
spear
starts to howl with pain,
and a reflection of the pain-causing instrument
begins to cast its spell on the earth
from one end to the other.

How will it come the day death comes.
Whether it comes like an assassin
or as merely the grace of the beloved.
My heart will utter these words,
my parting words of thanks.
'God be praised,'
for the way, it ended my heart's grief.
Thanks to the one whose lips
are filled with such sweetness.

(1972)

'Jis Roz Qaza Aayegi'

kis tarah aayegi jis roz qaza aayegi
shaayad is tarah k jis taur kabhi avval-e shab
betalab pehle-pahal marhamat-e bosa-e lab
jis se khulne lagein har samt talismaat ke dar
aur kahien duur se anjaan gulaabon ki bahaar
yak-b-yak siina-e mahtaab ko tarpaane lage
shaayad is tarah k jis taur kabhi aakhir-e shab
niim va kaliyon se sarsabz sahar
yak-b-yak hujra-e mahbuub mein lahraane lage
aur khaamosh dariichon se b-hangaam-e rahiil
jhanjhanaate hue taaron ki sada aane lage

kis tarah aayegi jis roz qaza aayegi
shaayad is tarah k jis taur tah-e nok-e sinaan
koi rag vaahma-e dard se chillaane lage
aur qazzaq-e sinaan dast ka dhundhla saaya
az-karaan-ta-b-karaan dahar pe mandlaane lage

jis tarah aayegi jis roz qaza aayegi
khawaah qaatil ki tarah aaye k mahbuub sifat
dil se bas ho gi yahi harf-e vid'a ki suurat
lillah-il hamd b-anjaam-e dil-e dil zadgaan
kalma-e shukar b-anaam-e lab-e shiiriin dahnaan

'जिस रोज़ क़ज़ा आयेगी'

किस तरह आएगी जिस रोज़ क़ज़ा आएगी
शायद इस तरह कि जिस तौर कभी अव्वल-ए शब
बेतलब पहले-पहल मर्हमत-ए बोसा-ए लब
जिस से खुलने लगें हर सम्त तिलिस्मात के दर
और कहीं दूर से अंजान गुलाबों की बहार
यक-ब-यक सीना-ए महताब को तड़पाने लगे

शायद इस तरह कि जिस तौर कभी आख़िर-ए शब
नीम-वा कलियों से सरसब्ज़ सहर
यक-ब-यक हुजरा-ए महबूब में लहराने लगे
और ख़ामोश दरीचों से ब-हंगाम-ए रहील
झनझनाते हुए तारों की सदा आने लगे

किस तरह आएगी जिस रोज़ क़ज़ा आएगी
शायद इस तरह कि जिस तौर तह-ए नोक-ए सिनाँ
कोई रग वाहिमा-ए दर्द से चिल्लाने लगे
और क़ज़्ज़ाक़-ए सिनाँ-दस्त का धुँदला साया
अज़-कराँ-ता-ब-कराँ दहर पे मंडलाने लगे

किस तरह आएगी जिस रोज़ क़ज़ा आएगी
ख़्वाह क़ातिल की तरह आए कि महबूब-सिफ़त
दिल से बस होगी यही हर्फ़-ए विदाअ की सूरत
लिल्लाहिल-हम्द ब-अनजाम-ए दिल-ए दिल-ज़दगाँ
कलमा-ए शुक्र ब-नाम-ए लब-ए शीरीं-दहनाँ

◆

GHAZAL

I have metamorphosed
and preserved in beautiful couplets
whatever heart-rending words
that you had voiced to me.

All those mysterious qualities
of colour and fragrance
were metaphors about you.

Before you committed yourself
to the relationship,
there were other sources
of support to me.

I took account
of those rubies and pearls
that your love's grief
bestowed upon me.

They fell into the lap
of my apparel
all those stars
that were shining
in the bowl of the sky.

A prayer for eternal life?
Faiz, I don't think
she was that much unto me.

(1972)

'Ham Ne Sab She'r Mein Sanvaare The'

ham ne sab she'r mein sanvaare the
ham se jitney sukhan tumhaare the

rang o khushbu ke husn o khuubi ke
tum se the jitney isti'aare the

tere qol o qaraar se pehle
apne kuchh aur bhi sahaare the

jab voh la'l o guhar hisaab kiye
jo tere gham pe dil ne vaare the

mere daaman mein aa gire saare
jitney tasht-e falak mein taare the

u'mr-e jaaved ki dua karte
Faiz itne voh kab hamaare the

'हम ने सब शे'र में सँवारे थे'

हम ने सब शे'र में सँवारे थे
हम से जितने सुख़न तुम्हारे थे

रंग ओ ख़ुशबू के हुस्न ओ ख़ूबी के
तुम से थे जितने इस्तिआरे थे

तेरे क़ौल ओ क़रार से पहले
अपने कुछ और भी सहारे थे

जब वो लाल ओ गुहर हिसाब किए
जो तेरे ग़म ने दिल पे वारे थे

मेरे दामन में आ गिरे सारे
जितने तश्त-ए फ़लक में तारे थे

उ'मर-ए जावेद की दुआ करते
'फ़ैज़' इतने वो कब हमारे थे

◆

QAT'A

One thousand agonies in the way of night's longings.
Tell me the place where the caravan can make a
stop.
Come closer so that my desire to see you is fulfilled.
Let me drink a little more to regain my normal
state.

(1972)

hazaar dard shab-e aarzu ki raah mein hai
koi thikaana bataao k qaafila utre
qariib aur bhi aaoo k shauq-e diid mite
sharaab aur pilaao k kuchh nasha utre

हज़ार दर्द शब-ए आरज़ू की राह में है
कोई ठिकाना बताओ कि क़ाफ़िला उतरे
क़रीब और भी आओ कि शौक़-ए दीद मिटे
शराब और पिलाओ कि कुछ नशा उतरे

◆

'IF MY GRIEF GETS ITS SAY'

This is a beautiful short poem written sometime in 1972. A. Sean Pue, who commented on this, compared it to someone delicately opening a shell and finding this little gem.

> Faiz celebrates individual experience, describing its necessity. For, as he writes, the individual experience of suffering is what opens up the possibility for a transformative self-awareness. This awareness is first of the individual self, the 'I', not of the collective. However, an appreciation of the individual reveals the nature of the 'outer' world—the 'world's order' (nazm-e jahaan)—while also unveiling the other 'inner' world, as well ... Faiz transverses the internal and the external, the individual and the collective. And so it would be a mistake to see this poet as ignoring the individual in favour of the collective; in fact, what he does is to articulate the relationship between the two.[55]

My grief is like a melody
that has never been sung.
My existence is like a particle

---

[55]Hameed, ed., *Daybreak*, p. 273.

that is lost without a trace.
If my grief gets its say
I will know my name and my roots.
If I know where my roots are,
I will find out the secret—
how the world works.
If I know the secret
how the world works,
my silence will have a reason
to express itself,
and I will be like a monarch
of the universe,
gaining the treasures
of two worlds.

'Mere Dard Ko Jo Zabaan Mili'

mera dard naghma-e besada
meri zaat zarra-e benishaan
mere dard ko jo zabaan mile
mujhe apna naam o nishaan mile
meri zaat ka jo nishaan mile
mujhe raaz-e nazm-e jahaan mile
jo mujhe ye raaz-e nihaan mile
meri khaamashi ko bayaaan mile
mujhe kaaenaat ki sarvari
mujhe daulat-e do jahaan mile

'मेरे दर्द को जो ज़बाँ मिले'

मेरा दर्द नग़मा-ए बेसदा
मेरी ज़ात ज़र्रा-ए बेनिशाँ
मेरे दर्द को जो ज़बाँ मिले
मुझे अपना नाम ओ निशाँ मिले
मेरी ज़ात का जो निशाँ मिले

मुझे राज़-ए नज़्म-ए जहाँ मिले
जो मुझे ये राज़-ए निहाँ मिले
मेरी ख़ामुशी को बयाँ मिले
मुझे काएनात की सरवरी
मुझे दौलत-ए दो-जहाँ मिले

◆

'WASH THE BLOOD FROM YOUR FEET'

Faiz wrote this poem in response to the criticism which
he was getting both from the left and the right sides of
the political spectrum. He knew that people will always
criticize you, no matter what you do. His solution: '*tum
dil ko sambhaalo jis mein abhi / sau tarah ke nashtar tuuteinge*
(You should take care of your heart / in which hundreds of
lancets / have yet to break)'.

> What could I do?
> Which way could I have gone?
> Each pathway had thorns
> of the broken relationships,
> of century-long friendships,
> that broke one after another,
> whichever way I took,
> whichever direction I chose,
> my feet were soaked with blood.
> All the observers were yelling:
> What is this new tradition?
> What is this new style?
> What about this henna
> on your feet?
>
> What were they saying?
> Why were they talking

about the famine of love?
Wipe off blood from your feet.
When these pathways
are ready to produce,
hundreds of new trails
will shoot from these tracks.
You should take care of your heart
in which hundreds of lancets
have yet to break.

(Delhi, September 1973)

'Paaon Se Lahu Ko Dho Dalo'

ham kya karte kis rah chalte
har raah mein kaante bikhre the
un rishton ke jo chhuut gaye
un saddiyon ke yaarano ke
jo ik ik karke tuut gaye
jis raah chale jis simt gaye
yuun paaon lahuluhaan hue
sab dekhne vaale kahte the
ye kaisi riit rachaaii hai
ye mehndi kyon lagaaii hai
voh kahte the kyon qaht-e vafa
ka na-haq charcha karte ho
paaon se lahu ko dho daalo
ye raahein jab at jaayeingi
sau raste in se phuuteinge
tum dil ko sambhaalo jis mein abhi
sau tarah ke nishtar tuuteinge

'पाँव से लहू को धो डालो'

हम क्या करते किस रह चलते
हर राह में काँटे बिखरे थे
इन रिश्तों के जो छूट गए
इन सदियों के यारानों के
जो इक इक कर के टूट गए
जिस राह चले जिस सम्त गए
यूँ पाँव लहूलुहान हुए
सब देखने वाले कहते थे
ये कैसी रीत रचाई है
ये मेहंदी क्यूँ लगाई है
वो कहते थे क्यूँ क़हत-ए वफ़ा
का नाहक़ चर्चा करते हो
पाँव से लहू को धो डालो
ये राहें जब अट जाएँगी
सौ रस्ते इन से फूटेंगे
तुम दिल को सँभालो जिस में अभी
सौ तरह के नश्तर टूटेंगे

◆

'LOVING AND MAKING A LIVING'

Faiz captures the feelings of every living human being in this short poem. Loving and labouring or working: these are the two things that we all do. Do we succeed in one or both? Not necessarily. Few lucky ones do, but for most of us, the poet's experience says it all: '*kaam i'shq ke aare aata raha / aur i'shq se kaam ulajhta raha / phir aakhir tang aa kar ham ne / donon ko adhuura chhor diya* (And my loving sometime complicated things for me. / Losing my composure in the end, / I left both of them somewhat unfinished)'.

Those people were blessed
who considered love as a kind of work.
They were in love with their calling.
Writing poetry, too, was like love.
I spent some of my time loving, some in action.
My work helped me become a better lover.
I kept myself busy as long as I lived.
But my loving eventually complicated things for me.
Losing my composure in the end,
I left both of them unfinished.

(1976)

'Kuchh I'shq Kiya Kuchh Kaam Kiya'

voh log bahut khush-qismat the
jo i'shq ko kaam samajhte the
ya kaam se aa'shqi karte the
ham jiite-ji masruuf rahe
kuchh i'shq kiya kuchh kaam kiya
kaam i'shq ke aade aata raha
aur i'shq se kaam ulajhta raha
phir aakhir tang aa kar ham ne
donon ko adhuura chhordiya

'कुछ इ'श्क़ किया कुछ काम किया'

वो लोग बहुत ख़ुश-क़िस्मत थे
जो इ'श्क़ को काम समझते थे
या काम से आ'शिक़ी करते थे
हम जीते-जी मसरूफ़ रहे
कुछ इ'श्क़ किया कुछ काम किया
काम इ'श्क़ के आड़े आता रहा
और इ'श्क़ से काम उलझता रहा
फिर आख़िर तंग आ कर हम ने
दोनों को अधूरा छोड़ दिया

◆

'TODAY ONCE AGAIN I AM SEARCHING FOR A WORD'

This poem, written in July 1977, is a commentary on the country's political situation. After a controversial election in early 1977 that resulted in civil unrest, the Bhutto government imposed martial law in several major cities. General Zia-ul-Haq took advantage of the situation and staged a coup on 5 July 1977 and declared himself the chief martial law administrator.

1

Today I am looking for a word—
a word of acclaim,
a name filled with poison.
A word that wins the heart,
a name that evokes horror.
A word of love like the beloved's eyes,
like a kiss on the lips.
Bright like a golden wave.
Sweet like a melody
at the start of a friends' gathering.
Or a word of detestation
with the sharpness of a sword
that destroys the city of oppressors.
So dark that it appears like the dreadful night
at the cremation grounds.
If I bring it to lips,
the lips will turn black.

2

Today my relationship with every note
of the melody was broken.
The voice was once again looking for the singer,
filled with agony like Majnun's torn garment.
Torn into pieces is every page
of the musical notes.
People are begging the tide of a breeze to bring
a melody, a voice, a prayer for peace, even an elegy.
There are cries for martyrdom,
or the awful call of the doomsday,
and the horrible call for the end of the world.

'Aaj Ik Harf Ko Phir Dhuundhta Phirta Hai Khayaal'

1

aaj ik harf ko phir dhuundhta phirta hai khayaal
madh bhara harf koi zahar bhara harf koi
dilnishiin harf koi qahr bhara harf koi
harf-e ulfat koi dildaar-e nazar ho jaise
jis se milti hai nazar bosa-e lab ki suurat
itna raushan k sar-e mauja-e zar ho jaise
sohbat-e yaar mein aaghaaz-e tarab ki suurat
harf nafrat koi shamshiir-e ghazab ho jaise
taa-abad shahr-e sitam jis se tabah ho jaaein
itna taariik k shamshaan ki shab ho jaise
lab pe laauun to mere hont siyaah ho jaaein

2

aaj har sur se ik raag ka naata tuuta
dhuundhti phirti hai mutrib ko phir us ki aavaaz

joshish-e dard se majnuun ke garebaan ki tarah
chaak dar chaak hua aaj har ik pardah-e saaz
aaj har mauj-e hava se hai savaali khalqat
laa koi naghma koi saut teri u'mr daraaz
nauha-e gham hi sahi shor-e shahadat hi sahi
suur-e mahshar hi sahi baang-e qiyamat hi sahi

'आज इक हर्फ़ को फिर ढूँडता फिरता है ख़याल'

1

आज इक हर्फ़ को फिर ढूँडता फिरता है ख़याल
मध भरा हर्फ़ कोई ज़हर भरा हर्फ़ कोई
दिल-नशीं हर्फ़ कोई क़हर भरा हर्फ़ कोई
हर्फ़-ए उल्फ़त कोई दिलदार-ए नज़र हो जैसे
जिस से मिलती है नज़र बोसा-ए लब की सूरत
इतना रौशन कि सर-ए मौजा-ए ज़र हो जैसे
सोहबत-ए यार में आग़ाज़-ए तरब की सूरत
हर्फ़-ए नफ़रत कोई शमशीर-ए ग़ज़ब हो जैसे
ता-अबद शहर-ए सितम जिस से तबह हो जाएँ
इतना तारीक कि शमशान की शब हो जैसे
लब पे लाऊँ तो मिरे होंट सियाह हो जाएँ

2

आज हर सुर से हर इक राग का नाता टूटा
ढूँडती फिरती है मुतरिब को फिर उस की आवाज़
जोशिश-ए दर्द से मजनूँ के गरेबाँ की तरह
चाक-दर-चाक हुआ आज हर इक पर्दा-ए साज़
आज हर मौज-ए हवा से है सवाली ख़िल्क़त
ला कोई नग़्मा कोई सौत तेरी उ'मर दराज़
नौहा-ए ग़म ही सही शोर-ए शहादत ही सही
सूर-ए महशर ही सही बाँग-ए क़यामत ही सही

◆

'BOUND BY LOYALTY'

Faiz often talked about his 'two loves'. His love for his country and its people was no less than his love for the beloved, a fascinating creation of his imagination. He was even trying to transcend these two loves and carve a vision that embraced all humanity, even all creation. But the reality was bitter and nasty. He was imprisoned, especially the second time, without any merit at all. His patriotism was questioned during the 1965 and 1971 wars. The poet wants an answer while he broadcasts his complaint desperately and touchingly to the country which he truly loved all his life: '*apne u'sh-shaaq se aisa bhi koi karta hai* (It is no way to treat those / who loved you deeply with their heart and soul)'. Those who control the levers of power make promises and break them. There is no accountability. It is the fate of the lovers of the land to suffer because their loyalty binds them. For them, betrayal is not an option.

How much blood and from how many people
do you still need, my dear land?
How much blood is still needed to make your
face
glow like blossoms?
How many sighs would calm your body's hunger?
How many tears are still needed to transform
your sweeping deserts into a garden of roses?

Tell me—
about the royal pledges
that were shredded in your palaces.
About the declarations
that were never followed up.

About the eyes that were gouged out
because of their innocence.
About the dreams that were shattered
and traumatized on your pathways.

Whatever happened to those
who suffered because of their sincere love,
let us not talk about it.
Whatever happened to me,
let us not talk about it.
Maybe one day, the culprits are seized by the
collar
and made to account for all their crimes
and miseries that they inflicted.
Better wash off those stains of bad blood
from the royal robes!
Whatever happened, let it go.

We were made helpless
by our loyalty, but the love of my life—
It is no way to treat those
who loved you deeply, heart and soul.
May God protect and bless you until eternity!
What of me? I was just a passerby,
and I will soon leave.

'Ham To Majbuur-e Vafa Hain'

tujh ko kitnon ka lahu chaahiye ai arz-e vatan
jo tere aariz-e berang ko gulnaar karein
kitni aahon se kaleja tera thanda hoga
kitne aansu tere sahraaon ko gulzaar karein

tere aivaanon mein purze hue paimaan kitne
kitne vaa'de jo n aasuuda-e iqraar hue

kitni aankhon ko nazar kha gaaii bad-khvaahon ki
khwaab kitne teri shah-raahon mein sangsaar hue

balaa-kashaan-e mohabbat pe jo hua so hua
jo mujh pe guzri mat us se kaho hua so hua
mabaada ho koi zaalim tera garebaan-giir
lahu ke daagh tu daaman se dho hua so hua

ham to majbuur-e vafa hain magar ai jaan-e jahaan
apne u'shshaaq se aisa bhi koi karta hai
teri mahfil ko khuda rakkhe abad tak qaaim
ham to mehmaan hain ghari bharke hamaara kya hai

'हम तो मजबूर-ए वफ़ा हैं'

तुझ को कितनों का लहू चाहिए ऐ अर्ज़-ए वतन
जो तेरे आरिज़-ए बेरंग को गुलनार करें
कितनी आहों से कलेजा तेरा ठंडा होगा
कितने आंसू तेरे सहराओं को गुलज़ार करें

तेरे ऐवानों में पुर्ज़े हुए पैमां कितने
कितने वा'दे जो ना आसूदा-ए इक़रार हुए
कितनी आँखों को नज़र खा गई बद-ख़्वाहों की
ख़्वाब कितने तेरी शह-राहों में संगसार हुए

बला-कशान-ए मोहब्बत पे जो हुआ सो हुआ
जो मुझ पे गुज़री मत उस से कहो हुआ सो हुआ
मबादा हो कोई ज़ालिम तेरा गरेबाँ-गीर
लहू के दाग़ तू दामन से धो हुआ सो हुआ

हम तो मजबूर-ए वफ़ा हैं मगर ऐ जान-ए जहाँ
अपने उश्'शाक़ से ऐसा भी कोई करता है
तेरी महफ़िल को ख़ुदा रखे अबद तक क़ायम
हम तो मेहमाँ हैं घड़ी भर के हमारा क्या है

◆

GHAZAL

Faiz wrote two ghazals in the memory of his dear friend and reputable Indian poet, Makhdoom Mohiuddin. He got the news of Makhdoom's death while he was in Moscow. Makhdoom had written the opening line of the following ghazal, which Faiz dedicated to Makhdoom.

Flashes of your memory appeared
and disappeared the whole night.
Moonlight continued to hurt
my heart the whole night.

Sometimes burning,
sometimes losing its breath,
the candle of grief
flickered the whole night.

Some fragrance stayed busy
changing garbs.
An image continued to resonate
the whole night.

Some gentle breeze
under the shade of the flower arcade,
continued to recite a story
the whole night.

The heart was pacified
with one hope.
A desire continued to nag
the whole night.

(Moscow, September 1978)

'Aapki Yaad Aati Rahi Raat Bhar'

'aapki yaad aati rahi raat bhar'
chaandni dil dukhaati rahi raat bhar

gaah jalti hui gaah bujhti hui
sham'a-e gham jhilmalaati rahi raat bhar

koi khushbu badalti rahi pairahan
koi tasviir gaati rahi raat bhar

phir saba saaya-e shaakh-e gul ke tale
koi qissa sunaati rahi raat bhar

ek ummid se dil bahalta raha
ik tamanna sataati rahi raat bhar

'आपकी याद आती रही रात भर'

'आपकी याद आती रही रात भर'
चाँदनी दिल दुखाती रही रात भर

गाह जलती हुई गाह बुझती हुई
शमा'-ए ग़म झिलमिलाती रही रात भर

कोई ख़ुशबू बदलती रही पैरहन
कोई तस्वीर गाती रही रात भर

फिर सबा साया-ए शाख़-ए गुल के तले
कोई क़िस्सा सुनाती रही रात भर

एक उम्मीद से दिल बहलता रहा
इक तमन्ना सताती रही रात भर

◆

GHAZAL

The pathway of life was easy,
but I spent time loving
every step of the way.

Rose gardens blossomed in my heart
whenever the spring season showed
any indifference to me.

I felt privileged like a royal
when I lived in your alley.
I have been wandering
like a beggar since my exit.

Only that one succeeded
who knew how to swim
in the river of blood.

'All the calamities
that were part of Dagh's life'[56]
are now the condition
of one and all.

(London 1979)

'Sahal Yuun Raah-e Zindagi Ki Hai'

sahal yuun raah-e zindagi ki hai
har qadam ham ne aa'shqi ki hai

ham ne dil mein saja liye gulshan
jab bahaaron ne berukhi ki hai

tere kuuche mein baadshaahi ki
jab se nikle gadaagari ki hai

bas vohi surkhuru hua jis ne
bahr-e khuun mein shanaavari ki hai

---

[56]The first line of the couplet was written by poet Dagh Dehlavi (1831–1905).

'jo guzarte the daagh par sadme'
ab vohi kaifiaat sabhi ki hai

'सहल यूँ राह-ए जिंदगी की है'

सहल यूँ राह-ए ज़िंदगी की है
हर क़दम हम ने आशिक़ी की है

हम ने दिल में सजा लिए गुलशन
जब बहारों ने बेरुख़ी की है

तेरे कूचे में बादशाही की
जब से निकले गदागरी की है

बस वही सुर्ख़-रू हुआ जिस ने
बहर-ए ख़ूँ में शनावरी की है

'जो गुज़रते थे दाग़ पर सदमे'
अब वही कैफ़ियत सभी की है

◆

GHAZAL

Everything is your bestowal—
all comfort, all sorrow.
Sometimes union, sometimes separation,
sometimes distance, sometimes closeness.

These verses that I have written are pages
of memories that you left behind.
One moment of the dawn of our union,
many remembrances of long durations
of the nights of our separations.

If I listen to your advice, dear preacher,
what will be left with me for joy or pleasure?
There will neither be the enmity of an enemy,
nor the affection of an idol.

Please come and let me show you
what has been spared
by the city's slaughterhouse.
Only the tombs and the shrines.
The shrines belong to the virtuous;
the tombs belong to the truthful.

Dear love, don't be anxious
about how the day will unfold.
It is possible that destiny
has written up by mistake
some joys in the future for us.

*'Sabhi Kuchh Hai Tera Diya Hua Sabhi Raahatein
Sabhi Kulfatein'*

*sabhi kuchh hai tera diya hua sabhi raahatein sabhi
kulfatein
kabhi sohbatein kabhi furqatein kabhi duuriyaan kabhi
qurbatein*

*ye sukhan jo ham ne raqam kiye ye hain sab varaq teri
yaad ke
koi lamha sub-h-e vasaal ka kaii shaam-e hijr ki muddatein*

*jo tumhaari maanlein naaseha to rahega daaman-e dil
mein kya
n kisi a'du ki a'daavatein n kisi sanam ki murravatein*

*chalo aao tum ko dikhaaein ham jo bacha hai maqtal-e
shahar mein
ye mazaar ahle safa ke hain ye hain ahle sidq ki turbatein*

*meri jaan aaj ka gham n kar k n jaane kaatib-e vaqt ne
kisi apne kal mein bhi bhuulkar kahien likh rakhi hon
mussartein*

'सभी कुछ है तेरा दिया हुआ'

सभी कुछ है तेरा दिया हुआ सभी राहतें सभी कुल्फ़तें
कभी सोहबतें कभी फ़ुरक़तें कभी दूरियाँ कभी कुर्बतें

ये सुख़न जो हम ने रक़म किये ये हैं सब वरक़ तेरी याद के
कोई लम्हा सुब्ह-ए विसाल का कई शाम-ए हिज्र की मुद्दतें

जो तुम्हारी मान लें नासेहा तो रहेगा दामन-ए दिल में क्या
न किसी अदू की अदावतें न किसी सनम की मुरव्वतें

चलो आओ तुम को दिखाएँ हम जो बचा है मक़्तल-ए शहर में
ये मज़ार अहल-ए सफ़ा के हैं ये हैं अहल-ए सिद्क़ की तुर्बतें

मेरी जान आज का ग़म ना कर कि ना जाने कातिब-ए वक़्त ने
किसी अपने कल में भी भूल कर कहीं लिख रखी हों मसर्रतें

◆

'TELL ME WHAT SHOULD WE DO'

This poem, written in London in 1981, shows the poet's continued dissatisfaction with the state of affairs in his country, which was being ruled by the oppressive regime of Gen. Zia-ul-Haq. But what makes this poem unique is its language. It is not Persianized Urdu which was Faiz's hallmark. Instead, it is written in Hindi, making it look like the work of a seasoned Hindi poet.

When we placed our boat of life to
float in the river,
our arms had the strength
and we had the stamina.
It appeared that when pushed with two hands
the boat will reach its journey's end.
But it did not end well.

In the downstream, we encountered
dark vortices, unseen dangers.
Some boatmen were new to the craft
and some rudders were untested.
You can analyse it any way you like.
We can blame as much as we want.
It is the same river, and it is the same boat.
Now, you tell me what we should do?
How are we going to land?
When we noticed some wounds on our hearts
about the direction of our country,
we had full faith in our vedas.[57]
And we knew many trickeries.
It seemed that within a few days
our turmoil would come to an end
and our wounds would heal.
But it did not happen.
Our disorders were old and chronic.
Vedas gave no clues about what to do.
Our schemes were rendered useless.
Now, we can think of any way we like.
We can blame anyone we want.
It is the same heart and the same wounds.
Now, tell me what we should do?
How do we heal the wounds and get well?

'Tum Hi Kaho Kya Karna Hai'

jab dukh ki nadiya mein ham ne

---

[57] The Vedas, Hindu scriptural texts, are treated as revelations witnessed by ancient sages after intense meditation. Faiz is using the word 'Vedas' in a generic sense rather than as religious texts of the Hindus, which would have little to do with Muslims living in Pakistan. It is an oblique metaphor to avoid any sort of political charge in a dictatorial regime.

jiivan ki nao daali thi
tha kitna kas-bal baanhon mein
lohu mein kitni laali thi
yuun lagta tha do haath lage
aur nao puuram paar lagi
aisa na hua har dhaare mein
kuchh andekhi manjdhaarein thiin
kuchh maanjhi the anjaan bahut
kuchh beparkhi parvaarein thiin
ab jo bhi chaaho chhaan karo
ab jitney chaaho dosh dharo
nadiya to vohi hai naav vohi
ab tum hi kaho kya karna hai
ab kaise paar utarna hai
jab apni chhaati mein ham ne
is des ke ghaav dekhe the
tha vedon par vishvaas bahut
aur yaad bahut se nuskhe the
yuun lagta tha bas kuchh din mein
saari bipta kat jaaegi
aur sab ghaav bhar jaaeinge
aisa n hua k rog apne
kuchh itne dher puraane the
ved inki toh ko paa n sake
aur totke sab bekaar gaae
ab jo bhi chaaho chhaan karo
ab jitney chaaho dosh dharo
chhaati to vohi hai ghaav vohi
ab tum hi kaho kya karna hai
ye ghaav kaise bharna hai

'तुम ही कहो क्या करना है'

जब दुख की नदिया में हम ने

जीवन की नाव डाली थी
था कितना कस-बल बाँहों में
लोहू में कितनी लाली थी
यूँ लगता था दो हाथ लगे
और नाव पूरम पार लगी
ऐसा न हुआ हर धारे में
कुछ अनदेखी मंझधारें थीं
कुछ माँझी थे अजान बहुत
कुछ बेपरखी पतवारें थीं
अब जो भी चाहो छान करो
अब जितने चाहो दोष धरो
नदिया तो वही है नाव वही
अब तुम ही कहो क्या करना है
अब कैसे पार उतरना है
जब अपनी छाती में हमने
इस देस के घाव देखे थे
था वेदों पर विश्वास बहुत
और याद बहुत से नुस्ख़े थे
यूँ लगता था बस कुछ दिन में
सारी बिपता कट जाएगी
और सब घाव भर जाएँगे
ऐसा न हुआ कि रोग अपने
कुछ इतने ढेर पुराने थे
वेद इन की टोह को पा न सके
और टोटके सब बेकार गए
अब जो भी चाहो छान करो
अब जितने चाहो दोष धरो
छाती तो वही है घाव वही
अब तुम ही कहो क्या करना है
ये घाव कैसे भरना है

◆

GHAZAL

If I don't see the journey's end,
then let me carry on my pursuit.
If the union is not possible,
then let me live by longing.

Neither there is sufficient supply of blood,
nor are there tears in my eyes.
If the prayer of love is still required,
I will have to perform it
without the ritualistic cleaning.

O the dwellers of the tavern,
let there be a spirited gathering.
There is no wine or glasses.
We can scream and yell.

If waiting is difficult,
then until something happens,
let us keep thinking
about the friend's promise to come
for sure.

If in the foreign land
there is no friend or a confidante,
then Faiz, please let me talk
about my land with my self, face to face.

(Lahore, February 1982)

'Nahien Nigaah Mein Manzil To Justuju Hi Sahi'

nahien nigaah mein manzil to justuju hi sahi
nahien visaal mayyassar to aarzu hi sahi

n tan mein khuun faraaham n ashk aankhon mein

namaaz-e shauq to vaajab hai bevazu hi sahi

kisi tarah to jame bazm maikade vaalo
nahien jo baadah o saaghar to haa o huu hi sahi

agar intizaar kathin hai to jab talak ae dil
kisi ke vaa'da-e farda ki guftugu hi sahi

dyaar-e ghair mein mahram agar nahien koi
to Faiz zikre vatan apne ru-b-ru hi sahi

'नहीं निगाह में मंज़िल तो जुस्तुजू ही सही'

नहीं निगाह में मंज़िल तो जुस्तुजू ही सही
नहीं विसाल मयस्सर तो आरज़ू ही सही

न तन में ख़ून फ़राहम न अश्क आँखों में
नमाज़-ए शौक़ तो वाजिब है बेवज़ू ही सही

किसी तरह तो जमे बज़्म मयकदे वालो
नहीं जो बादा ओ साग़र तो हाव-हू ही सही

गर इंतिज़ार कठिन है तो जब तलक ऐ दिल
किसी के वा'दा-ए फ़र्दा की गुफ़्तुगू ही सही

दयार-ए ग़ैर में महरम अगर नहीं कोई
तो 'फ़ैज़' ज़िक्र-ए वतन अपने रू-ब-रू ही सही

'THIS MOMENT IT FEELS'

In early 1982, Faiz had another close encounter with death. He was in Lahore, preparing for another foreign trip. He started to have breathing problems. He was taken to the hospital, where he stayed in intensive care for 10 days. He wrote this poem while he was recovering in the hospital. He also recited it at the BBC Mushaira in 1984, his last appearance at a poetical symposium.

At this moment, it feels
that everything is coming to an end.
No moon, no sun, no darkness, no daybreak.
In the panel of my eyes,
I can see the beauty
hiding behind a Venetian blind.
In the depths of my heart,
pain has dug its big tent.
It is possible that
it is just an apprehension,
something that I heard somewhere.
There is sound coming
from the streets
as if someone is making his last round.
In the branches of an overgrown tree
of my thoughts,
no dream shall land and make a nest.
No malice, no kindness,
no connection, no bond.
Yours is not mine.
No stranger is mine.
Agreed that this desolate time
is tough for me.
But dear heart,
it is just one point in time.
Forget it, and there is a whole life ahead of you.

(Mayo Hospital, Lahore, March 1982)

'Is Vaqt To Yuun Lagta Hai'

is vaqt to yuun lagta hai ab kuchh bhi nahien hai
mahtaab n suraj n andhera n savera
aankhon ke darichon pe kisi husn ki chilman

aur dil ki panaahon mein kisi dard ka dera
mumkin hai koi vahm tha mumkin hai suna ho
galiyon mein kisi chaap ka aakhri phera
shaakhon mein khayaalon ke ghane per ki shaayad
ab aa ke karega n koi khwaab basera
ik bair n ik mehr n ik rabt n rishta
tera koi apna n paraya koi mera
mana k ye sunsaan ghari sakht ghari hai
lekin mere dil ye to faqat ik hi ghari hai
himmat karo jiine ko to ik u'mr pari hai

'इस वक़्त तो यूँ लगता है'

इस वक़्त तो यूँ लगता है अब कुछ भी नहीं है
महताब न सूरज न अँधेरा न सवेरा
आँखों के दरीचों पे किसी हुस्न की चिलमन
और दिल की पनाहों में किसी दर्द का डेरा
मुमकिन है कोई वहम था मुमकिन है सुना हो
गलियों में किसी चाप का इक आख़िरी फेरा
शाख़ों में ख़यालों के घने पेड़ की शायद
अब आ के करेगा न कोई ख़्वाब बसेरा
इक बैर न इक मेहर न इक रब्त न रिश्ता
तेरा कोई अपना न पराया कोई मेरा
माना कि ये सुनसान घड़ी सख़्त घड़ी है
लेकिन मेरे दिल ये तो फ़ुक़त इक ही घड़ी है
हिम्मत करो जीने को तो इक उम्र पड़ी है

GHAZAL

I am a traveller,
I will spend time travelling.
If I lost my way in the city,
then I shall quietly return home.

There will be a lot of hue and cry
about the death of love and constancy,
the day I am no longer
a part of your loving memory.

Jewelers are shutting down
their stores of gems of poetry.
Where shall I go to sell
my diamonds and pearls?

How will I repay this debt
of the gift of life?
When I am overtaken
by the worrisome thought,
I would say: I am dying.

Faiz, there are hard places
in the path of love.
But please tell those
who are following me
that I am a wanderer
and I will pass away.

'Ham Musaafir Yuunhi Masruuf-e Safar Jaaeinge'

ham musaafir yuunhi masruuf-e safar jaaeinge
benishaan ho gaye jab shahar to ghar jaaeinge

kis qadar ho gaya haan mehr o vafa ka maatam
ham teri yaad se jis roz utar jaaeinge

jauhari band kiye jaate hain baazaar-e sukhan
ham kise bechne almaas o guhar jaaeinge

ne'mat-e ziist ka ye qarz chuke ga kaise
laakh ghabra ke ye kahte rahein mar jaaeinge

Faiz aate hain rah-e i'shq mein jo sakht muqaam
aane vaalon se kaho ham to guzar jaaeinge

'हम मुसाफ़िर यूँही मसरूफ़-ए सफ़र जाएँगे'

हम मुसाफ़िर यूँ ही मसरूफ़-ए सफ़र जाएँगे
बेनिशाँ हो गए जब शहर तो घर जाएँगे

किस क़दर होगा यहाँ मेहर ओ वफ़ा का मातम
हम तेरी याद से जिस रोज़ उतर जाएँगे

जौहरी बंद किए जाते हैं बाज़ार-ए सुख़न
हम किसे बेचने अलमास ओ गुहर जाएँगे

नेमत-ए जीस्त का ये क़र्ज़ चुकेगा कैसे
लाख घबरा के ये कहते रहें मर जाएँगे

'फ़ैज़' आते है रह-ए इ'श्क़ में सख़्त मक़ाम
आने वालों से कहो हम तो गुज़र जाएँगे

'THIS RELATIONSHIP ... YOURS AND MINE'

This poem, included in the posthumous collection of Faiz's verse titled *Ghubaar-e Ayyaam,* was written sometime in 1984, just before his death. Faiz wrote many poems on romantic relationships. This one is special because in eight poignant lines he makes an important point: every romantic relationship is unique. Each moment of bliss and each moment of grief due to separation is also unique: '*magar ye kaifiiyat apni raqam nahien hai kahien* (But this condition that we have / is not narrated anywhere)'.

What can I write
about the relationship we have?
In the language of passionate love,
it is not described anywhere.

Much has been written
about the pleasures of the union
and the torment caused by separation.
But this condition that we have
is not described anywhere.
This love of ours in which union
and separation embrace each other;
this pain that has persisted
over months and years;
this special love of ours
which we have been keeping it a secret.
'Much time has passed,
but this mutual obsession
has survived.'

'Jo Mera Tumhara Rishta Hai'

main kya likhuun k jo mera tumhara rishta hai
voha aa'shiqi ki zabaan mein kahiin bhi darj nahien

likha gaya hai bahut lutf o vasl o dard-e firaaq
magar ye kaifiiyat apni raqam nahien hai kahien

ye apna i'shq ham-aaghosh jis mein hijr o visaal
ye apna dard k hai kab se hamdam-e mah o saal

is i'shq-e khaas ko har ek se chhupa-e hue
'guzar gaya hai zamaana gale lagaaye hue'

'जो मेरा तुम्हारा रिश्ता है'

मैं क्या लिखूँ कि जो मेरा तुम्हारा रिश्ता है
वो आ'शिक़ी की ज़बाँ में कहीं भी दर्ज नहीं
लिखा गया है बहुत लुत्फ़-ए वस्ल ओ दर्द-ए फ़िराक़
मगर ये कैफ़ियत अपनी रक़म नहीं है कहीं
ये अपना इ'श्क़-ए हम-आग़ोश जिस में हिज्र ओ विसाल

ये अपना दर्द कि है कब से हमदम-ए मह ओ साल
इस इ'श्क़-ए ख़ास को हर एक से छुपाए हुए
'गुज़र गया है ज़माना गले लगाए हुए'

THE LAST GHAZAL

This is the last ghazal that Faiz wrote a few days before his
death in November 1984. For this, he used the 'zamiin'
created a century ago by Mirza Ghalib. In the fourth
couplet, he talks about death sending a message. The fifth
and last couplet (without his nom de plume) sounds like
a parting message for his followers and admirers: '*sajaao
bazm-e ghazal gaao jaam taaza karo*' (Prepare yourself for a
gathering, / sing a ghazal, freshen up wine glasses). This
is a message of love and peace for all human beings. Like
the great American poet Walt Whitman (1819–1892) before
him, Faiz holds every human, be it a man or woman, young
and old, fair or dark, believer or an atheist, in his embrace.
If people engage in friendly conversations, they sing and
dance and seek the little joys of life, that is a design for a
world free of conflict.

If life gave me either more or less,
how does it matter?
When there is so much pain to go by—
more or less means nothing.

I have known life well,
no patience for any more lessons.
My kind-hearted friend,
I know what the pleasure is
and what constitutes oppression.

If it doesn't create flare,

what is the purpose of a couplet?
If it doesn't generate mayhem in the city,
of what use is the moist eye?

The hand of death
is carrying a message.
Wonder what is written
in today's do-list!

Prepare yourself for a gathering,
sing a ghazal, freshen up wine glasses.
'The sufferings of this world are boundless,
but we are not short on wine.'[58]

'Bahut Mila N Mila Zindagi Se Gham Kya Hai'

bahut mila n mila zindagi se gham kya hai
mata-e dard baham hai to besh o kam kya hai

ham ek u'mr se vaaqif hain ab n samjhaao
k lutf kya hai mere mehrabaan sitam kya hai

kare n jag mein aalaao to sh'er kis masraf
kare n shahar mein jal thal to chashm-e nam kya hai

ajal ke haath koi aa raha hai parvaana
n jaane aaj ki fahrist mein raqam kya hai

sajaao bazm-e ghazal gaao jaam taaza karo
'bahut sahi gham-e giit ishara ab kam kya hai'

'बहुत मिला न मिला ज़िंदगी से ग़म क्या है'

---

[58]This line is the matl'a of a ghazal written by Mirza Ghalib: '*bahut sahi gham-e giiti sharaab kam kya hai / ghulaam-e saaqi-e kausar huun mujh ko gham kya hai* (There is lot of sorrow in the world, / but there is no shortage of wine. / I am like a slave of Saqi / who lives in paradise. / Do I need to worry about anything?)'. Deol, *The Treasure*, p. 416.

बहुत मिला न मिला ज़िंदगी से ग़म क्या है
मता-ए दर्द बहम है तो बेश ओ कम क्या है

हम एक उम्र से वाक़िफ़ हैं अब न समझाओ
कि लुत्फ़ क्या है मेरे मेहरबां सितम क्या है

करे न जग में आलाओ तो शे'र किस मसरफ़
करे न शहर में जलथल तो चश्म-ए नम क्या है

अजल के हाथ कोई आ रहा है परवाना
न जाने आज की फ़हरिस्त में रक़म क्या है

सजा ओ बज़्म-ए ग़ज़ल गाओ जाम ताज़ा करो
'बहुत सही ग़म-ए गीती शराब कम क्या है'

EPILOGUE

Several years ago I spent some time with Faiz Ahmad Faiz, the greatest of contemporary Urdu poets. He was exiled from his native Pakistan by Zia's military regime, and found a welcome of sorts in strife-torn Beirut. Naturally, his closest friends were Palestinian, but I sensed that although there was an affinity of spirit between them, nothing quite matched—language, poetic convention or life-history. Only once, when Iqbal Ahmad, a Pakistani friend and fellow-exile, came to Beirut, did Faiz seem to overcome his sense of constant estrangement. The three of us sat in a dingy Beirut restaurant late one night, while Faiz recited poems. After a time, he and Iqbal stopped translating his verses for my benefit, but as the night wore on, it did not matter. What I watched required no translation: it was an enactment of a homecoming, expressed through defiance and loss, as if to say, 'Zia, we are here.'

—Edward Said[59]

Faiz had contemplated his encounter with death for a very long time. In a poem written many years ago, he had asked the question: 'How will it come the day death comes?' And only a couple of years before his death, he

---

[59]Kassamali, Sumayya. 'You Had No Address', *The Caravan*, 1 June 2016, https://caravanmagazine.in/reviews-essays/you-had-no-address-faiz-beirut. Accessed on 2 June 2021.

had written: 'At this moment, it feels / that everything is coming to an end'. We have an authentic account of his death from his grandson, Ali Madeeh Hashmi, who wrote an authorized biography of the poet.[60] He makes our task easier by giving us a moment-by-moment account of how the end came and how the family and the world reacted to this tragedy.

Although Faiz deeply loved his family and adored his city (Lahore), he was a frequent traveller and sometimes he was gone for months. But on the fateful day of 19 November 1984, he was in Lahore. A few days earlier, he had done something unusual. He had taken out time to go to village Kala Qader, near Sialkot, the place of his birth, and his mother's village, Jessar. The people received him with pride and great affection. No one had any idea that they would be seeing him for the last time. On his return from this trip, he jokingly told Salima, his eldest daughter, that he had happened to see a woman in the village who used to be a great beauty in her younger days (and possibly his heart had missed a beat on seeing her!) but now she was an old crone. Laughingly, he had added, 'I wonder what I looked like to her.'

During these last days, Faiz also saw three of his old friends: Sher Muhammad Hameed, whom he had met in 1929 during his college days; Khwaja Khurshid Anwar, who was a filmmaker but had been a member of the Ghadar Party in his younger days and Chiragh Deen or Ustad Daman, a Punjabi poet and mystic.

Moneeza, his younger daughter, was preparing to celebrate her wedding anniversary, and a dinner had been arranged for the extended family. Faiz came to the

---

[60]Hashmi, *Love and Revolution.*

celebration but he looked sick. He was offered Scotch, which he refused. He didn't stay long and walked back home, which was just next door. A short time later, Moneeza got a call from Alys, saying that her dad was unconscious. He was taken to Mayo Hospital, where doctors took immediate steps to give him relief. This is how Salima remembers his last moments:

> Mizu [Moneeza] had stepped out of the room, he was lying in bed gasping for air as he had been all night and all of a sudden, he sat bolt upright, eyes wide open and staring at the ceiling. I rushed to him and threw my arms around him and felt him go limp. I screamed for the doctors, and they all rushed in and pushed me away. They shooed us out of the room and started working on him.[61]

Faiz died on 20 November 1984, as 'the afternoon calls for prayers had started ringing out from the mosques.'[62] Both BBC and Doordarshan TV in India broadcast the news of Faiz's demise, but PTV, Pakistan's state TV, did not announce his death until late night. Hundreds of people, friends, admirers and ordinary folk gathered for the funeral. He was laid to rest in a simple grave in Model Town, Lahore. The man who had roamed the world, spreading his message of peace and love, had come back home, finally.

> How will it come the day death comes.
> Whether it comes like an assassin
> or as merely the grace of the beloved.
> My heart will utter these words,

---

[61]Hashmi, *Love and Revolution*, p. 7.
[62]Hashmi, *Love and Revolution*, pp. 7–8.

my parting words of thanks.
'God be praised,'
for the way, it ended my heart's grief.
Thanks to the one whose lips
are filled with such sweetness.

(From 'The Day Death Comes')

As we conclude this literary odyssey, it is time to summarize some key arguments. All poets go through some form of evolutionary development. For Faiz, the lines of the thresholds that he crossed are easily discernible. The young college student that we meet towards the end of the 1920s, was a bleary-eyed romantic, or to quote N.M. Rashed, 'a poet fond of decadence'. For a 20 year old, the romance was all his reality. He would walk on the same ground until mid-1930s, when a breakthrough moment came in the form of the realization that other things mattered besides 'love for the beloved'. The first major expression of this new thinking was found in the poem 'Not the Same Old Love (Mujh Se Pehli Si Mohabbat Meri Mahbuub N Maang)'. Kanahiya Lal Kapoor captured this new poet in these memorable words: 'Faiz rose like a black cloud and within a short period he had the whole literary world under his spell.' We know that this transformation was not easy. Faiz considered his remarkable first collection of poems *Naqsh-e Faryadi* a 'defeat'. Notwithstanding this subjective assessment, it was a fact that everyone around him realized that he had found not only a new direction but also a unique style and a new voice.

The voice that we heard in *Naqsh-e Faryadi* was artistic, mellow, soft and lyrical, yet it was full of compassion for the downtrodden and the exploited. Even his compassion had a distinctive aesthetic touch. The relaxed pace made space for short pauses or moments of poetic silences. The lyrical flair, aesthetic sensibility, colourful imagery and rich language overflowing with metaphors and similes were characteristics that readers of Urdu verse had not seen in any other poet since Ghalib. Faiz had internalized a powerful lesson, principally from his mentor (Ghalib): that when a poet uses language infused with innovative metaphors, it not only helps him to hide his layered depths but also to create a text that has a magical effect on the reader. There are many examples to illustrate this point. Purposeful metaphorical ambiguity in 'Loneliness (Tanhaaii)' opened the door to many interpretations. Faiz's most controversial work 'The Dawn of Freedom (Sub-h-e Aazaadi)' does not contain words like freedom, independence, India, Pakistan or partition, though it is about all these things and more. We can remove the title and put a new title of our choice, and the poem will still make sense. Similarly, neither of the two Bangladesh poems—'Keep Yourself at Some Distance from Me (Hazar Karo Mere Tan Se)' and 'Layer after Layer (Tah B Tah)'—contain the words 'Bangladesh', 'genocide' or 'war'. 'Blackout', written about the India–Pakistan war of 1965, does not contain the word 'war' or the names of the entities engaged in warfare.

In addition to the mastery over the use of metaphors, Faiz developed the exceptional skill of creating stunning imagery with the use of tender words and bonded phrases. It is seen in poem after poem, but some examples are in order. 'The Night Music (Surud-e Shabana)', 'Vista (Manzar)', 'An Evening in the Jailhouse (Zindaan Ki Ek Shaam)' and 'A Morning in the Jailhouse (Zindaan Ki Ek Sub-h)' can be read as we read any other poem or they can be visually experienced with our eyes closed.

Faiz was in love with the world and the beauty it

represented. But at the same, he was conscious of the fact that economic inequality and deprivation was keeping a large number of people from fully accessing this beauty. Therefore, a majority of these lives were pushed into perpetual darkness, first by foreign rule and then after Independence by politicians, the army and the fundamentalists, who were using their hold on power to exploit people in the name of religion or fake patriotism to promote their vested interests. His idea of revolution was not something that would happen through the force of ideology or violence or the rise of a messianic figure. It will come, he said, from the realization that people are the masters of their destiny. They have to organize and demand change and social justice. This message comes out clearly in 'No Saviour for the Broken Glasses (Shiishon Ka Masiha Koi Nahien)'.

While Faiz was a messenger of social and political change, he had a deep reverence for cultural tradition. He felt that there were things that must be preserved. He was probably the only one who asked hard questions about Pakistan's cultural history and identity. Did it start with Pakistan's resolution, Iqbal's poetic vision of an independent Muslim nation, Sir Syed's efforts at social and educational reform, foreign invasions that brought with it Muslim faith or did it start with its pre-Islamic civilization, ancient history and culture? Faiz was convinced that it was wrong to look at the cultural identity of a nation solely through the lens of one's religious beliefs. Belief systems change over time, but the history of a place is linked to ancient footprints, folk heritage and the people and the archaeological evidence they left behind. As chairperson of the PNCA, he proposed the idea of establishing the International University of Taxila, named after the ancient city of Taxila. The proposal got no traction for obvious political reasons.

There was, at all times, a perfect synchronicity between Faiz the poet and Faiz the person. His gentleness or gentlemanliness was always the talk of the town. He never raised his voice at anyone. Even when someone said something offensive, he answered it by way of silence. Arguing about things was not his nature. He accomplished a lot but never lost his penchant for humility. In one of the letters, he told Alys: 'My talent is limited. There are many more people who are much more talented than me. But hard work counts, and it makes a difference.'

As Professor Gopi Chand Narang has beautifully summed up Faiz's poetic evolution in his foreword, we need to pay attention to his *three* (not just *two*) evolutionary stages of love. While the two loves are easily discernable (passionate love for the beloved and compassionate love for the land and its people), the third love (a love that embraces everyone and everything) finds expression in selected poems, speeches and other writings in the later part of his life. This universal or cosmic love was not Faiz's creation, it flows from India's ancient scriptures and the heritage of Sufi and mystic poets like Amir Khusrau, Sheikh Baba Farid, Kabir, Guru Nanak, Bulleh Shah and Waris Shah. It was always there: Faiz simply channelled its existence and transformed it into his soul-touching creative lyricism.

One reading of Faiz is never enough. His work prods us to go back to his compositions time and again. Every time we pick up any of his poetry collections, the sheer beauty of his words engages us. New images continuously shine like new stars appearing on the dark horizon. This also has to do with the freshness of his work that is hard to describe in words. It is the freshness of a dawn that brings with it a gentle breeze, spreading fragrance in its path. Faiz does not avoid the dark side of life, but he promises a better future, that is created by the combined effort of the people themselves. Time and again, he tells us that it is important to retain one's hope in periods of despair.

It is difficult to encapsulate the work of a poet, whether it is Ghalib or Iqbal, Whitman or Naruda, but Faiz left behind a few lines that synopsized his life and work in pure and heartful penetrating words.

> Those people were blessed
> who considered love as a kind of work.
> They were in love with their calling.
> Writing poetry, too, was like love.
> I spent some of my time loving, some in action.
> My work helped me become a better lover.
> I kept myself busy as long as I lived.
> But my loving eventually complicated things for me.
> Losing my composure in the end,
> I left both of them unfinished.

BIBLIOGRAPHY

Abedi, Syed Taqi, ed. *Faiz Fahmi*, Lahore: Multi Media Affairs, 2011.

Ali, Agha Shahid. *The Rebel's Silhouette: Selected Poems Faiz Ahmed Faiz*, Amherst: University of Massachusetts Press, 1991.

Anjum, Khaleeq, ed. *Faiz Ahmed Faiz: Tanqeedi Jaaeza*, New Delhi: Anjuman Tarraqi Urdu (Hind), 1985.

Azmi, Anees, ed. *Aiwan-e-Urdu: Shumara Number-004*, Delhi: Urdu Akademi, 2011.

Begum, Sadiqa, ed. *Adab-e Latiif: Shumara Number-003,004*, 1985.

Bhat, Mohammad Hamid Ullah, ed. *Fikr o Tahqeeq: Shumara Number-001*, New Delhi: National Council for Promotion of Urdu Language, 2011.

Chowdhary, Supriya. *Poetry, Protest and Politics: A Study of Progressive Urdu Poetry*, Lahore: Sang-e Meel Publications, 2016.

Coppola, Carlo. *Urdu Poetry, 1935–1970: The Progressive Episode*, Karachi: Oxford University Press, 2017.

Death House Letters of Ethel and Julius Rosenberg, New York: Jero Pub. Co. 1953.

Dehlavi, Idrees, ed. *Shabistan*, Faiz Number, New Delhi: Sham'a Publication, n.d.

Deol, Surinder. *Sahir: A Literary Portrait*, New Delhi: Oxford University Press, 2019.

Deol, Surinder, *The Treasure: A Modern Rendition of Ghalib's Lyrical Love Poetry*, 2nd ed., New Delhi: Partridge Publishing, 2018.

Dutt, Sabar and Salma Saddiqi. *Fan aur Shakhsiat*, Faiz Ahmed Faiz Number, Bombay: Nargis Publications, 1981.

Faiz, Alys. *Dear Heart: To Faiz in Prison—1951–1955*, Lahore: Ferozesons Ltd, 1985.

Faiz, Alys. *Over My Shoulder*, Lahore: The Frontier Post Publications, 1993.

Faiz, Faiz Ahmed. *Dast-e Saba*, Delhi: Azad Kitab Ghar, 1953.

Faiz, Faiz Ahmed. *Dast-e Tah-e Sang*, Aligarh: Educational Book House, 1979.

Faiz, Faiz Ahmed. *Mah o Saal-e Aashnaii*, Karachi: Maktaba Daniyal, 2008.

Faiz, Faiz Ahmed. *Meezan*, Karachi: Urdu Academy Sindh, 1987.

Faiz, Faiz Ahmed. *Mere Dil Mere Musafir*, Karachi: Maktaba Dinyal, 1981.

Faiz, Faiz Ahmed. *Naqsh-e Fariyadi*, Lahore: Maktaba Urdu, 1941.

Faiz, Faiz Ahmed. *Nuskha Haae Wafa*, Lahore: Maktaba Karvaan, 1985.

Faiz, Faiz Ahmed. *Saare Sukhan Hamaare*, London: Hosain's Books, 1982.

Faiz, Faiz Ahmed. *Saleebeinn Mere Darichay Mein*, Karachi: Maktaba Daniyal, 2011.

Faiz, Faiz Ahmed. *Sar-e Vaadiy-e Saina*, Lucknow: Kitabi Duniya, n.d.

Faiz, Faiz Ahmed. *Shaam-e Shahar Yaaraan*, New Delhi: Maktaba Jamia, 1978.

Faiz, Faiz Ahmed. *The True Subject: Selected Poems of Faiz Ahmed Faiz*, edited and translated by Naomi Lazard, Princeton, N.J.: Princeton University Press, 2014.

Faiz, Faiz Ahmed. *Zindaan Nama*, Aligarh: Anjuman Taraqqi Urdu Hind, 1958.

Farooqi, Baran. *Faiz Ahmed Faiz: The Colours of My Heart*, Gurgaon, Haryana: Penguin Random House India, 2017.

Forche, Carolyn, ed. *Against Forgetting: Twentieth Century Poetry of Witness*, New York: W.W. Norton & Co, 1993.

Hameed, Yasmeen, ed. *Daybreak: Writings on Faiz*, Karachi: Oxford University Press, 2013.

Hamilton, Lillias. *A Vizier's Daughter: A Tale of Hazara War*, London: John Murray, 1900.

Hasan, Khalid, ed. 'A Conversation with Faiz', *The Unicorn and the Dancing Girl*, New Delhi: Allied Publishers, 1988.

Hashmi, Ali Madeeh. *Love and Revolution: Faiz Ahmed Faiz—The Authorized Biography*, New Delhi: Rupa Publications India Private Ltd, 2016.

Housden, Roger. *10 Poems to Last a Lifetime*, New York: Harmony Books, 2004.

Husain, Ashfaq. *Faiz Ke Maghrabi Havaale*, Karachi: Pakistan Study Center, 2011.

Jalil, Rakhshanda. *Liking Progress, Loving Change: A Literary History of the Progressive Writers' Movement in Urdu*, New Delhi: Oxford University Press, 2014.

Jama, Mahmood, trans. *Faiz Fifty Poems*, Karachi: Oxford University Press, 2013.

Javed, Azhar. *Takhleeq*, Gosha-e Faiz: Lahore, 2005.

Karkaria, Bachi. 'Alys and Faiz', *Erratica, Times of India* (Blog), 17 October 2012. Available at https://timesofindia.indiatimes.com/blogs/erratica/alys-and-faiz/. Accessed on 2 June 2021.

Kassamali, Sumayya. 'You Had No Address', *The Caravan*, 1 June 2016. Available at https://caravanmagazine.in/reviews-essays/you-had-noaddress-faiz-beirut. Accessed on 2 June 2021.

Khan, M. Habeeb, ed. *Urdu Adab*, Faiz Number, New Delhi: Anjuman Taraqqi Urdu Hind, 1985.

Kiernan, V.G. *Poems by Faiz*, New Delhi: Oxford University Press, 1971.

Lakhnavi, Sehba and Kashish Siddiqi. *Afkar*, Faiz Number, Karachi: Maktaba-e Afkar, 1965.

Majeed, Sheema, ed. *Coming Back Home: Selected Articles, Editorials and Interviews of Faiz Ahmed Faiz*, Karachi: Oxford University Press, 2008.

Majeed, Sheema. *Culture and Identity: Selected English Writing of Faiz*, Karachi: Oxford University Press, 2005.

Malik, Abdur Rauf. *Faiz Shanaasi*, Karachi: Pakistan Study Center, Karachi Unversity, 2011.

Meeropol, Michael, ed. *The Rosenberg Letters*, London: D. Dobson, 1953.

Mir, Ali Husain and Raza Mir. *Anthems of Resistance: A Celebration of Progressive Urdu Poetry*, New Delhi: Roli, 2006.

Mirza, Ayub. *Faiz Nama*, Lahore: Classic Publishers, 2005.

Moyers, Bill and Joseph Campbell. *The Power of Myth*, New York: Doubleday, 1988.

Narang, Gopi Chand. 'Tradition and Innovation in Faiz Ahmed Faiz', *Urdu Language and Literature: Critical Perspectives*, New Delhi: Sterling Publishers, 1991.

Narang, Gopi Chand, trans. Baidar Bakht, 'How Not To Read Faiz Ahmed Faiz', *Indian Literature I*, vol. 53 no. 1 (249), January/ February 2009, pp. 44–56.

Narang, Gopi Chand, trans. Surinder Deol. *Ghalib: Innovative Meanings and the Ingenious Mind*, New Delhi: Oxford University Press, 2017.

Narang, Gopi Chand, trans. Surinder Deol. *The Urdu Ghazal: A Gift of India's Composite Culture*, New Delhi: Oxford University Press, 2020.

Rahmani, Abrar, ed. *AajKal*, Faiz Ahmed Faiz Number, New Delhi: Publication Division, Government of India, 2011.

Rushdie, Salman and Elizabeth West, eds. *Mirrorwork: 50 years of Indian Writing 1947–1997*, New York: Henry Holt and Company, 1997.

Sibt-e Hasan, Syed. *Sukhandar Sukhan*, Karachi: Maktaba Daniyal, 2009.

Vasilieva, Ludmila. *Parvarish-e Lauh O Qalam: Faiz Hayaataur Takhleeqaat*, Karachi: Oxford University Press, 2006.

Zaheer, Syed Sajjad. *Roshnaaii*, New Delhi: Seema Publications, 1985.

Zaheer, Syed Sajjad. *The Light*, trans. Amina Azfar, Karachi: Oxford University Press, 2006.

QAT'AS, GHAZALS AND POEMS

2. A Blemished Sunrise

3. Dawns and Dusks of the Jailhouse